Street by Street

RICHMOND
KINGSTON UPON THAMES
HOUNSLOW, NEW MALDEN, SURBITON,
TEDDINGTON, TWICKENHAM

Barnes, Brentford, Chessington, Feltham, Ham, Hampton Court, Isleworth, Kew, Putney, Raynes Park, Stoneleigh, Sunbury, Wimbledon, Worcester Park

C000047265

1st edition September 2002

© Automobile Association Developments Limited 2002

Ordnance Survey® This product includes map data licensed from Ordnance Survey® with the permission of the Controller of Her Majesty's Stationery Office. © Crown copyright 2002. All rights reserved. Licence No: 399221.

Published by AA Publishing (a trading name of Automobile Association Developments Limited, whose registered office is Millstream, Maidenhead Road, Windsor, Berkshire SL4 5GD. Registered number 1878835).

The Post Office is a registered trademark of Post Office Ltd. in the UK and other countries.

Schools address data provided by Education Direct.

One-way street data provided by:

Tele Atlas   © Tele Atlas N.V.

Mapping produced by the Cartographic Department of The Automobile Association. A01100

A CIP Catalogue record for this book is available from the British Library.

Printed by GRAFIASA S.A., Porto, Portugal

The contents of this atlas are believed to be correct at the time of the latest revision. However, the publishers cannot be held responsible for loss occasioned to any person acting or refraining from action as a result of any material in this atlas, nor for any errors, omissions or changes in such material. This does not affect your statutory rights. The publishers would welcome information to correct any errors or omissions and to keep this atlas up to date. Please write to Publishing, The Automobile Association, Fanum House (FH17), Basing View, Basingstoke, Hampshire, RG21 4EA.

Ref: ML212

Key to map pages ii-iii

Key to map symbols iv-1

Enlarged scale pages 2-3

Street by Street 4-45

Index – towns & villages 46

Index – streets 47-63

Index – featured places 63-66

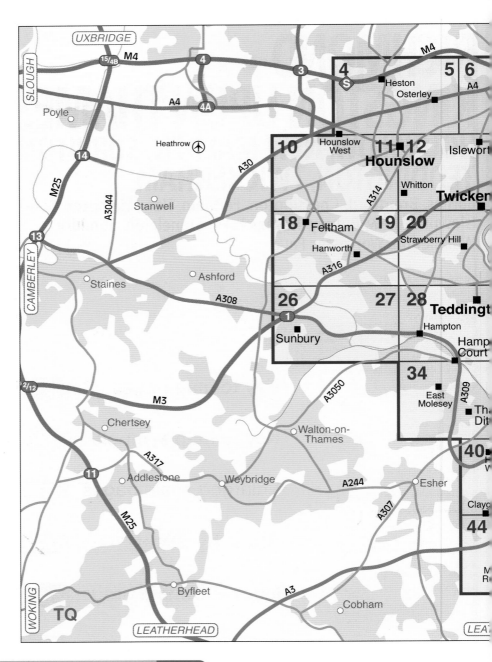

Enlarged scale pages 1:10,000 6.3 inches to 1 mile

| 0 | | 1/4 | miles | 1/2 |
| 0 | 1/4 | 1/2 | kilometres 3/4 | 1 |

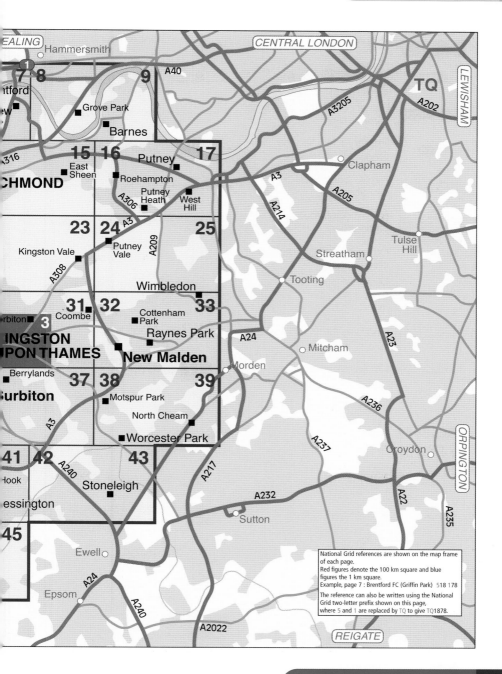

EALING
Hammersmith
CENTRAL LONDON
LEWISHAM
7 8 9 A40
TQ A202
ntford
w
Grove Park
A3205
Barnes
A316 15 16 Putney 17
East Sheen
Roehampton
Clapham
CHMOND
A306
Putney Heath
West Hill
A3
A205
A214
23 24 A3 25
Kingston Vale
A308
Putney Vale
A209
Tulse Hill
Streatham
Wimbledon
Tooting
31 32 33
Coombe
rbiton 3
Cottenham Park
Raynes Park
A24
A23
A237
A236
Mitcham
INGSTON
PON THAMES
New Malden
Morden
A237
37 38 39
Berrylands
urbiton
Motspur Park
North Cheam
A3
Croydon
ORPINGTON
A235
A22
Worcester Park
41 42 43
Hook
A240
Stoneleigh
A217
A232
A232
essington
Sutton
45
Ewell
A24
Epsom
A240
A2022
REIGATE

National Grid references are shown on the map frame of each page.
Red figures denote the 100 km square and blue figures the 1 km square.
Example, page 7 : Brentford FC (Griffin Park) 518 178
The reference can also be written using the National Grid two-letter prefix shown on this page, where 5 and 1 are replaced by TQ to give TQ1878.

4.2 inches to 1 mile **Scale of main map pages 1:15,000**

0   1/4   miles   1/2   3/4   1
0   1/4   1/2   kilometres 3/4   1   1 1/4   1 1/2

iv

Motorway & junction	Underground station
Motorway service area	Light railway & station
Primary road single/dual carriageway	Preserved private railway
Primary road service area	Level crossing
A road single/dual carriageway	Tramway
B road single/dual carriageway	Ferry route
Other road single/dual carriageway	Airport runway
Minor/private road, access may be restricted	County, administrative boundary
One-way street	Mounds
Pedestrian area	Page continuation 1:15,000
Track or footpath	Page continuation to enlarged scale 1:10,000
Road under construction	River/canal, lake, pier
Road tunnel	Aqueduct, lock, weir
AA Service Centre	Peak (with height in metres)
Parking	Beach
Park & Ride	Woodland
Bus/coach station	Park
Railway & main railway station	Cemetery
Railway & minor railway station	Built-up area

Junction 9 — Motorway & junction
Services — Motorway service area
Services — Primary road service area
LC — Level crossing
465 Winter Hill — Peak (with height in metres)
I7 — Page continuation 1:15,000
3 — Page continuation to enlarged scale 1:10,000

	Featured building		Abbey, cathedral or priory
	City wall		Castle
A&E	Hospital with 24-hour A&E department		Historic house or building
PO	Post Office	Wakehurst Place NT	National Trust property
	Public library		Museum or art gallery
i	Tourist Information Centre		Roman antiquity
	Petrol station Major suppliers only		Ancient site, battlefield or monument
†	Church/chapel		Industrial interest
	Public toilets		Garden
	Toilet with disabled facilities		Arboretum
PH	Public house AA recommended		Farm or animal centre
	Restaurant AA inspected		Zoological or wildlife collection
	Theatre or performing arts centre		Bird collection
	Cinema		Nature reserve
	Golf course		Visitor or heritage centre
▲	Camping AA inspected		Country park
	Caravan Site AA inspected		Cave
	Camping & caravan site AA inspected		Windmill
	Theme park		Distillery, brewery or vineyard

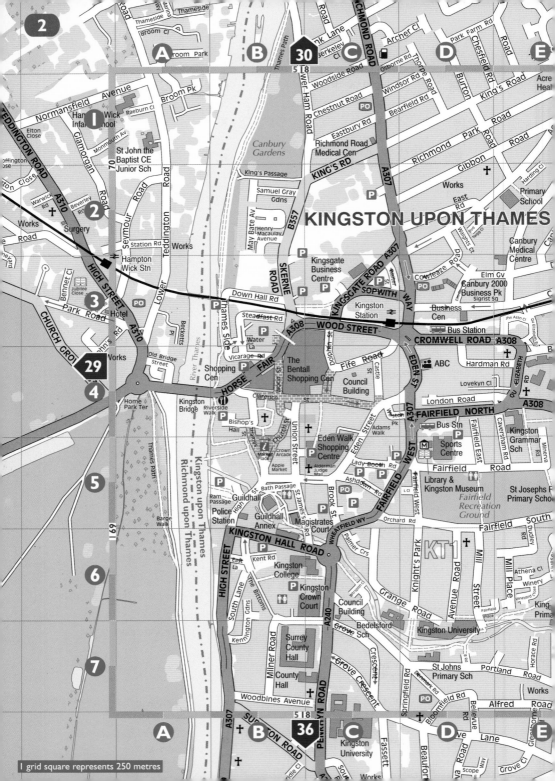

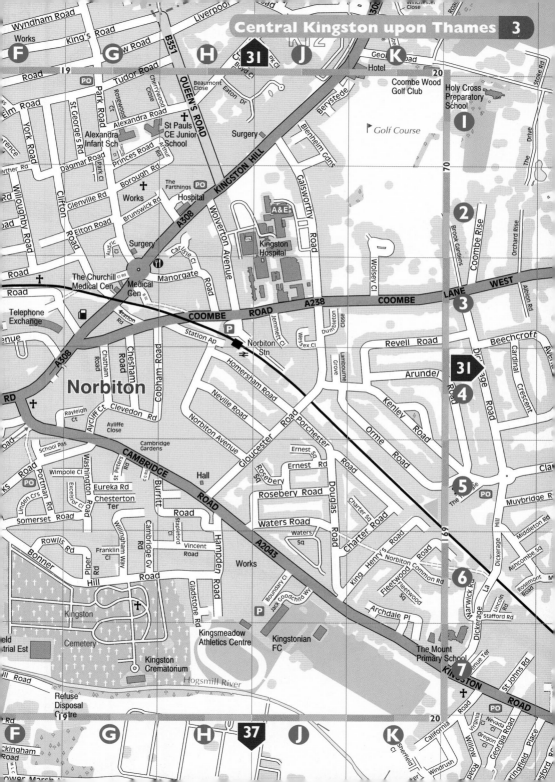

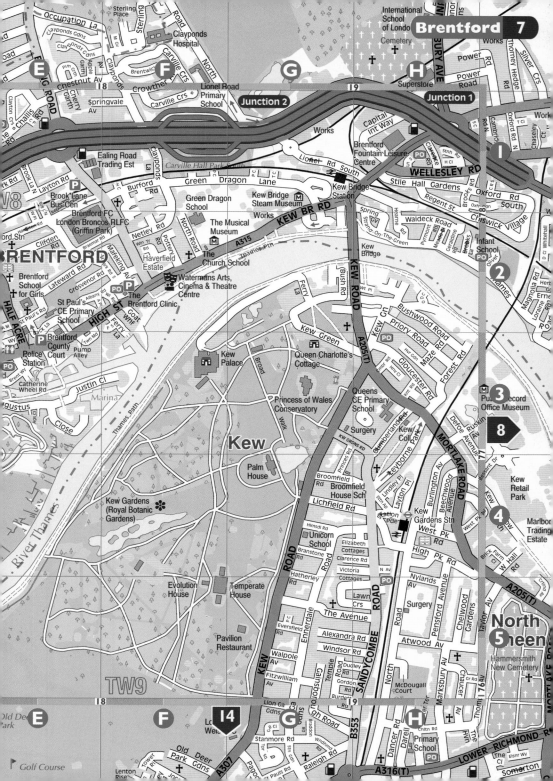

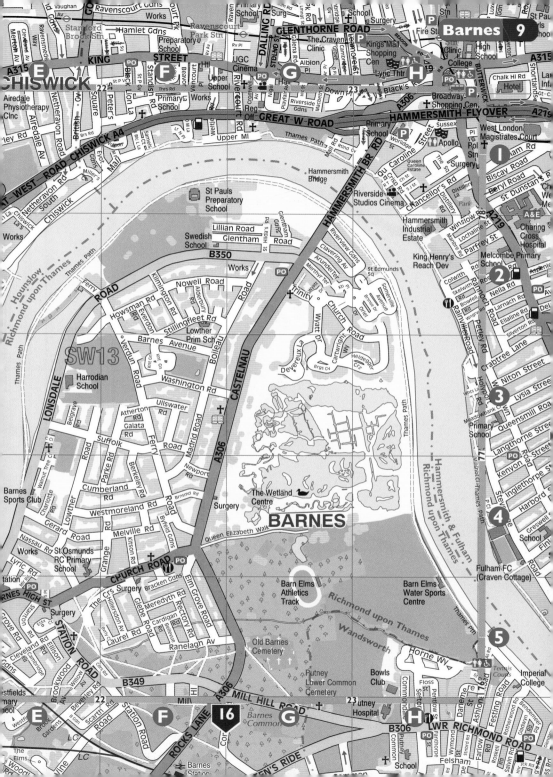

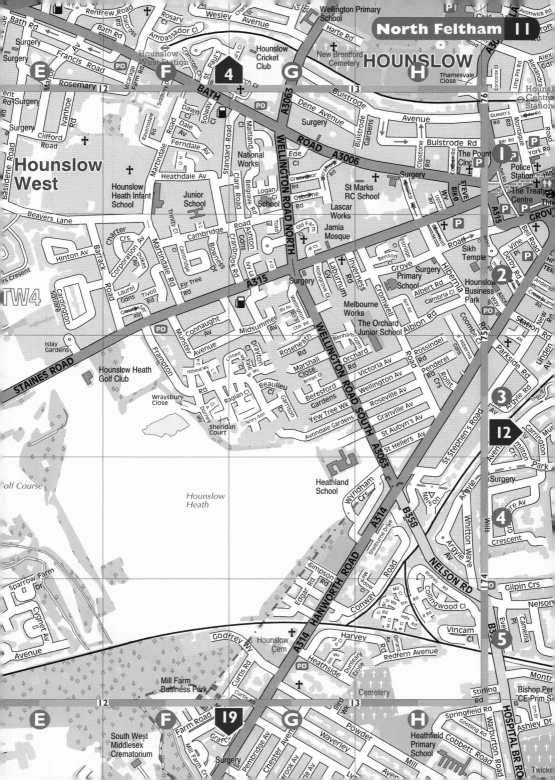

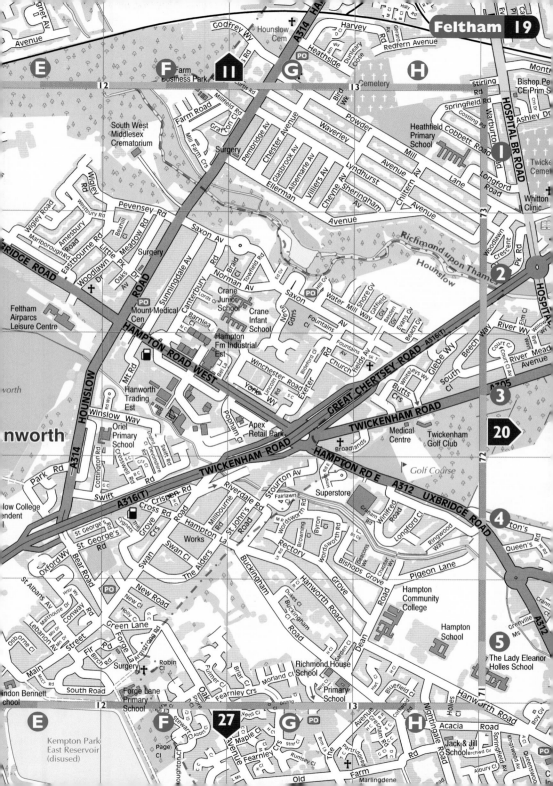

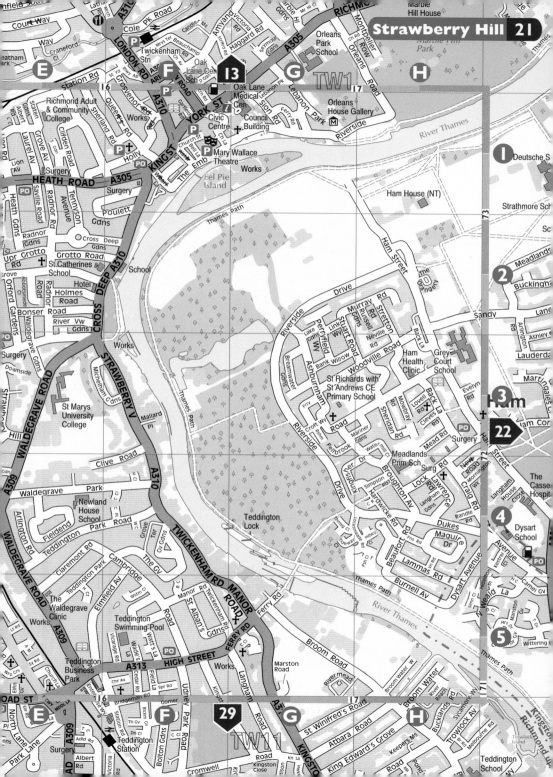

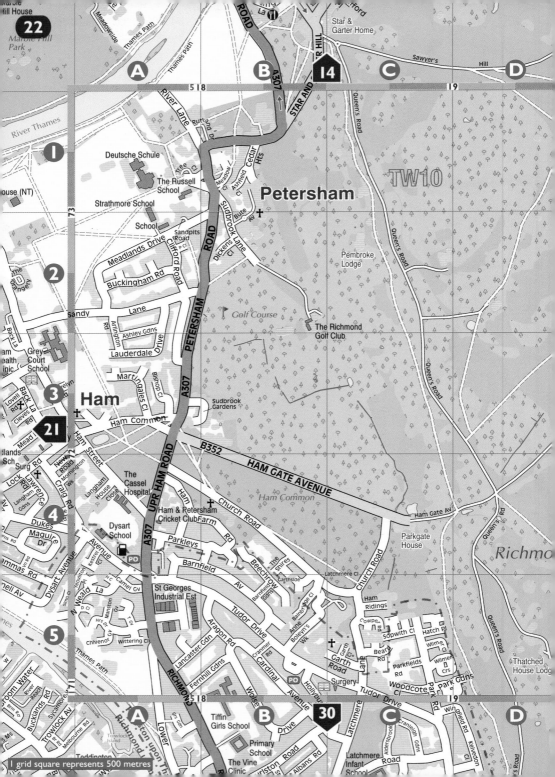

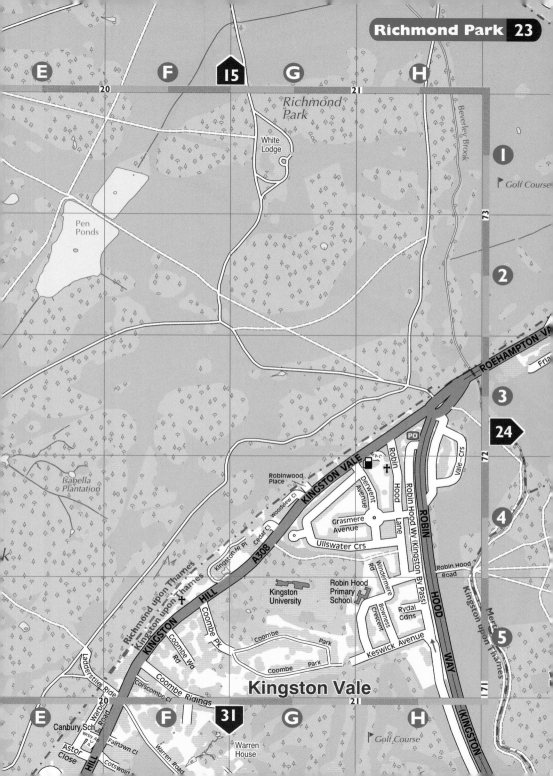

E F **15** G H

20 21

Richmond Park

White Lodge

I

Golf Course

73

Pen Ponds

2

ROEHAMPTON VA

Frla

3

Isabella Plantation

PO

24

72

KINGSTON VALE

Robinwood Place

Robin Hood Wy (Kingston By Pass)

Derwent Avenue

Robin Hood Lane

Vale Crs

4

Woodview Cl

Cedar Cl

Grasmere Avenue

Ullswater Crs

Robin Hood Road

Kingston Hi Pl

A308

Kingston upon Thames

Windermere Rd

Richmond upon Thames

KINGSTON HILL

Robin Hood Primary School

Bowness Crescent

Rydal Gdns

Kingston upon Thames

Mert

5

71

Kingston University

Coombe Pk

Coombe Wa

Coombe

Park

Keswick Avenue

ROBIN

HOOD

WAY

Ladderstile Ride

Coombe Rd

Coombe

Park

Kingston Vale

Corscombe Cl

Coombe Ridings

E F **31** G H

20 21

Canbury Sch

Watb

Road

Wrby Ab

Fairlawn Cl

Warren House

Golf Course

KINGSTON

Astor Close

HILL

Cotswold

Warren Road

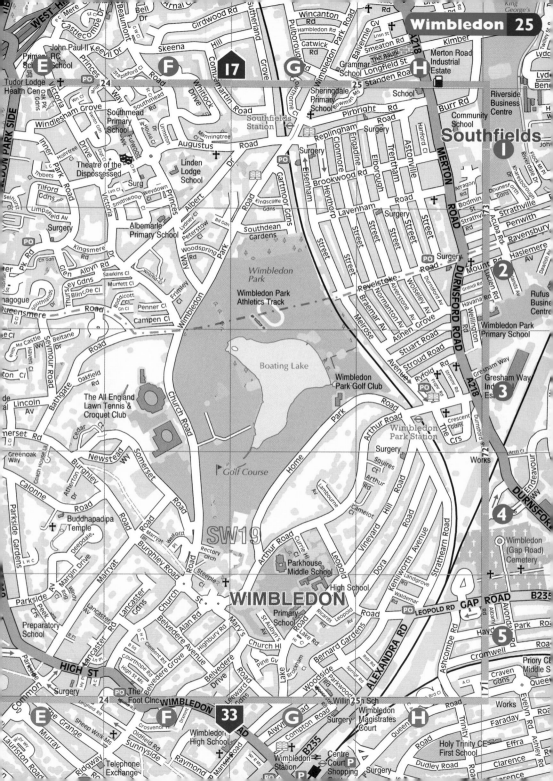

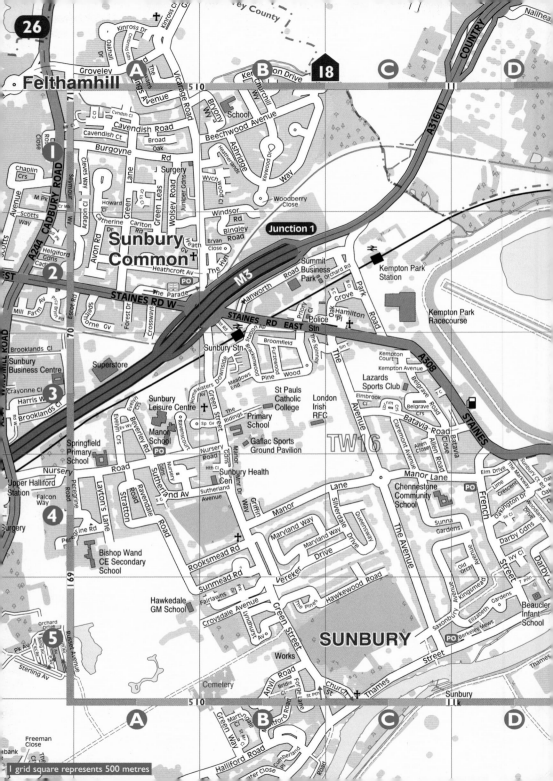

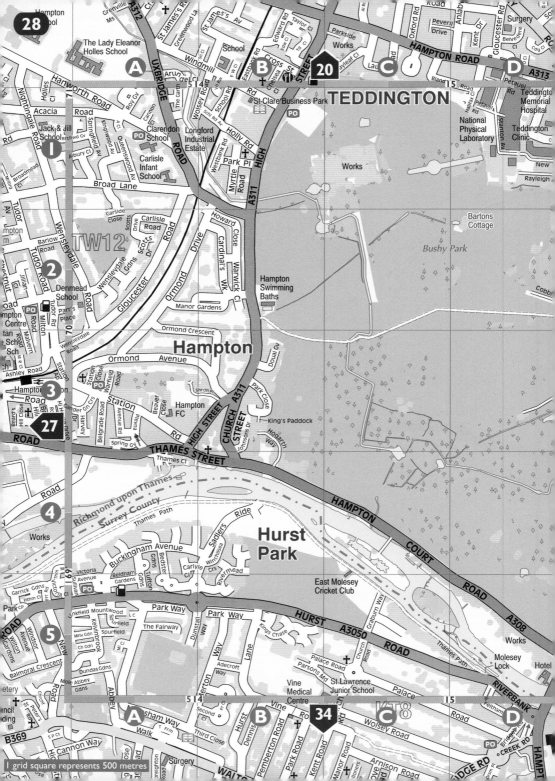

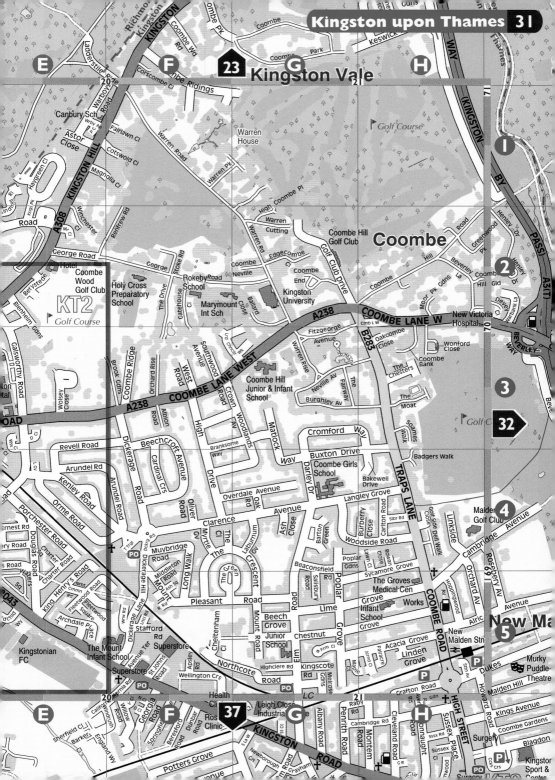

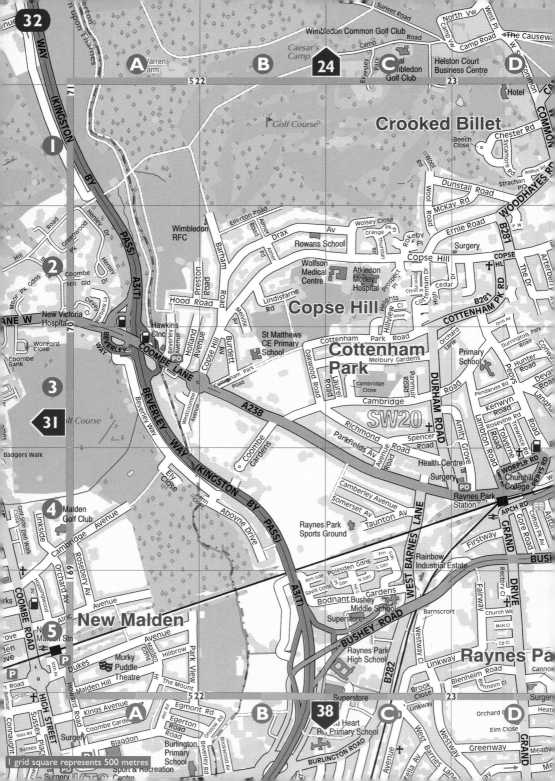

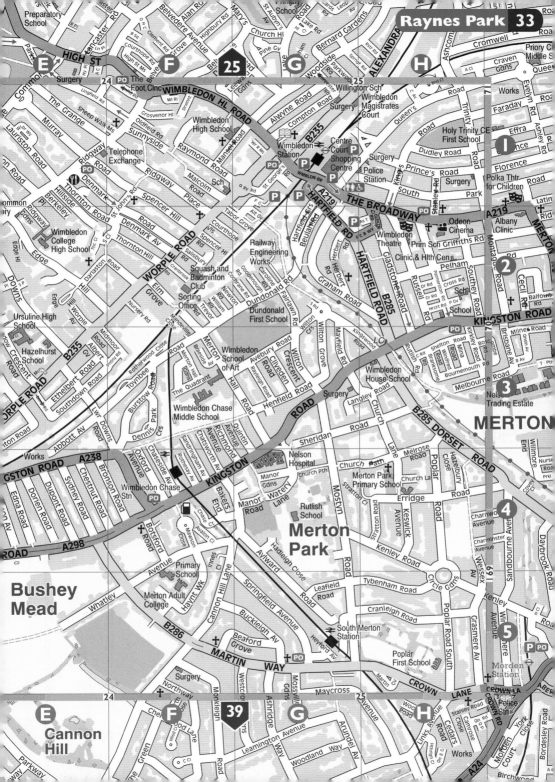

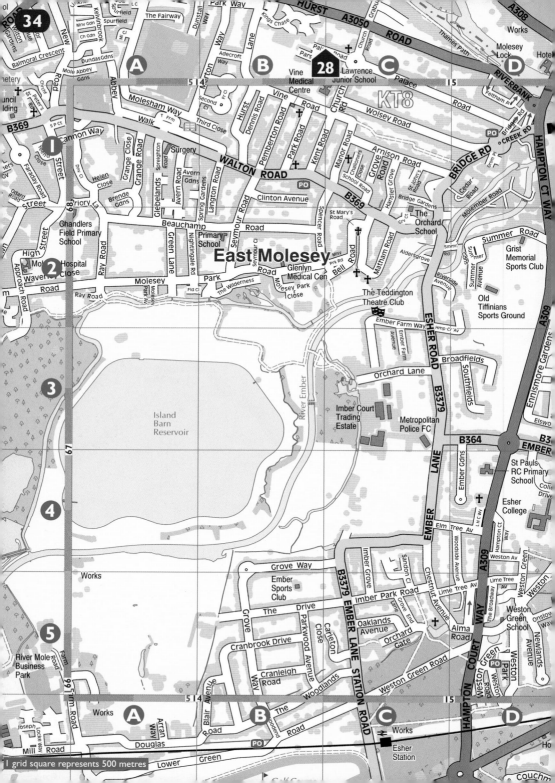

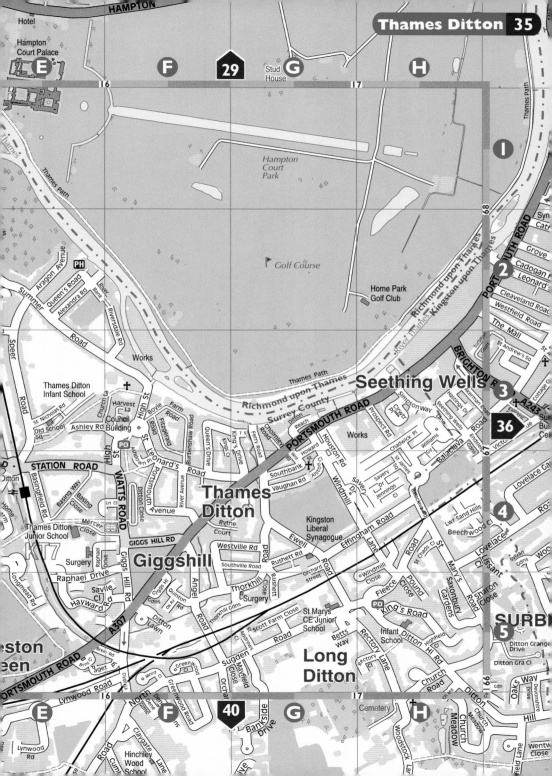

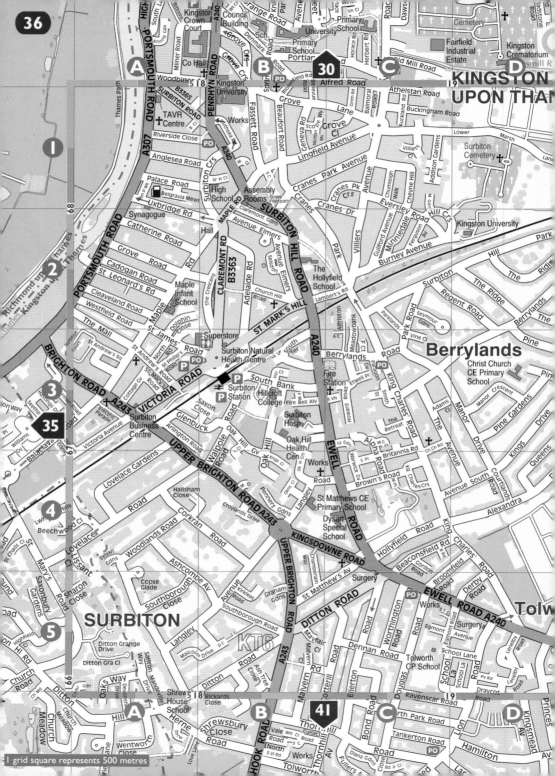

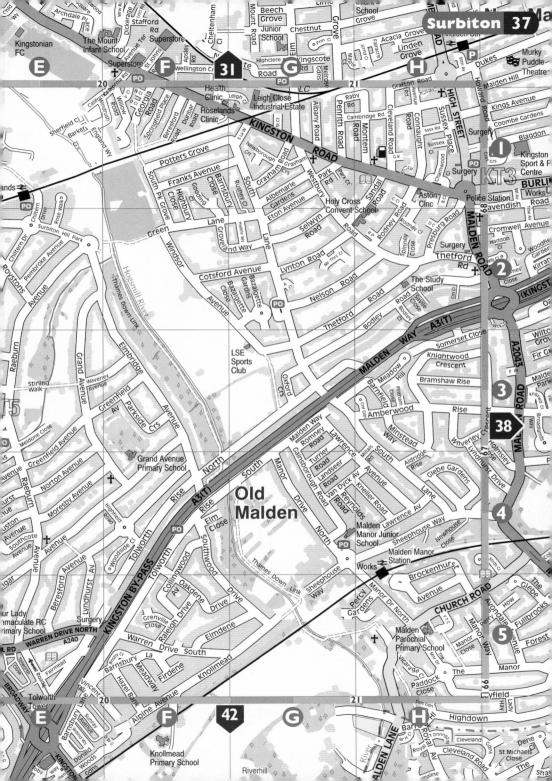

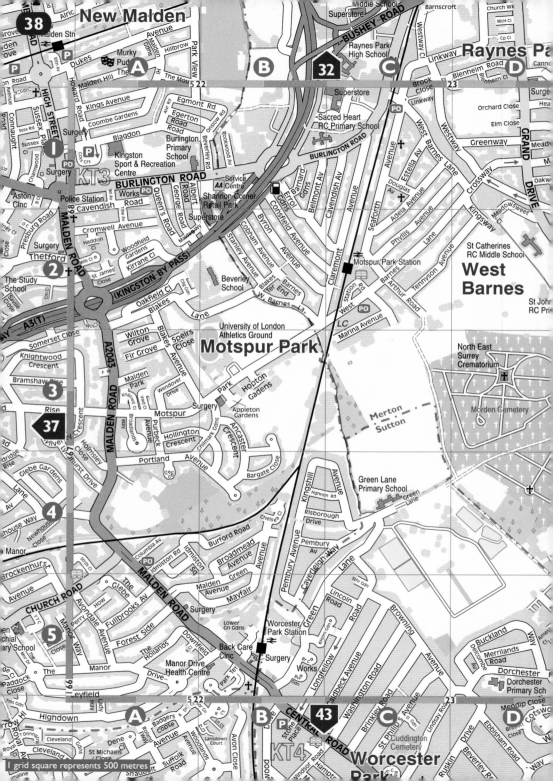

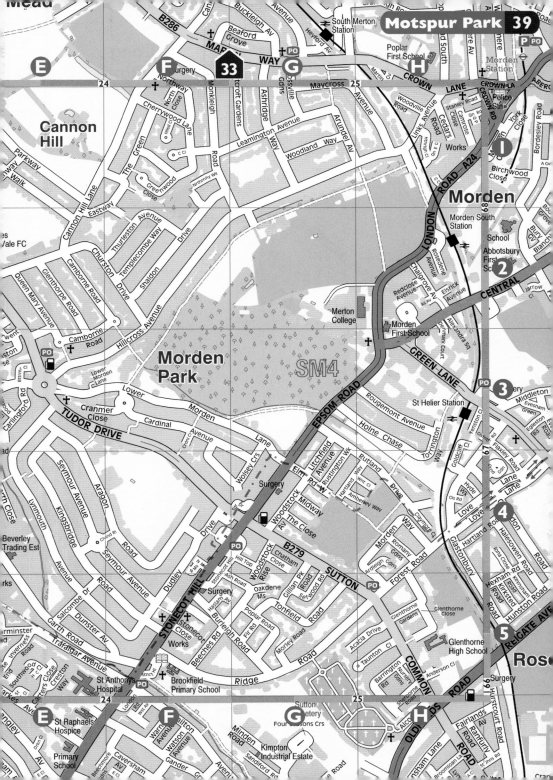

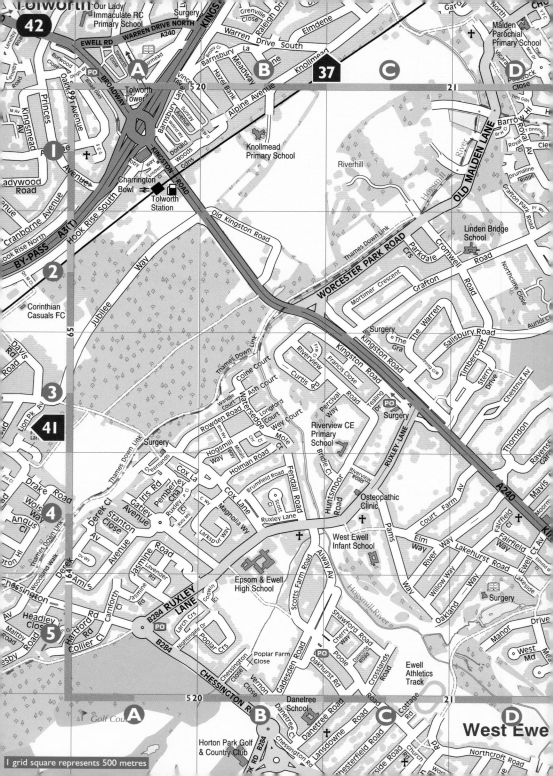

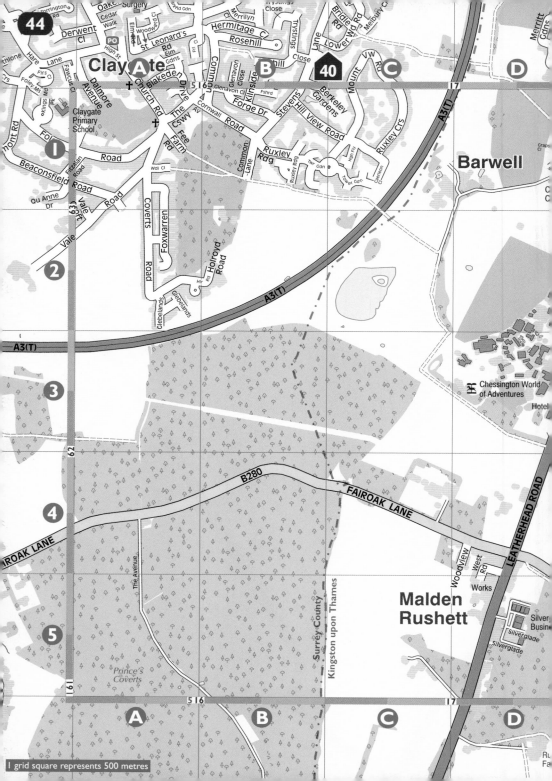

Barnes 9 G4	Hampton 28 A3	Morden Park 39 F3	Southfields 2⁹
Barwell 44 D1	Hampton Hill 20 B4	Mortlake 8 B5	Spring Grove ....
Berrylands 36 C3	Hampton Wick 29 C3	Motspur Park 38 B3	Stoneleigh 4³
Brentford 7 E2	Hanworth 19 E3	New Malden 32 A5	Strawberry Hill 2⁶
Brentford End 6 C2	Heston 4 C3	Norbiton 3 G4	Sunbury 2⁶
Bushey Mead 33 E5	Hinchley Wood 40 A2	North Feltham 10 C3	Sunbury Common 2⁶
Cannon Hill 39 E1	Hook 41 F4	North Hyde 4 B1	Surbiton 3⁶
Chessington 41 F5	Hounslow 4 D5	North Sheen 8 A5	Teddington 2⁶
Claygate 40 A5	Hounslow West 11 E1	Old Malden 37 G4	Thames Ditton 3
Cole Park 13 F4	Hurst Park 28 B4	Osterley 5 F3	Tolworth 3⁶
Coombe 31 H2	Isleworth 13 G1	Petersham 22 B1	Twickenham 2⁶
Copse Hill 32 B2	Kew 7 G3	Putney 17 E3	Wandsworth 1⁷
Cottenham Park 32 C3	Kingston upon Thames 2 B2	Putney Heath 16 D5	West Barnes 3⁴
Crooked Billet 32 C1	Kingston Vale 23 G5	Putney Vale 24 B3	West Hill 1⁷
East Molesey 34 B2	Lampton 5 E4	Raynes Park 32 D5	Weston Green 3⁶
East Sheen 15 G3	Long Ditton 35 G5	Richmond 14 B3	Whitton 1
Feltham 18 C2	Malden Rushett 44 C5	Richmond Hill 14 B4	Wimbledon 2⁹
Giggshill 35 F4	Merton 33 H3	Roehampton 16 A3	Woodlands 1²
Grove Park 8 C4	Merton Park 33 G4	St Margarets 13 H4	Worcester Park 1⁷
Ham 22 A3	Morden 39 H1	Seething Wells 35 G3	

USING THE STREET INDEX

Street names are listed alphabetically. Each street name is followed by its postal town or area locality, the Postcode District, the page number, and the reference to the square in which the name is found.

Standard index entries are shown as follows:

Abbey Wk *E/WMO/HCT* KT8 ....**28** A5

Street names and selected addresses not shown on the map due to scale restrictions are shown in the index with an asterisk:

Abbotts Md *RCHPK/HAM* * TW10 ....**21** H4

GENERAL ABBREVIATIONS

ACC ....ACCESS	E ....EAST	LDG ....LODGE	R ....RIV
ALY ....ALLEY	EMB ....EMBANKMENT	LGT ....LIGHT	RBT ....ROUNDABC
AP ....APPROACH	EMBY ....EMBASSY	LK ....LOCK	RD ....RO
AR ....ARCADE	ESP ....ESPLANADE	LKS ....LAKES	RDG ....RID
ASS ....ASSOCIATION	EST ....ESTATE	LNDG ....LANDING	REP ....REPUB
AV ....AVENUE	EX ....EXCHANGE	LTL ....LITTLE	RES ....RESERV(
BCH ....BEACH	EXPY ....EXPRESSWAY	LWR ....LOWER	RFC ....RUGBY FOOTBALL CL
BLDS ....BUILDINGS	EXT ....EXTENSION	MAG ....MAGISTRATE	RI ....R
BND ....BEND	F/O ....FLYOVER	MAN ....MANSIONS	RP ....RAI
BNK ....BANK	FC ....FOOTBALL CLUB	MD ....MEAD	RW ....RW
BR ....BRIDGE	FK ....FORK	MDW ....MEADOWS	S ....SOU
BRK ....BROOK	FLD ....FIELD	MEM ....MEMORIAL	SCH ....SCHC
BTM ....BOTTOM	FLDS ....FIELDS	MKT ....MARKET	SE ....SOUTH EA
BUS ....BUSINESS	FLS ....FALLS	MKTS ....MARKETS	SER ....SERVICE AR
BVD ....BOULEVARD	FLS ....FLATS	ML ....MALL	SH ....SHC
BY ....BYPASS	FM ....FARM	ML ....MILL	SHOP ....SHOPPI
CATH ....CATHEDRAL	FT ....FORT	MNR ....MANOR	SKWY ....SKYW
CEM ....CEMETERY	FWY ....FREEWAY	MS ....MEWS	SMT ....SUMM
CEN ....CENTRE	FY ....FERRY	MSN ....MISSION	SOC ....SOCIE
CFT ....CROFT	GA ....GATE	MT ....MOUNT	SP ....SP
CH ....CHURCH	GAL ....GALLERY	MTN ....MOUNTAIN	SPR ....SPRI
CHA ....CHASE	GDN ....GARDEN	MTS ....MOUNTAINS	SQ ....SQUA
CHYD ....CHURCHYARD	GDNS ....GARDENS	MUS ....MUSEUM	ST ....STRE
CIR ....CIRCLE	GLD ....GLADE	MWY ....MOTORWAY	STN ....STATI
CIRC ....CIRCUS	GLN ....GLEN	N ....NORTH	STR ....STREA
CL ....CLOSE	GN ....GREEN	NE ....NORTH EAST	STRD ....STRA
CLFS ....CLIFFS	GND ....GROUND	NW ....NORTH WEST	SW ....SOUTH WE
CMP ....CAMP	GRA ....GRANGE	O/P ....OVERPASS	TDG ....TRADI
CNR ....CORNER	GRG ....GARAGE	OFF ....OFFICE	TER ....TERRA
CO ....COUNTY	GT ....GREAT	ORCH ....ORCHARD	THWY ....THROUGHW
COLL ....COLLEGE	GTWY ....GATEWAY	OV ....OVAL	TNL ....TUNN
COM ....COMMON	GV ....GROVE	PAL ....PALACE	TOLL ....TOLL
COMM ....COMMISSION	HGR ....HIGHER	PAS ....PASSAGE	TPK ....TURNP
CON ....CONVENT	HL ....HILL	PAV ....PAVILION	TR ....TRA
COT ....COTTAGE	HLS ....HILLS	PDE ....PARADE	TRL ....TR
COTS ....COTTAGES	HO ....HOUSE	PH ....PUBLIC HOUSE	TWR ....TOW
CP ....CAPE	HOL ....HOLLOW	PK ....PARK	U/P ....UNDERPA
CPS ....COPSE	HOSP ....HOSPITAL	PKWY ....PARKWAY	UNI ....UNIVERSI
CR ....CREEK	HRB ....HARBOUR	PL ....PLACE	UPR ....UPP
CREM ....CREMATORIUM	HTH ....HEATH	PLN ....PLAIN	V ....VA
CRS ....CRESCENT	HTS ....HEIGHTS	PLNS ....PLAINS	VA ....VALL
CSWY ....CAUSEWAY	HVN ....HAVEN	PLZ ....PLAZA	VIAD ....VIADU
CT ....COURT	HWY ....HIGHWAY	POL ....POLICE STATION	VIL VIL
CTRL ....CENTRAL	IMP ....IMPERIAL	PR ....PRINCE	VIS ....VIS
CTS ....COURTS	IN ....INLET	PREC ....PRECINCT	VLG ....VILLA
CTYD ....COURTYARD	IND EST ....INDUSTRIAL ESTATE	PREP ....PREPARATORY	VLS VILL
CUTT ....CUTTINGS	INF ....INFIRMARY	PRIM ....PRIMARY	VW ....VIE
CV ....COVE	INFO ....INFORMATION	PROM ....PROMENADE	W ....WE
CYN ....CANYON	INT ....INTERCHANGE	PRS ....PRINCESS	WD ....WO
DEPT ....DEPARTMENT	IS ....ISLAND	PRT ....PORT	WHF ....WHA
DL ....DALE	JCT ....JUNCTION	PT ....POINT	WK ....WA
DM ....DAM	JTY ....JETTY	PTH ....PATH	WKS ....WAL
DR ....DRIVE	KG ....KING	PZ ....PIAZZA	WLS ....WEI
DRO ....DROVE	KNL ....KNOLL	QD ....QUADRANT	WY ....W
DRY ....DRIVEWAY	L ....LAKE	QU ....QUEEN	YD ....Y
DWGS ....DWELLINGS	LA ....LANE	QY ....QUAY	YHA ....YOUTH HOST

OSTCODE TOWNS AND AREA ABBREVIATIONS

...Barnes	EW..................Ewell	KUT.............Kingston upon Thames
DS................Berrylands	FELT..................Feltham	KUTN/CMB...Kingston upon Thames north/
................Brentford	FUL/PGN.......Fulham/Parsons Green	Coombe
AM................Cheam	HEST..................Heston	LHD/OX............Leatherhead/Oxshott
GTN..............Chessington	HMSMTH..........Hammersmith	MORT/ESHN....Mortlake/East Sheen
WK................Chiswick	HNWL..................Hanwell	MRDN..................Morden
MO/HCT.......East & West Molesey/	HOR/WEW.......Horton/West Ewell	NWDGN............Norwood Green
Hampton Court	HPTN..................Hampton	NWMAL..............New Malden
................Ealing	HSLW..................Hounslow	PUT/ROE.........Putney/Roehampton
/NFELT....East Bedfont/North Feltham	HSLWW..............Hounslow west	RCH/KEW.........Richmond/Kew
M................Epsom	HTHAIR.............Heathrow Airport	RCHPK/HAM....Richmond Park/Ham
CLAY.............Esher/Claygate	ISLW..................Isleworth	RYNPK..............Raynes Park

SUN..................Sunbury	
SURB................Surbiton	
SUT..................Sutton	
TEDD................Teddington	
THDIT..............Thames Ditton	
TWK..................Twickenham	
WAND/EARL......Wandsworth/Earlsfield	
WHTN................Whitton	
WIM/MER.........Wimbledon/Merton	
WOT/HER..........Walton-on-Thames/	
Hersham	
WPK..................Worcester Park	

Index - streets

Abb - Ave

A

The Alders *FELT* TW13 ....**19** F5
  NWDGN UB2 ....**4** C2
Alderwick Dr *HSLW* TW3 ....**12** C1
Aldridge Ri *NWMAL* KT3 ....**37** H4
Alexander Cl *WHTN* TW2 ....**20** D2
Alexandra Dr *BRYLDS* KT5 ....**36** D4
Alexandra Gdns *HSLW* TW3 ....**5** E5
Alexandra Rd *BTFD* * TW8 ....**7** E2
  HSLW TW3 ....**5** E5
  KUTN/CMB KT2 ....**3** C1
  MORT/ESHN SW14 ....**15** C1
  RCH/KEW TW9 ....**7** G5
  THDIT KT7 ....**35** E2
  TWK TW1 ....**13** H4
  WIM/MER SW19 ....**25** H5
Alexandra Sq *MRDN* SM4 ....**39** H2
Alfred Rd *FELT* TW13 ....**18** D2
  KUT KT1 ....**2** D7
Alfreton Cl *WIM/MER* SW19 ....**25** E3
Alfriston *BRYLDS* KT5 ....**36** C3
Alfriston Cl *BRYLDS* KT5 ....**36** C3
Algar Rd *ISLW* TW7 ....**13** F1
Alice Ms *TEDD* TW11 ....**21** E5
Alice Wy *HSLW* TW3 ....**12** A2
Alkerden Rd *CHSWK* W4 ....**8** D1
Allan Cl *NWMAL* KT3 ....**37** G2
Allbrook Cl *TEDD* TW11 ....**20** D5
Allcot Cl *EBED/NFELT* TW14 ....**18** A1
Allen Cl *SUN* TW16 ....**26** C3
Allen Rd *SUN* TW16 ....**26** C3
Alleyn Pk *NWDGN* UB2 ....**4** C1
Allgood Cl *MRDN* SM4 ....**39** E4
Allington Cl *WIM/MER* SW19 ....**25** E5
All Saints Pas
  WAND/EARL * SW18 ....**17** H3
Alma Rd *ESH/CLAY* KT10 ....**34** D5
Almer Rd *RYNPK* SW20 ....**32** B2
Almond Gv *BTFD* TW8 ....**6** C3
Almorah Rd *HEST* TW5 ....**4** A4
Almshouse La *CHSGTN* KT9 ....**44** D2
Alpha Pl *MRDN* * SM4 ....**39** E4
Alpha Rd *BRYLDS* KT5 ....**36** C3
  HPTN TW12 ....**20** C5
Alpine Av *BRYLDS* KT5 ....**42** B1
Alric Av *NWMAL* KT3 ....**31** H5
Alsom Av *HOR/WEW* KT19 ....**43** E3
Alston Cl *THDIT* KT7 ....**35** G4
Alt Gv *WIM/MER* SW19 ....**33** G2
Alton Cl *ISLW* TW7 ....**6** A5
Alton Gdns *WHTN* TW2 ....**12** C5
Alton Rd *PUT/ROE* SW15 ....**24** B1
  RCH/KEW TW9 ....**14** B2
Alverstone Av
  WAND/EARL SW18 ....**25** H2
Alverstone Rd *NWMAL* KT3 ....**38** A1
Alway Av *HOR/WEW* KT19 ....**42** B4
Alwyn Av *CHSWK* W4 ....**8** C1
Alwyne Rd *WIM/MER* SW19 ....**33** G1
Amalgamated Dr *BTFD* TW8 ....**6** B2
Ambassador Cl *HSLW* TW3 ....**4** B5
Amberley Gdns *HOR/WEW* KT19 ....**43** E3
Amberley Wy *HSLWW* TW4 ....**10** D3
  MRDN SM4 ....**39** G4
Amberside Cl *ISLW* TW7 ....**12** C4
Amberwood Ri *NWMAL* KT3 ....**37** H3
Ambleside Dr
  EBED/NFELT TW14 ....**18** A1
Amerland Rd *WAND/EARL* SW18 ....**17** G4
Amesbury Cl *WPK* KT4 ....**38** D5
Amesbury Rd *FELT* TW13 ....**19** E2
Amhurst Gdns *ISLW* TW7 ....**6** A4
Amis Av *HOR/WEW* KT19 ....**41** H5
Amity Gv *RYNPK* SW20 ....**32** D3
Amyand Cottages *TWK* TW1 ....**13** C4
Amyand Park Gdns *TWK* TW1 ....**13** C5
Amyand Park Rd *TWK* TW1 ....**13** F5
Ancaster Crs *NWMAL* KT3 ....**38** B3

Anchorage Cl *WIM/MER* SW19 ....**25** H5
Anderson Cl *CHEAM* SM3 ....**39** H5
Anderson's Pl *HSLW* TW3 ....**12** A2
Andover Cl *EBED/NFELT* TW14 ....**18** A1
Andover Rd *WHTN* TW2 ....**20** C1
Angelfield *HSLW* TW3 ....**12** A3
Angel Rd *THDIT* KT7 ....**35** F5
Anglers Reach *SURB* * KT6 ....**36** A1
Anglesea Rd *KUT* KT1 ....**36** A1
Angus Cl *CHSGTN* KT9 ....**41** H4
Anlaby Rd *TEDD* TW11 ....**20** D5
Anne Boleyn's Wk
  KUTN/CMB KT2 ....**22** B5
Anne Case Ms *NWMAL* * KT3 ....**31** G5
Anstice Cl *CHSWK* W4 ....**8** D3
Anvil Rd *SUN* TW16 ....**26** B5
Aplin Wy *ISLW* TW7 ....**5** H4
Appleby Cl *WHTN* TW2 ....**20** C2
Appleby Gdns
  EBED/NFELT * TW14 ....**18** A2
Applegarth *ESH/CLAY* KT10 ....**40** A1
Apple Gv *CHSGTN* KT9 ....**41** F3
Apple Market *KUT* KT1 ....**2** B5
Appleton Gdns *NWMAL* KT3 ....**38** B3
Approach Rd *RYNPK* SW20 ....**32** D4
April Cl *FELT* TW13 ....**18** B3
Apsley Rd *NWMAL* KT3 ....**31** F5
Aquarius *TWK* * TW1 ....**21** G1
Arabella Dr *PUT/ROE* SW15 ....**15** H2
Aragon Av *THDIT* KT7 ....**35** E2
Aragon Cl *SUN* TW16 ....**26** A2
Aragon Rd *KUTN/CMB* KT2 ....**22** B5
  MRDN SM4 ....**39** E4
Arcade Pde *CHSGTN* * KT9 ....**41** F3
Archdale Pl *NWMAL* KT3 ....**3** K6
Archer Cl *KUTN/CMB* KT2 ....**30** B2
Archway St *BARN* SW13 ....**15** H1
Ardleigh Gdns *CHEAM* SM3 ....**39** G5
Ardmay Gdns *SURB* * KT6 ....**36** B2
Ardrossan Gdns *WPK* KT4 ....**43** E1
Ardshiel Cl *PUT/ROE* SW15 ....**17** E1
Argent Cl *SURB* * KT6 ....**41** H1
Argyle Av *HSLW* TW3 ....**11** H4
Argyle Rd *HSLW* TW3 ....**12** A3
Ariel Wy *HSLWW* TW4 ....**10** C1
Arlington Cl *TWK* * TW1 ....**13** H4
Arlington Gdns *CHSWK* W4 ....**8** B1
Arlington Rd
  RCHPK/HAM TW10 ....**26** A3
  SURB KT6 ....**36** A3
  TEDD TW11 ....**21** E4
  TWK TW1 ....**13** H4
Armadale Rd *EBED/NFELT* TW14 ....**10** B3
Armoury Wy *WAND/EARL* SW18 ....**17** H3
Armstrong Rd *FELT* TW13 ....**19** F5
Armytage Rd *HEST* TW5 ....**4** A3
Arnal Crs *WAND/EARL* SW18 ....**17** F5
Arnewood Cl *PUT/ROE* SW15 ....**24** B1
Arnison Rd *E/WMO/HCT* KT8 ....**34** C1
Arnold Crs *ISLW* TW7 ....**12** C3
Arnold Dr *CHSGTN* KT9 ....**41** E5
Arosa Rd *TWK* TW1 ....**14** C5
Arragon Rd *TWK* TW1 ....**13** F5
  WAND/EARL SW18 ....**25** G4
Arterberry Rd *RYNPK* SW20 ....**32** D2
Arthur Rd *KUTN/CMB* KT2 ....**3** G1
  NWMAL KT3 ....**38** C2
  WIM/MER SW19 ....**25** G4
Arundel Av *MRDN* SM4 ....**39** H3
Arundel Cl *HPTN* TW12 ....**20** A5
Arundel Rd *HSLWW* TW4 ....**10** C3
  KUT KT1 ....**3** K4
Arundel Ter *BARN* SW13 ....**9** H4
Ashbourne Gv *CHSWK* W4 ....**8** C1
Ashbourne Ter *WIM/MER* SW19 ....**33** H2
Ashburnham Rd
  RCHPK/HAM TW10 ....**21** G3
Ashby Av *CHSGTN* KT9 ....**41** H5

Ash Cl *NWMAL* KT3 ....**31** G4
Ashcombe Av *SURB* KT6 ....**36** A4
Ashcombe Rd *WIM/MER* SW19 ....**25** H5
Ashcombe Sq *NWMAL* KT3 ....**31** F5
Ash Ct *HOR/WEW* KT19 ....**42** B3
Ashcroft Rd *CHSGTN* KT9 ....**41** G2
Ashdale Cl *WHTN* TW2 ....**12** A5
Ashdown Pl *THDIT* KT7 ....**35** F3
Ashdown Rd *KUT* KT1 ....**2** C5
Ashen Gv *WIM/MER* SW19 ....**25** H3
Ashfield Av *FELT* TW13 ....**18** C1
Ashfield Cl *RCHPK/HAM* TW10 ....**22** B1
Ashford Rd *FELT* TW13 ....**18** A3
Ash Gv *HEST* TW5 ....**4** A4
Ashleigh Rd *MORT/ESHN* SW14 ....**15** H1
Ashley Av *MRDN* SM4 ....**39** H2
Ashley Dr *ISLW* TW7 ....**5** H2
  WHTN TW2 ....**20** A1
Ashley Gdns *RCHPK/HAM* TW10 ....**22** A3
Ashley Rd *HPTN* TW12 ....**27** H3
  RCH/KEW TW9 ....**14** B1
  THDIT KT7 ....**35** E3
Ashlone Rd *PUT/ROE* SW15 ....**16** D1
Ashlyns Wy *CHSGTN* KT9 ....**41** E5
Ashmead Rd *EBED/NFELT* TW14 ....**18** B1
Ashridge Wy *MRDN* SM4 ....**39** G1
  SUN TW16 ....**26** B1
Ash Rd *MRDN* SM4 ....**39** F5
Ashton Gdns *HSLWW* TW4 ....**11** G2
Ash Tree Cl *SURB* KT6 ....**36** B5
Askill Dr *PUT/ROE* SW15 ....**17** F3
Aspen Wy *FELT* TW13 ....**18** C3
Aston Rd *RYNPK* SW20 ....**32** D4
Astonville St *WAND/EARL* SW18 ....**25** H1
Astor Cl *KUTN/CMB* KT2 ....**31** E1
Atbara Rd *TEDD* TW11 ....**29** G1
Atcham Rd *HSLW* TW3 ....**12** B2
Athelstan Rd *KUT* KT1 ....**36** C1
Athena Cl *KUT* KT1 ....**2** E7
Atherley Wy *HSLWW* TW4 ....**11** G5
Atherton Dr *WIM/MER* SW19 ....**25** E4
Atherton Rd *BARN* SW13 ....**9** F3
Atney Rd *PUT/ROE* SW15 ....**17** F2
Atwood Av *RCH/KEW* TW9 ....**7** H5
Aubyn Sq *PUT/ROE* SW15 ....**16** B2
Auckland Rd *KUT* KT1 ....**36** C1
Auden Pl *CHEAM* * SM3 ....**43** H5
Audley Rd *RCHPK/HAM* TW10 ....**14** C3
Audric Cl *KUTN/CMB* KT2 ....**3** G2
Augusta Cl *E/WMO/HCT* KT8 ....**27** G5
Augusta Rd *WHTN* TW2 ....**20** B2
Augustus Cl *BTFD* TW8 ....**7** E3
Augustus Rd *WIM/MER* SW19 ....**25** F1
Auriol Cl *HOR/WEW* KT19 ....**42** D2
Auriol Park Rd *WPK* KT4 ....**42** D2
Austyn Gdns *BRYLDS* * KT5 ....**37** E5
Avalon Cl *RYNPK* SW20 ....**33** F4
Avebury Pk *SURB* * KT6 ....**36** A3
Avebury Rd *WIM/MER* SW19 ....**33** G3
Avening Rd *WAND/EARL* SW18 ....**17** H5
Avening Ter *WAND/EARL* SW18 ....**17** H4
The Avenue *BRYLDS* KT5 ....**36** C3
  HPTN TW12 ....**27** G1
  HSLW TW3 ....**12** A3
  LHD/OX KT22 ....**44** A5
  RCH/KEW TW9 ....**7** G5
  SUN TW16 ....**26** C3
  TWK TW1 ....**13** G4
  WPK KT4 ....**43** E1
Avenue Elmers *SURB* KT6 ....**36** B2
Avenue Gdns
  MORT/ESHN SW14 ....**15** H1
  TEDD TW11 ....**29** E2
Avenue Pde *SUN* * TW16 ....**26** C3
Avenue Rd *BTFD* TW8 ....**6** D1
  FELT TW13 ....**18** A3
  HPTN TW12 ....**28** A3
  ISLW TW7 ....**5** H4

ey Wk *E/WMO/HCT* KT8 ....**28** A5
ots Av *HOR/WEW* KT19 ....**45** H4
otsmede Cl *TWK* TW1 ....**21** E2
otstone Rd *PUT/ROE* SW15 ....**16** D1
ott Av *RYNPK* SW20 ....**33** E4
ott Cl *HPTN* TW12 ....**27** F1
otts Md *RCHPK/HAM* * TW10 ....**21** H4
ger Gdns *ISLW* TW7 ....**12** D1
yne Dr *RYNPK* SW20 ....**32** B4
cia Av *BTFD* TW8 ....**6** C3
cia Dr *CHEAM* SM3 ....**39** G5
cia Gv *NWMAL* KT3 ....**31** H5
cia Rd *HPTN* TW12 ....**27** H1
Pde *CHSGTN* * KT9 ....**41** F2
rn Cl *HPTN* TW12 ....**28** A1
n Cl *KUTN/CMB* KT2 ....**2** E1
ms Cl *BRYLDS* KT5 ....**36** C3
ms Wk *KUT* KT1 ....**2** C4
m Wk *FUL/PGN* * SW6 ....**9** H3
son Av *HSLW* TW3 ....**5** F4
son Gdns *BRYLDS* KT5 ....**36** C1
son Rd *TEDD* TW11 ....**29** G1
croft Wy *E/WMO/HCT* KT8 ....**28** B5
a Av *NWMAL* KT3 ....**38** C2
aide Rd *HEST* TW5 ....**4** B4
CH/KEW* TW9 ....**14** C2
RB* KT6 ....**36** B2
DD* TW11 ....**29** E1
AND/EARL* SW18 ....**17** H3
aide Ter *BTFD* * TW8 ....**7** E1
airalty Rd *TEDD* TW11 ....**29** E1
r Cl *SURB* KT6 ....**41** G1
a Av *TWK* TW1 ....**13** F3
a Rd *TWK* TW1 ....**13** G3
dale Av *CHSWK* W4 ....**9** E1
nan Dr *CHSWK* * W4 ....**7** H1
hurst St *PUT/ROE* SW15 ....**16** B4
rman Rd *SURB* KT6 ....**35** H3
 Rd *WIM/MER* SW19 ....**25** F5
ny Cl *MORT/ESHN* SW14 ....**15** C2
ny Ms *KUTN/CMB* * KT2 ....**30** A1
ny Park Rd *KUTN/CMB* KT2 ....**30** A1
ny Pl *BTFD* * TW8 ....**7** E2
ny Rd *BTFD* TW8 ....**7** E2
WMAL* KT3 ....**37** G1
ny Ter *RCHPK/HAM* * TW10 ....**14** C3
HPK/HAM* * TW10 ....**14** C3
TW1 ....**21** E1
on Rd *HSLW* TW3 ....**11** H2
TN/CMB* KT2 ....**31** F3
HTN* TW2 ....**20** D1
ry Av *ISLW* TW7 ....**6** A3
ry Cl *HPTN* TW12 ....**27** H1
ry Rd *CHSGTN* KT9 ....**41** F4
ck Rd *HEST* TW5 ....**4** A3
rbury Rd *BARN* SW13 ....**9** F2
rman Judge Ml *KUT* KT1 ....**2** C5
rney Av *HEST* TW5 ....**5** E3
r Rd *MORT/ESHN* SW14 ....**15** G1
rsbrook Dr *KUTN/CMB* KT2 ....**30** C1
rsgrove *E/WMO/HCT* KT8 ....**34** C2

KUT KT1 ....2 D6
NWMAL KT3 ....31 H5
RYNPK SW20 ....32 C4
TEDD TW11 ....29 F2
Avenue South *BRYLDS* TW6 ......36 C4
Avenue Ter *NWMAL* KT3 ....31 H5

Avern Gdns *E/WMO/HCT* TW8 ....34 A1
Avern Rd *E/WMO/HCT* TW8 ....34 A1
Avon Cl *WPK* KT4 ....43 F1
Avondale Av *ESH/CLAY* KT10 ....40 B2
WPK KT4 ....38 A5
Avondale Gdns *HSLWW* TW4 .....11 G3
Avondale Rd *MORT/ESHN* SW14 ...15 C1
Avon Rd *SUN* TW16 ....29 H4
Avonwick Rd *HSLW* TW3 ....5 E5
Aycliff Ct *KUT* KT1 ....3 C4
Aylett Rd *ISLW* TW7 ....5 H5
Ayliffe Cl *KUT* KT1 ....3 C4
Aylward Rd *RYNPK* SW20 ....33 G4

B

Babbacombe Cl *CHSGTN* KT9 .....41 E4
Baber Bridge Pde
EBED/NFELT * TW14 ....10 D4
Baber Dr *EBED/NFELT* TW14 ....10 D4
Back La *BTFD* TW8 ....7 E3
RCHPK/HAM TW10 ....21 H2
Back Rd *TEDD* TW11 ....28 D2
Baden Powell Cl *SURB* KT6 ......41 G1
Badger Cl *FELT* TW13 ....18 C3
HSLWW TW4 ....10 D1
Badgers Copse *WPK* KT4 ....43 E1
Badgers Ct *WPK* * KT4 ....43 E1
Badgers Wk *NWMAL* KT3 ....31 H4
Bainbridge Cl *KUTN/CMB* KT2 ...22 B5
Bakers End *RYNPK* SW20 ....33 F4
Bakewell Dr *NWMAL* KT3 ....31 H4
Balaclava Rd *SURB* KT6 ....35 H4
Baldwin Gdns *HSLW* TW3 ....5 F4
Balfern Gv *CHSWK* W4 ....8 D1
Balfour Rd *HSLW* TW3 ....12 A1
Balgowan Cl *NWMAL* KT3 ....37 H1
Ballard Cl *KUTN/CMB* KT2 ....31 G2
Balmoral Cl *PUT/ROE* * SW15 ....17 E4
Balmoral Crs *E/WMO/HCT* KT8 ...27 H5
Balmoral Rd *KUT* KT1 ....36 C1
WPK KT4 ....43 G2
Balmuir Gdns *PUT/ROE* SW15 ....16 D2
Balvernie Gv *WAND/EARL* SW18 ...17 C5
Bangalore St *PUT/ROE* SW15 ....16 F1
Bank La *KUTN/CMB* KT2 ....30 B2
PUT/ROE SW15 ....15 H3
Bankside Cl *ISLW* TW7 ....13 E2
Bankside Dr *THDIT* KT7 ....40 C1
Bank Willow *RCHPK/HAM* TW10 ...21 G3
Bardolph Rd *RCH/KEW* TW9 ......14 C2
Bargate Cl *NWMAL* KT3 ....38 B4
Barge Wk *KUT* KT1 ....2 A5
Barham Rd *RYNPK* SW20 ....32 B2
Barker Cl *KUT* KT1 ....37 E1
Barley Mow Pas *CHSWK* W4 ....8 C1
Barlow Rd *HPTN* TW12 ....27 H2
Barnard Cl *SUN* TW16 ....26 C2
Barnard Gdns *NWMAL* KT3 ....38 B1
Barnes Av *BARN* SW13 ....9 F3
Barnes Br *CHSWK* W4 ....8 D5
Barnes End *NWMAL* KT3 ....38 B2
Barnes High St *BARN* SW13 ......9 E5
Barnfield *NWMAL* KT3 ....37 H3
Barnfield Av *KUTN/CMB* KT2 ....22 A4
Barnfield Gdns *KUTN/CMB* KT2 ...22 B5
Barnlea Cl *FELT* TW13 ....19 F2
Barnsbury Cl *NWMAL* KT3 ....37 F1
Barnsbury Crs *BRYLDS* KT5 ......37 F1
Barnsbury La *BRYLDS* KT5 ....42 A1
Barnscroft *RYNPK* SW20 ....32 C5
Baronsfield Rd *TWK* * TW1 .....13 G4
Baronsmead Rd *BARN* SW13 ......9 F4
The Barons *TWK* TW1 ....13 G4
Barrack Rd *HSLWW* TW4 ....11 E2
Barrington Rd *CHEAM* SM3 ....H5
Barrowgate Rd *CHSWK* W4 ....8 B1
Barrow Hl *WPK* KT4 ....42 D1
Barrow Hill Cl *WPK* KT4 ....42 D1
Barton Gn *NWMAL* KT3 ....37 H2
Barwell Ct *CHSGTN* * KT9 ....44 D1
Basden Gv *FELT* TW13 ....19 H2
Basildene Rd *HSLWW* TW4 ....11 E4
Basing Cl *THDIT* KT7 ....35 E4
Basingfield Rd *THDIT* KT7 ......35 E4
Basing Wy *THDIT* KT7 ....35 E4
Bassett Gdns *ISLW* TW7 ....5 F3
Batavia Cl *SUN* TW16 ....26 C3
Batavia Rd *SUN* TW16 ....26 C3

Bathgate Rd *WIM/MER* SW19 ....25 E3
Bath Pas *KUT* KT1 ....2 B5
Bath Rd *HEST* TW5 ....4 A5
The Baulk *WAND/EARL* SW18 ....17 H5
Bayleaf Cl *HPTN* TW12 ....20 C5
Bazalgette Cl *NWMAL* KT3 ......37 F2
Bazalgette Gdns *NWMAL* KT3 ....37 G2
Beach Gv *FELT* TW13 ....19 H3
Beaconsfield Cl *CHSWK* W4 ....8 D1
Beaconsfield Rd *BRYLDS* KT5 ....36 C4
NWMAL KT3 ....31 G4
TWK TW1 ....13 G5
Beaford Gv *RYNPK* SW20 ....33 F5
Beagle Cl *FELT* TW13 ....18 C4
Beard Rd *RCHPK/HAM* TW10 .....22 C5
Beard's Hl *HPTN* TW12 ....27 H5
Beards Hill Cl *HPTN* TW12 ......27 H3
Bearfield Rd *KUTN/CMB* KT2 .....2 C1
Bear Rd *FELT* TW13 ....19 E4
Beatrice Rd *RCHPK/HAM* TW10 ...14 C3
Beattie Cl *EBED/NFELT* TW14 ...18 A1
Beauchamp Rd
E/WMO/HCT KT8 ....34 A2
TWK TW1 ....13 F5
Beauchamp Ter *PUT/ROE* SW15 ...16 C1
Beauclerk Cl *FELT* TW13 ....18 C1
Beaufort Cl *PUT/ROE* SW15 .....24 D1
Beaufort Gdns *HEST* TW5 ....4 B4
Beaufort Rd *KUT* KT1 ....36 B1
RCHPK/HAM TW10 ....21 H4
TWK TW1 ....13 H5
Beaulieu Cl *HSLWW* TW4 ....11 G3
TWK TW1 ....14 A4
Beaumont Av *RCH/KEW* TW9 .....14 C2
Beaumont Cl *KUTN/CMB* KT2 ......3 H1
Beaumont Pl *ISLW* TW7 ....13 E3
Beaumont Rd *WIM/MER* SW19 ....17 F5
Beaver Cl *HPTN* TW12 ....28 A3
Beavers Crs *HSLWW* TW4 ....11 E2
Beavers La *HSLWW* TW4 ....10 C4
Becketts Cl *EBED/NFELT* TW14 ...10 D1
Becketts Pl *KUT* KT1 ....2 C3
Bective Rd *PUT/ROE* SW15 ......17 G2
Bedfont La *EBED/NFELT* TW14 ...18 B1
Bedfont Rd *FELT* TW13 ....18 A3
Bedford Cl *CHSWK* W4 ....8 D2
Bedford Rd *WHTN* TW2 ....20 C3
WPK KT4 ....43 H1
Bedford Vls *KUT* * KT1 ....3 F5
Bedgebury Gdns
WIM/MER SW19 ....25 F2
Bedster Gdns *E/WMO/HCT* KT8 ...28 A4
Beech Av *BTFD* TW8 ....6 C3
Beech Cl *PUT/ROE* SW15 ....16 B5
RYNPK SW20 ....32 D5
SUN TW16 ....27 E4
Beechcroft Av *NWMAL* KT3 ......31 H5
Beechcroft Cl *HEST* TW5 ....4 B3
Beechcroft Rd *CHSGTN* KT9 ....41 G5
MORT/ESHN * SW14 ....15 F1
Beechen Cliff Wy *ISLW* TW7 .....6 A4
Beeches Rd *CHEAM* SM3 ....39 F5
Beeches Av *NWMAL* KT3 ....31 G5
Beechrow *KUTN/CMB* KT2 ....22 B4
Beech Wy *FELT* * TW13 ....19 H3
Beechwood Av *RCH/KEW* TW9 .....7 H4
SUN TW16 ....26 B1
Beechwood Cl *SURB* KT6 ....35 H4
Beeston Wy *EBED/NFELT* TW14 ...10 D4
Begonia Pl *HPTN* TW12 ....27 H1
Beldham Gdns *E/WMO/HCT* KT8 ...28 A5
Belgrade Rd *HPTN* TW12 ....28 A3
Belgrave Crs *SUN* TW16 ....26 C3
Belgrave Rd *BARN* SW13 ....9 E3
HSLWW TW4 ....11 G1
SUN TW16 ....26 C3
Belgravia Ms *KUT* KT1 ....36 A1
Bel La *FELT* TW13 ....19 F3
Bell Dr *WAND/EARL* SW18 ....17 F5
Bellevue Rd *BARN* SW13 ....9 F5
KUT KT1 ....2 D7
Bell La *TWK* TW1 ....21 F1
Bell Pde *HSLW* * TW3 ....12 A2
Bell Rd *E/WMO/HCT* KT8 ....34 C2
HSLW TW3 ....12 A1
Belmont Av *NWMAL* KT3 ....38 B2
Belmont Rd *WHTN* TW2 ....20 C2
Beloe Cl *BARN* SW13 ....16 B2
Beltane Dr *WIM/MER* SW19 .....24 C3
Belvedere Av *WIM/MER* SW19 ...25 E3
Belvedere Cl *TEDD* TW11 ....20 D5
Belvedere Dr *WIM/MER* SW19 ...25 F5
Belvedere Gv *WIM/MER* SW19 ...25 E5
Belvedere Rd *WIM/MER* SW19 ...25 E5
Belvedere Sq *WIM/MER* SW19 ...25 E5
Bemish Rd *PUT/ROE* SW15 ......17 E1
The Bench *RCHPK/HAM* * TW10 ...21 H3
Bendemeer Rd *PUT/ROE* SW15 ...17 E1
Benham Cl *CHSGTN* KT9 ....40 D5

Benham Gdns *HSLWW* TW4 ....11 G3
Bennet Cl *KUT* KT1 ....29 H3
Bennett St *CHSWK* W4 ....8 D2
Bensbury Cl *PUT/ROE* SW15 ....16 C5
Benson Cl *HSLW* TW3 ....11 H2
Benwell Ct *SUN* * TW16 ....26 B3
Beresford Av *BRYLDS* KT5 ......37 E5
TWK TW1 ....13 H4
Beresford Gdns *HSLWW* TW4 ....11 G3
Beresford Rd *KUTN/CMB* KT2 .....2 E2
NWMAL KT3 ....37 F1
Berestede Rd *HMSMTH* W6 ....9 E1
Berkeley Cl *KUTN/CMB* KT2 .....30 B2
Berkeley Dr *E/WMO/HCT* KT8 ....27 C5
Berkeley Gdns *ESH/CLAY* KT10 ...44 B1
Berkeley Ms *SUN* TW16 ....26 D5
Berkeley Pl *WIM/MER* SW19 ....33 E1
Berkeley Waye *HEST* TW5 ....4 B3
Berkley Cl *WHTN* * TW2 ....20 D3
Bernard Gdns *WIM/MER* SW19 ...25 C5
Berrylands *BRYLDS* KT5 ....36 D2
RYNPK SW20 ....32 D5
Berrylands Rd *BRYLDS* KT5 .....36 C3
Bertram Rd *KUTN/CMB* KT2 .....30 D2
Berwyn Av *HSLW* TW3 ....5 E4
Berwyn Rd *RCHPK/HAM* TW10 ...15 E2
Berystede *KUTN/CMB* KT2 ....3 J1
Bessant Dr *RCH/KEW* TW9 ....8 A4
Bessborough Rd
PUT/ROE SW15 ....24 B1
Betts Wy *THDIT* KT7 ....35 G5
Beulah Rd *WIM/MER* SW19 ......33 G2
Beverley Av *HSLWW* TW4 ....11 G2
RYNPK SW20 ....32 A3
Beverley Cl *BARN* SW13 ....9 F5
CHSGTN KT9 ....40 D3
Beverley Gdns *BARN* SW13 ......16 A1
WPK KT4 ....38 B5
Beverley La *KUTN/CMB* KT2 .....31 H2
Beverley Rd *BARN* SW13 ....16 A1
CHSWK W4 ....9 E1
KUT KT1 ....29 H3
NWMAL KT3 ....38 B1
SUN TW16 ....26 A3
WPK KT4 ....43 H1
Beverley Wy *NWMAL* KT3 ....32 A3
Beverley Wy (Kingston By-Pass)
NWMAL KT3 ....32 A3
Bexhill Cl *FELT* TW13 ....19 F2
Bexhill Rd *MORT/ESHN* SW14 ...15 F1
Bicester Rd *RCH/KEW* TW9 .....14 D1
Bideford Cl *FELT* TW13 ....19 G3
Bigg's Rw *PUT/ROE* SW15 ......17 E1
Billockby Cl *CHSGTN* KT9 .....41 G5
Bingley Rd *SUN* TW16 ....26 B2
Binns Rd *CHSWK* W4 ....8 D1
Birch Cl *BTFD* TW8 ....6 C1
HSLW TW3 ....12 C1
TEDD TW11 ....21 F5
The Birches *HSLWW* * TW4 .....11 G5
Birchington Rd *BRYLDS* KT5 ....36 C4
Birch Rd *FELT* TW13 ....19 E5
Birchwood Gv *HPTN* TW12 ......27 H1
Bird Wk *WHTN* TW2 ....19 C1
Birdwood Cl *TEDD* TW11 ....20 D4
Birkenhead Av *KUTN/CMB* KT2 ...2 E4
Biscoe Cl *HEST* TW5 ....4 D2
Bishop Cl *RCHPK/HAM* TW10 ....22 A3
Bishops Cl *CHSWK* W4 ....8 B1
Bishops Gv *HPTN* TW12 ....19 G4
Bishop's Hall *KUT* KT1 ....2 B4
Bisley Cl *WPK* KT4 ....38 D5
Bittoms Ct *KUT* * KT1 ....2 B6
The Bittoms *KUT* KT1 ....2 B6
Blackberry Farm Cl *HEST* TW5 ...4 B3
Blackett St *PUT/ROE* SW15 .....17 E1
Blackmore's Gv *TEDD* TW11 .....29 F1
Black's Rd *HMSMTH* W6 ....9 H1
Blackthorn Ct *HEST* TW5 ....4 B3
Blagdon Rd *NWMAL* KT3 ....38 A1
Blagdon Wk *TEDD* TW11 ....29 H1
Blakeden Dr *ESH/CLAY* KT10 ....44 A1
Blakes Av *NWMAL* KT3 ....38 A2
Blakes La *NWMAL* KT3 ....38 A2
Blakes Ter *NWMAL* KT3 ....38 B2
Blakewood Cl *FELT* TW13 ....18 D4
Blandford Av *WHTN* TW2 ....20 A1
Blandford Rd *TEDD* TW11 ....20 C5
Blenheim Cl *RYNPK* SW20 ......32 D5
Blenheim Gdns *KUTN/CMB* KT2 ...3 J1
Blenheim Rd *RYNPK* SW20 ......32 D5
Blenheim Wy *ISLW* TW7 ....6 B4
Blincoe Cl *WIM/MER* SW19 .....25 E2
Bloomfield Rd *KUT* KT1 ....36 B1
Blossom Waye *HEST* TW5 ....4 B3
Bloxham Crs *HPTN* TW12 ....27 G3
Bluefield Cl *HPTN* TW12 ....19 H5

Blyth Cl *TWK* TW1 1
Bockhampton Rd
KUTN/CMB KT2 3
Boddicott Cl *WIM/MER* SW19 2
Bodley Cl *NWMAL* KT3 3
Bodley Rd *NWMAL* KT3 3
Bodmin St *WAND/EARL* SW18 2
Bodnant Gdns *RYNPK* SW20 3
Boileau Rd *BARN* SW13 ....
Boleyn Dr *E/WMO/HCT* KT8 2
Bolton Cl *CHSGTN* KT9 4
Bolton Gdns *TEDD* TW11 4
Bolton Rd *CHSGTN* KT9 4
CHSWK W4 ....
Bond Rd *SURB* KT6 4
Bonner Hill Rd *KUT* KT1 ....
Bonser Rd *TWK* TW1 ....
Bordon Wk *PUT/ROE* SW15 1
Borland Rd *TEDD* TW11 1
Borneo St *PUT/ROE* SW15 1
Borough Rd *ISLW* TW7 ....
KUTN/CMB KT2 ....
Boscombe Rd *WIM/MER* SW19 3
WPK KT4 ....
Boston Gdns *CHSWK* W4 ....
Boston Park Rd *BTFD* TW8 ......
Botsford Rd *RYNPK* SW20 3
Boucher Cl *TEDD* TW11 2
Boundaries Rd *FELT* TW13 1
Boundary Cl *KUT* KT1 ....
NWDGN UB2 ....
Bournemouth Rd
WIM/MER SW19 3
Bourne Wy *HOR/WEW* KT19 4
Bowfell Rd *HMSMTH* W6 ....
Bowling Green Cl
PUT/ROE SW15 1
Bowman Ms *WAND/EARL* SW18 ...2
Bowness Crs *PUT/ROE* SW15 2
Bowness Dr *HSLWW* TW4 ....
Bowsley Ct *FELT* TW13 ....
Boyd Cl *KUTN/CMB* KT2 ....
Boyle Farm Rd *THDIT* KT7 ......
Bracken Cl *HSLWW* TW4 1
SUN * TW16 ....
Brackendale Cl *HEST* TW5 ......
Bracken End *ISLW* TW7 1
Bracken Gdns *BARN* SW13 ......
Brackenwood *SUN* TW16 1
Brackley Ter *CHSWK* W4 ....
Braddock Cl *ISLW* TW7 1
Braddon Rd *RCH/KEW* TW9 1
Bradford Dr *HOR/WEW* KT19 4
Bradshaw Cl *WIM/MER* SW19 3
Bradstock Rd *EW* KT17 ....
Braemar Av *WIM/MER* SW19 2
Braemar Rd *BTFD* TW8 ....
WPK KT4 4
Braeside Av *WIM/MER* SW19 3
Bragg Rd *TEDD* TW11 2
Braid Cl *FELT* TW13.............
Brainton Av *EBED/NFELT* TW14 ...1
Bramble La *HPTN* TW12 1
Brambles Cl *BTFD* TW8 ....
The Brambles *WIM/MER* * SW19 ..2
Bramcote Rd *PUT/ROE* SW15 1
Bramham Gdns *CHSGTN* * KT9 4
Bramley Cl *WHTN* TW2 1
Bramley Wy *HSLWW* TW4 1
Bramshaw Ri *NWMAL* KT3 3
Bramwell Cl *SUN* TW16 2
Brandlehow Rd *PUT/ROE* SW15 ...1
Brandon Rd *NWDGN* UB2 ....
Branksome Rd *WIM/MER* SW19 ...3
Branksome Wy *NWMAL* KT3 3
Bransby Rd *CHSGTN* KT9 ....
Branstone Rd *RCH/KEW* TW9 ....
Brantwood Av *ISLW* TW7 1
Brasenose Dr *BARN* SW13 ....
Brassey Cl *EBED/NFELT* * TW14 ...1
Brathway Rd *WAND/EARL* SW18 ...1
Braybourne Dr *ISLW* TW7 ....
Breamore Ct *PUT/ROE* SW15 2
Breamwater Gdns
RCHPK/HAM TW10 2
Breasley Cl *PUT/ROE* SW15 1
Brecon Cl *WPK* KT4 1
Brende Gdns *E/WMO/HCT* KT8 ...2
Brent Lea *BTFD* TW8 ....
Brent Rd *BTFD* TW8 ....
Brentside *BTFD* TW8 ....
Brent Wy *BTFD* TW8 ....
Brewhouse St *PUT/ROE* SW15 ...1
Briar Cl *HPTN* TW12 1
ISLW TW7 ....
Briar Rd *WHTN* TW2 ....
Briar Wk *PUT/ROE* SW15 1
Briarwood Ct *WPK* * KT4 ....

...wood Rd EW KT17.....43 F5
. Farm CI RCH/KEW TW9 ....8 A4
...field CI BTFD TW8 ....6 D3
...ge Av HMSMTH W6 .....9 H1
...ge Gdns E/WMO/HCT KT8 ...34 C1
...ge Rd CHSGTN KT9 .....41 F4
...WMO/HCT KT8.....34 D1
...LW TW3 .....12 C1
...ge St TWK TW1 .....14 A4
...geview HMSMTH W6 .....9 H1
...ge Vls WIM/MER * SW19 ....25 H5
...ge Wy WHTN TW2 .....12 B5
...gewood Rd WPK KT4.....43 F3
...e CI HOR/WEW KT19 .....42 B3
...KT1 .....36 A1
...N TW16 .....26 B5
...e La TWK TW1 .....13 G4
...e Rd ESH/CLAY KT10 .....40 C5
...nton Rd SURB KT6 .....35 H3
...kley Rd WPK KT4.....43 C1
...sworth CI WHTN TW2.....20 C1
...ow Rd HSLW TW3 .....12 A1
...nnia Rd BRYLDS KT5 .....36 C4
...sh Gv CHSWK W4 .....9 F1
...sh Grove Pas CHSWK * W4 ....9 F1
...dfields E/WMO/HCT KT8 ...34 C3
...dlands FELT TW13 .....19 G3
...dlands Wy NWMAL KT3 .....38 A3
...d La HPTN TW12.....27 G2
...dmead Av WPK KT4.....38 B4
...dmead CI HPTN TW12 .....27 H1
...d Oak SUN TW16 .....26 A1
...d Oaks SURB KT6 .....37 E5
...d St TEDD TW11 .....29 E1
...d Wk HEST TW5 .....4 C4
...'H/KEW TW9.....7 G3
...dway SURB KT6.....37 E5
...dway Av TWK TW1 .....13 G4
...dway Ct WIM/MER * SW19 ...33 H1
...Broadway THDIT KT7.....34 D5
...M/MER SW19 .....33 G1
...kenhurst Av WPK KT4.....37 H5
...kham CI WIM/MER SW19 ...25 G5
...kshot CI BTFD TW8 .....7 E2
...npton CI HSLWW TW4 .....11 G3
...ason Rd RYNPK SW20.....33 E4
...k CI RYNPK SW20.....32 C5
...kfield Gdns ESH/CLAY KT10 ..40 A5
...kd Gdns BARN SW13 .....16 A1
...TN/CMB KT2 .....31 F3
...klands Rd THDIT KT7.....35 E5
...Brooklands ISLW * TW7 .....5 G4
...ket La North BTFD TW8 .....7 E1
...ket Md HOR/WEW KT19 .....42 D5
...ket Rd SURB KT6 .....41 F1
...VK TW1 .....13 F4
...ket Rd South BTFD * TW8 ....7 E1
...kside CI FELT TW13 .....18 B3
...kside Crs WPK KT4.....38 B5
...ks La CHSWK W4 .....7 H2
...ks Rd CHSWK W4 .....7 H1
...ks St KUT KT1 .....2 C5
...kwood Av BARN SW13 ...16 A1
...kwood Rd HSLW TW3 .....5 E5
...AND/EARL SW18.....25 G1
...om CI TEDD TW11 .....30 A2
...ome Rd HPTN TW12 .....27 G3
...omfield SUN TW16 .....26 B3
...omfield Rd BRYLDS KT5 .....36 C5
...CH/KEW TW9.....7 G4
...DD TW11 .....29 H1
...omhill Rd WAND/EARL SW18 ....17 H5
...om Lock TEDD * TW11 .....21 H5
...om Pk KUT KT1.....2 A1
...DD TW11 .....30 A2
...om Rd TEDD TW11 .....21 G5
...om Water TEDD TW11 .....29 H1
...om Water West TEDD TW11 ...21 H5
...ugh CI KUTN/CMB * KT2 ...22 A5
...ughton Av
...CHPK/HAM TW10 .....21 H4
...well's La FELT TW13.....18 C2
...wning Av WPK KT4.....38 C5
...wning CI HPTN TW12 .....19 G4
...wning Wy HEST TW5.....4 A4
...wn's Rd BRYLDS KT5 .....36 C4
...nfield Rd HOR/WEW KT19...42 B4
...nel Wk HSLWW TW4 .....11 H5
...nswick CI THDIT KT7.....35 E5
...HTN TW2.....20 C3
...nswick Rd KUTN/CMB KT2 ....3 G2
...an CI SUN TW16 .....26 B5
...anston Av WHTN TW2.....20 A1
...ony Wy SUN TW16 .....26 B1
...khold Rd WAND/EARL SW18 ....17 H4

Buckingham Av
  E/WMO/HCT KT8.....28 A4
  EBED/NFELT TW14.....10 A4
Buckingham CI HPTN TW12.....19 G5
Buckingham Rd FELT TW13.....19 G4
  KUT KT1 .....36 C1
  RCHPK/HAM TW10 .....22 A2
Buckland Rd CHSGTN KT9.....41 G4
Bucklands Rd TEDD TW11.....29 H1
Bucklands Whf KUT * KT1.....2 B4
Buckleigh Av RYNPK SW20.....33 C5
Bullard Rd TEDD * TW11 .....29 E1
Bulls Aly MORT/ESHN * SW14...15 C1
Bulstrode Av HSLW TW3 .....11 G1
Bulstrode Gdns HSLW TW3 .....11 H1
Bulstrode Rd HSLW TW3 .....11 H1
Burberry CI NWMAL KT3 .....31 H4
Burden CI BTFD TW8 .....6 D1
Burdenshott Av
  RCHPK/HAM TW10 .....15 E2
Burdett Av RYNPK SW20.....33 E4
Burdett Rd RCH/KEW TW9 .....7 G5
Burford Rd BTFD TW8 .....7 F1
  WPK KT4.....38 B4
Burges Gv BARN SW13 .....9 G3
Burgess CI FELT TW13 .....19 F4
Burghley Av NWMAL KT3 .....31 G3
Burghley Hall CI
  WIM/MER * SW19 .....25 F1
Burghley Rd WIM/MER SW19 ...25 E4
Burgoyne Rd SUN TW16.....26 A1
Burke CI PUT/ROE SW15.....15 H2
Burleigh PI PUT/ROE SW15 .....17 E3
Burleigh Rd CHEAM SM3.....39 F5
Burlington Av RCH/KEW TW9 .....7 H4
Burlington Gdns CHSWK W4 .....8 B1
Burlington La CHSWK W4 .....8 B1
Burlington Rd CHSWK * W4 .....8 B1
  ISLW TW7 .....5 G4
  NWMAL KT3 .....38 A1
Burnaby Crs CHSWK W4 .....8 A2
Burnaby Gdns CHSWK W4 .....8 A2
Burnell Av RCHPK/HAM TW10 ...21 H5
Burney Av BRYLDS KT5 .....36 C2
Burnham St KUTN/CMB KT2.....3 G3
Burns Av EBED/NFELT TW14 .....10 B4
Burnside CI TWK TW1 .....13 F4
Burns Wy HEST TW5.....4 A4
Burritt Rd KUT KT1.....3 G5
Burr Rd WAND/EARL SW18 .....25 H1
Burstock Rd PUT/ROE SW15 .....17 F2
Burston Rd PUT/ROE SW15 .....17 E3
Burtenshaw Rd THDIT KT7.....35 F4
Burton CI CHSGTN KT9.....45 E1
Burton Gdns HEST TW5.....4 C4
Burton Rd KUTN/CMB KT2 .....2 D1
Burton's Rd HPTN TW12.....20 A4
Burwood CI SURB KT6.....36 D5
Busch CI ISLW TW7.....6 C4
Bush Cottages
  WAND/EARL SW18.....17 H3
Bushey Rd RYNPK SW20.....32 D4
Bush Rd RCH/KEW TW9.....7 G2
Bushwood Rd RCH/KEW TW9 .....7 H2
Bushy Park Gdns HPTN * TW12...20 C5
Bushy Park Rd TEDD TW11.....29 G2
Bushy Rd TEDD TW11 .....28 D1
Bute Av RCHPK/HAM TW10 .....22 B2
Bute Gdns RCHPK/HAM * TW10...22 B1
Butterfield CI TWK TW1 .....13 E4
Buttermere CI
  EBED/NFELT TW14.....18 A1
  MRDN SM4.....39 E3
Buttermere Dr PUT/ROE SW15 ...17 F3
Butts Crs FELT TW13 .....19 H3
The Butts BTFD TW8 .....7 E2
Buxton Dr NWMAL KT3.....31 G4
Buxton Rd MORT/ESHN SW14...15 H1
Bychurch End TEDD * TW11.....21 E5
The Byeway MORT/ESHN SW14...15 F1
The Byeways BRYLDS KT5.....36 C5
Bye Ways WHTN TW2.....20 A3
Byfeld Gdns BARN SW13.....9 F4
Byfield Rd ISLW TW7 .....13 F1
Byron Av NWMAL KT3 .....38 B2
Byron CI HPTN TW12 .....19 G4
Byward Av EBED/NFELT TW14...10 D4
The Byways HOR/WEW KT19 ...43 E3

C

Cadbury CI ISLW TW7 .....6 B4
Cadmer CI NWMAL KT3 .....37 H1
Cadogan CI TEDD TW11 .....20 D5

Cadogan Rd SURB KT6 .....36 A2
Caerleon CI ESH/CLAY KT10 .....44 C1
Caldbeck Av WPK KT4.....43 C1
California Rd NWMAL KT3.....37 E1
Calonne Rd WIM/MER SW19 .....25 E4
Calverley Rd EW KT17.....43 F5
Camac Rd WHTN TW2 .....20 C1
Cambalt Rd PUT/ROE SW15.....17 E3
Camberley Av RYNPK SW20.....32 C4
Camborne Rd MRDN SM4.....39 E2
  WAND/EARL SW18.....17 H5
Camborne Wy HEST TW5.....4 D4
Cambria CI HSLW TW3 .....11 H2
Cambria Ct EBED/NFELT TW14...10 C5
Cambrian Rd RCHPK/HAM TW10...14 C4
Cambridge Av NWMAL KT3 .....31 H4
Cambridge CI HSLWW TW4 .....11 F2
  RYNPK SW20.....32 C3
Cambridge Crs TEDD * TW11.....21 F5
Cambridge Gdns KUT KT1.....3 G5
Cambridge Grove Rd KUT KT1.....3 G5
Cambridge Pk TWK TW1.....14 A5
Cambridge Rd BARN SW13.....9 F4
  HPTN TW12.....27 G2
  HSLWW TW4.....11 F2
  KUT KT1 .....3 G5
  NWMAL KT3 .....37 G1
  RCH/KEW TW9.....7 H3
  RYNPK SW20.....32 C3
  TEDD TW11 .....21 F4
  TWK TW1 .....14 A5
Cambridge Rd North CHSWK W4 ...8 A1
Cambridge Rd South CHSWK W4 ...8 A1
Camden Av FELT TW13 .....18 D2
Camel Gv KUTN/CMB KT2 .....22 A5
Camellia PI WHTN TW2 .....12 A5
Camelot CI WIM/MER SW19 .....25 G4
Camm Gdns KUT KT1.....3 F4
  THDIT KT7.....34 D4
Campbell CI WHTN TW2 .....20 C1
Campbell Rd WHTN TW2.....20 C2
Campden Ter CHSWK * W4.....8 D1
Campen CI WIM/MER SW19 .....25 F2
Campion Rd ISLW TW7 .....6 A4
  PUT/ROE SW15.....16 D2
Camp Rd WIM/MER SW19 .....24 C5
Camp Vw WIM/MER SW19 .....24 C5
Camrose Av FELT TW13 .....18 C4
Camrose CI MRDN SM4.....39 H1
Canbury Av KUTN/CMB KT2 .....2 E2
Canbury Park Rd KUTN/CMB KT2...2 E3
Candler Ms TWK TW1.....13 H5
Canford Gdns NWMAL KT3.....37 H3
Canford PI TEDD TW11 .....29 H1
Cannizaro Rd WIM/MER SW19 ...32 D1
Cannon CI HPTN TW12 .....28 A1
  RYNPK SW20.....32 D5
Cannon Hill La MRDN SM4.....39 E2
Canterbury Rd FELT TW13 .....19 F2
Capital Interchange Wy
  CHSWK 7 H1
Cardigan Rd BARN SW13 .....9 F5
  RCHPK/HAM TW10 .....14 B4
  MRDN SM4.....39 H1
Cardinal Av KUTN/CMB KT2 .....22 B5
  MRDN SM4.....39 F3
Cardinal CI MRDN SM4.....39 F3
  WPK KT4.....43 E3
Cardinal Crs NWMAL KT3 .....31 F4
Cardinal Dr PUT/ROE SW15.....17 E3
Cardinal PI FELT TW13 .....18 C1
Cardinal's Wk HPTN TW12 .....28 B2
Cardington Sq HSLWW TW4.....11 E2
Carleton CI ESH/CLAY KT10.....34 C5
Carlingford Rd MRDN SM4.....39 E3
Carlisle CI KUTN/CMB KT2.....3 F2
Carlisle Rd HPTN TW12 .....28 B2
Carlton Av EBED/NFELT TW14 ...10 D4
Carlton CI CHSGTN KT9.....41 E5
Carlton Dene EW * KT17.....43 G4
Carlton Dr PUT/ROE SW15 .....17 E3
Carlton Park Av RYNPK SW20...32 D4
Carlton Rd MORT/ESHN SW14...15 F1
  NWMAL KT3 .....31 H4
  SUN TW16 .....26 A2
Carlyle CI E/WMO/HCT KT8.....28 A4
Carmalt Gdns PUT/ROE SW15...16 D2
Carnegie CI SURB KT6.....41 G1
Carnegie PI WIM/MER SW19 .....25 E3
Carnforth CI HOR/WEW KT19 ...42 A5
Carnwath Rd FUL/PGN SW6...17 H1
Caroline Rd WIM/MER SW19 .....25 F3
Carrick CI ISLW TW7.....13 F1
Carrington Av HSLW TW3.....12 A3
Carrington Rd
  RCHPK/HAM TW10 .....14 D2
Carslake Rd PUT/ROE SW15.....16 D4
Carters Yd WAND/EARL * SW18...17 H3
  WAND/EARL SW18.....17 H3

Cartwright Wy BARN SW13 .....9 G3
Carville Crs BTFD TW8 .....7 F1
Cassilis Rd TWK TW1 .....13 G4
Cassiobury Av
  EBED/NFELT TW14.....10 A5
Castello Av PUT/ROE SW15.....16 D3
Castelnau BARN SW13.....9 G3
Castle CI WIM/MER SW19 .....25 E3
Castlecombe Dr
  WIM/MER SW19 .....17 E5
Castlegate RCH/KEW TW9 .....14 C1
Castle Rd ISLW TW7.....6 A5
Castle Rw CHSWK * W4.....8 C1
Castle St KUT KT1.....2 C4
Castle Wk SUN * TW16 .....26 B5
Castle Wy FELT TW13.....18 D4
  WIM/MER SW19 .....25 E3
Castle Yd RCHPK/HAM TW10 .....14 A3
Catherine Dr RCH/KEW TW9 .....14 B2
  SUN TW16 .....26 A2
Catherine Gdns HSLW TW3.....12 C2
Catherine Rd SURB KT6 .....36 A2
Catherine Vls RYNPK * SW20 ...32 C2
Catherine Wheel Rd BTFD TW8 ....7 E3
The Causeway CHSGTN KT9.....41 F3
  ESH/CLAY KT10 .....44 A1
  TEDD TW11 .....29 E1
  WIM/MER SW19 .....24 D5
Causeway EBED/NFELT TW14 ...10 C2
Cavalry Crs HSLWW TW4 .....11 E2
Cavalry Gdns PUT/ROE SW15...17 F3
Cavel Wy HOR/WEW KT19 .....45 H4
Cavendish Av NWMAL KT3 .....38 C2
Cavendish CI SUN TW16 .....26 A1
Cavendish Ct SUN TW16 .....26 A1
Cavendish Pde HSLWW * TW4 .....4 B5
Cavendish Rd CHSWK W4 .....8 B3
  NWMAL KT3 .....38 A2
  SUN TW16 .....26 A1
Cavendish Ter FELT * TW13 .....18 B2
Caverleigh Wy WPK KT4.....38 B5
Cave Rd RCHPK/HAM TW10 .....21 H4
Caversham Rd KUT KT1.....2 E4
Caxton Ms BTFD * TW8 .....7 E3
Cecil CI CHSGTN KT9.....41 E3
Cecil Rd HSLW TW3 .....12 B1
Cedar Av WHTN TW2 .....12 A4
Cedar CI KUTN/CMB KT2 .....23 G4
Cedar Ct WIM/MER SW19 .....25 E3
Cedarcroft Rd CHSGTN KT9.....41 G3
Cedar Hts RCHPK/HAM TW10...22 B1
Cedar Rd E/WMO/HCT KT8.....34 D1
  TEDD TW11 .....21 F5
The Cedars TEDD TW11.....29 E1
Cedars Cottages
  PUT/ROE * SW15.....16 B4
Cedars Rd BARN SW13.....9 E5
  E/WMO/HCT KT8.....29 H3
  MRDN SM4.....39 H1
Cedar Ter RCH/KEW TW9 .....14 B2
Cedar Wk ESH/CLAY KT10.....40 A5
Centaur Ct BTFD * TW8.....7 F1
Central Av HSLW TW3 .....12 B2
Central Pde SURB * KT6 .....36 B3
Central Park Est HSLWW * TW4...11 E2
Central Rd WPK KT4.....43 G4
Central Wy EBED/NFELT TW14...10 C3
The Centre FELT TW13.....18 B2
Chadacre Rd EW KT17.....43 G4
Chadwick Av WIM/MER SW19 ...33 H1
Chadwick CI TEDD TW11.....29 F1
Chadwick PI SURB KT6.....35 H4
Chaffinch CI SURB KT6.....41 H2
Chailey CI HEST TW5.....4 A4
Chalcott Gdns SURB * KT6.....35 H5
Chalgrove Av MRDN SM4.....39 H2
Chalky La CHSGTN KT9.....45 E2
Challis Rd BTFD TW8.....7 E2
Challoners CI E/WMO/HCT KT8 ...34 C1
Chalmers Wy EBED/NFELT TW14...10 C3
Chamberlain Gdns HSLW TW3 .....5 F4
Chamberlain Wy SURB KT6.....36 B4
Chancellor's Rd HMSMTH W6 .....9 H1
Chancellors St HMSMTH W6 .....9 H1
Chancellors Whf HMSMTH * W6...9 H1
Chandler CI HPTN TW12.....27 G3
Chandlers CI EBED/NFELT TW14 ...10 A5
Channel CI HEST TW5.....4 D4
Chantry Rd CHSGTN KT9.....41 G4
Chapel Rd HSLW TW3 .....12 B1
  TWK TW1 .....13 G5
Chapman Sq WIM/MER SW19 ...25 E2
Chapter Wy HPTN TW12 .....19 H4
Chara PI CHSWK W4.....8 C2
Charles Babbage CI CHSGTN KT9...44 D1
Charles Rd WIM/MER SW19 .....33 H3
Charles St BARN SW13.....15 H1
  HSLW TW3 .....4 C5

Charleston Cl FELT TW13 ....18 B3
Charlotte Rd BARN SW13 ....9 E4
Charlwood Rd PUT/ROE SW15 .....17 E2
Charlwood Ter PUT/ROE SW15 .....17 E2
Charminster
  WIM/MER SW19 ....33 H4
Charminster Rd WPK KT4 ....39 E5
Charnwood Av WIM/MER SW19 .....33 H4
Charnwood Cl NWMAL KT3 ....37 H1
Charter Crs HSLWW TW4 ....11 F2
Charter Rd KUT KT1 ....3 J6
Charter Sq KUT KT1 ....3 K5
Chartfield Av PUT/ROE SW15 .....16 C3
Chartfield Sq PUT/ROE * SW15 .....17 E3
Chase Ct RYNPK SW20 ....33 F4
Chase Gdns WHTN TW2 ....12 C4
Chaseley Ct CHSWK W4 ....8 A1
Chaseside Av RYNPK SW20 ....33 F5
The Chase SUN TW16 ....26 C3
Chatham Av CHEAM SM3 ....39 G4
Chatham Rd KUTN/CMB KT2 ....3 G4
Chatsworth Av WIM/MER SW19 .....33 H4
Chatsworth Cl CHSWK * W4 ....8 B2
Chatsworth Crs HSLW TW3 ....12 C2
Chatsworth Gdns NWMAL * KT3 .....38 A2
Chatsworth Pl TEDD TW11 ....21 F4
Chatsworth Rd CHSWK W4 ....8 B2
Chaucer Av RCH/KEW TW9 ....7 H5
Cheam Common Rd WPK KT4 .....43 G1
Cheeseman Cl HPTN TW12 ....27 F1
Chelsea Cl HPTN TW12 ....28 B1
  WPK KT4 ....38 B4
Cheltenham Av TWK TW1 ....13 F5
Cheltenham Av NWMAL KT3 .....31 F5
Chelverton Rd PUT/ROE SW15 .....17 E2
Chelwood Gdns RCH/KEW TW9 .....7 H5
Chepstow Cl PUT/ROE SW15 .....17 E3
Cherimoya Gdns
  E/WMO/HCT KT8 ....28 A5
Cherry Cl MRDN SM4 ....39 F1
Cherry Crs BTFD TW8 ....6 C3
Cherry Garth BTFD TW8 ....7 E1
Cherry Orchard Gdns
  E/WMO/HCT KT8 ....27 H5
Cherry Orchard Rd
  E/WMO/HCT KT8 ....27 H5
Cherry Wy HOR/WEW KT19 ....42 C5
Cherrywood Cl KUTN/CMB KT2 .....3 G1
Cherrywood Dr PUT/ROE SW15 .....17 E3
Cherrywood La MRDN SM4 ....39 F1
Chertsey La HOR/WEW KT19 .....45 H5
Chertsey Rd TWK TW1 ....13 F4
  WHTN TW2 ....20 B1
Chervil Cl FELT TW13 ....18 B3
Cherwell Ct HOR/WEW KT19 .....42 B3
Chesfield Rd KUTN/CMB KT2 .....30 B2
Chesham Rd KUTN/CMB KT2 .....3 G3
Cheshire Gdns CHSGTN KT9 .....41 H5
Chessington Cl HOR/WEW KT19 .....42 B5
Chessington Hall Gdns
  CHSGTN KT9 ....45 E1
Chessington Hill Pk CHSGTN KT9...41 H5
Chessington Pde CHSGTN * KT9 .....41 E4
Chessington Rd CHSGTN KT9 .....41 H5
Chester Av RCHPK/HAM TW10...14 C4
  WHTN TW2 ....19 G1
Chester Cl BARN * SW13 ....16 C1
Chesterfield Dr ESH/CLAY KT10...40 B1
Chesterfield Rd CHSWK W4 ....8 B2
Chester Rd HSLWW TW4 ....10 C1
  WIM/MER SW19 ....32 D1
The Chesters NWMAL KT3 ....31 H3
Chesterton Cl
  WAND/EARL SW18 ....17 H3
Chesterton Ter KUT KT1 ....3 G5
Chestnut Av BTFD TW8 ....7 E1
  E/WMO/HCT KT8 ....29 E5
  ESH/CLAY KT10 ....34 C4
  HOR/WEW KT19 ....42 D3
  HPTN TW12 ....27 H2
  MORT/ESHN * SW14 ....15 G1
  TEDD TW11 ....29 E2
Chestnut Cl SUN TW16 ....26 A1
Chestnut Gv ISLW TW7 ....13 F2
  NWMAL KT3 ....31 G5
Chestnut Rd KUTN/CMB KT2 .....2 C1
  RYNPK SW20 ....33 G4
  WHTN TW2 ....20 D2
Chestnut Wy FELT TW13 ....18 C3
Cheyne Av WHTN TW2 ....19 G1
Cheyne Hl BRYLDS KT5 ....36 C1
Chichester Cl HPTN TW12 ....27 G1
Chichester Wy
  EBED/NFELT TW14 ....10 D5
Chillingworth Gdns TWK * TW1 .....21 E2
Chilmark Gdns NWMAL KT3 ....38 A3
Chiltern Av WHTN TW2 ....19 H1
Chiltern Cl WPK KT4 ....43 H1

Chiltern Dr BRYLDS KT5 ....37 E2
Chilton Rd RCH/KEW TW9 ....14 D1
Chilvers Cl WHTN TW2 ....20 D2
Chisholm Rd RCHPK/HAM TW10 ...14 C4
Chislehurst Rd
  RCHPK/HAM TW10 ....14 B4
Chiswick Br MORT/ESHN SW14 .....8 B5
Chiswick High Rd CHSWK W4 .....8 C1
Chiswick House Grounds
  CHSWK * W4 ....8 C2
Chiswick La CHSWK W4 ....8 D1
Chiswick La South CHSWK W4...9 E1
Chiswick Ml CHSWK W4 ....9 E1
Chiswick Pier CHSWK * W4 ....9 E3
Chiswick Quay CHSWK W4 ....8 D2
Chiswick Sq CHSWK W4 ....8 D2
Chiswick Staithe CHSWK W4 .....8 A4
Chiswick Village CHSWK W4 .....7 H2
Chivenor Gv KUTN/CMB KT2 .....22 A5
Chobham Gdns WIM/MER SW19 .....25 E3
Cholmley Rd THDIT KT7 ....35 G3
Cholmley Ter THDIT * KT7 ....35 G4
Cholmley Vls THDIT * KT7 ....35 G4
Christabel Cl ISLW TW7 ....12 D1
Christchurch Av TEDD TW11 .....21 F5
Christ Church Rd BRYLDS KT5 .....36 C4
  EPSOM KT18 ....45 F5
Christchurch Rd
  MORT/ESHN SW14 ....15 E3
Chudleigh Rd WHTN TW2 ....12 D4
Chumleigh Wk BRYLDS KT5 ....36 C1
Church Av MORT/ESHN SW14 .....15 G2
Church Cl HSLW TW3 ....4 C5
Churchfields E/WMO/HCT KT8 .....27 H5
Churchfields Av FELT TW13 ....19 G3
Church Ga FUL/PGN SW6 ....17 F1
Church Gv KUT KT1 ....29 H3
Church Hl WIM/MER SW19 ....25 G5
Church Hill Rd SURB KT6 ....36 B2
Churchill Cl EBED/NFELT TW14 .....18 A1
Churchill Rd HOR/WEW KT19 .....45 H4
Churchill Wy SUN TW16 ....18 B5
Church La CHSGTN KT9 ....41 G5
  TEDD TW11 ....21 E5
  THDIT KT7 ....35 E3
  TWK TW1 ....21 F1
  WIM/MER SW19 ....33 H4
Church Meadow SURB KT6 ....40 D1
Church Pth RYNPK SW20 ....33 G4
Church Ri CHSGTN KT9 ....41 G5
Church Rd BARN SW13 ....9 F5
  E/WMO/HCT KT8 ....28 C5
  ESH/CLAY KT10 ....40 A5
  FELT TW13 ....19 E5
  HEST TW5 ....4 D3
  ISLW TW7 ....5 H5
  KUT KT1 ....2 E4
  RCHPK/HAM TW10 ....14 B3
  RCHPK/HAM TW10 ....22 B4
  SURB KT6 ....35 H5
  TEDD TW11 ....20 D4
  WIM/MER SW19 ....25 F4
  WPK KT4 ....37 H5
Church Rw WAND/EARL * SW18...17 H3
Church St CHSWK W4 ....8 D2
  HPTN TW12 ....28 B3
  HSLW TW3 ....12 B3
  ISLW TW7 ....13 F1
  KUT KT1 ....2 B5
  SUN TW16 ....26 B5
  TWK TW1 ....21 F1
Church St RCHPK/HAM TW10...14 A3
Churchview Rd WHTN TW2 ....20 C1
Church Wk BTFD TW8 ....6 D2
  RYNPK SW20 ....32 D5
Churston Dr MRDN SM4 ....39 E2
Churton Pl CHSWK * W4 ....8 A2
Circle Gdns WIM/MER SW19 .....33 H5
Clairvale Rd HEST TW5 ....4 A4
Clandon Cl EW KT17 ....43 E5
Clandon Ter RYNPK * SW20 .....33 E4
Clare Lawn Av
  MORT/ESHN SW14 ....15 G3
Claremont Av NWMAL KT3 ....38 C2
  SUN TW16 ....26 C3
Claremont Gdns SURB KT6 ....36 B1
Claremont Gv CHSWK W4 ....8 D3
Claremont Rd SURB KT6 ....36 B2
  TEDD TW11 ....21 E5
  TWK TW1 ....13 G5
Claremont Ter THDIT * KT7 ....35 G4
Claremont Vls KUT * KT1 ....3 F5
Clarence Av NWMAL KT3 ....31 H4
Clarence La PUT/ROE SW15 .....16 A4
Clarence Rd CHSWK W4 ....7 H1
  RCH/KEW TW9 ....7 H4
  TEDD TW11 ....29 E1
Clarence St KUT KT1 ....2 B4

  RCH/KEW TW9 ....14 B2
Clarence Ter HSLW TW3 ....12 A2
Clarence Vls KUT * KT1 ....3 F5
Clarendon Crs WHTN TW2 ....20 C5
Clarendon Dr PUT/ROE SW15 .....16 D2
Clare Rd HSLWW TW4 ....11 G1
Clarkes Av WPK KT4 ....39 E5
Clark Wy HEST TW5 ....4 A3
Claudia Pl WIM/MER SW19 ....25 F1
Clavering Av BARN SW13 ....9 G2
Clavering Cl TWK TW1 ....21 F4
Claygate La ESH/CLAY KT10 .....40 B1
  THDIT KT7 ....35 F5
Claymore Cl MRDN SM4 ....39 H4
Claypole Dr HEST TW5 ....4 A2
Clayponds La BTFD TW8 ....7 F1
Clayton Crs BTFD TW8 ....7 E1
Clayton Rd CHSGTN KT9 ....40 D3
  ISLW TW7 ....12 D1
Clearwater Pl SURB KT6 ....35 H3
Cleaveland Rd SURB KT6 ....36 A2
Clement Rd WIM/MER SW19 .....25 F5
Clements Pl BTFD TW8 ....7 E1
Clevedon Rd KUT KT1 ....3 G4
  TWK TW1 ....14 A4
Cleveland Av HPTN TW12 ....27 G2
Cleveland Gdns BARN SW13 .....9 E5
  WPK KT4 ....42 D1
Cleveland Ri MRDN SM4 ....39 E4
Cleveland Rd BARN SW13 ....9 E5
  ISLW TW7 ....13 F2
  NWMAL KT3 ....37 H1
  WPK KT4 ....42 D1
Cleves Rd RCHPK/HAM TW10 .....21 H3
Cleves Wy HPTN TW12 ....27 G2
  SUN TW16 ....26 A1
Clifden Rd BTFD TW8 ....7 E2
  TWK TW1 ....21 E1
Clifford Av MORT/ESHN SW14 .....8 B5
  RCH/KEW TW9 ....15 E1
Clifford Rd HSLWW TW4 ....11 E1
  RCHPK/HAM TW10 ....22 A2
Clifton Av FELT TW13 ....18 D3
Clifton Pde FELT * TW13 ....18 D4
Clifton Park Av RYNPK SW20 .....32 D4
Clifton Pl KUTN/CMB KT2 ....3 G3
Clifton Rd ISLW TW7 ....5 H5
  KUTN/CMB KT2 ....3 F2
  TEDD TW11 ....20 D4
  WIM/MER SW19 ....33 E1
Clinton Av E/WMO/HCT KT8 .....34 B1
Clippesby Cl CHSGTN * KT9 .....41 G5
Clipstone Br HSLW TW3 ....11 H1
Clitherow Rd BTFD TW8 ....6 C1
Cliveden Rd WIM/MER SW19 .....33 G1
Clive Rd EBED/NFELT TW14 .....10 B4
  TWK TW1 ....21 E4
Clockhouse Cl WIM/MER SW19 .....24 D3
Clockhouse Pl PUT/ROE SW15...17 F3
Clock Tower Rd ISLW TW7 ....13 E1
Cloister Cl TEDD TW11 ....21 G5
Clonmel Rd HPTN TW12 ....20 C4
Clonmore St WAND/EARL SW18...25 G1
The Close CHEAM SM3 ....39 G4
  ISLW TW7 ....5 G5
  NWMAL KT3 ....31 F4
  RCH/KEW TW9 ....15 G1
  SURB KT6 ....36 B4
Clovelly Rd HSLW TW3 ....4 D5
Clunbury Av NWDGN UB2 ....4 C1
Clydesdale Cl ISLW TW7 ....13 E1
Clydesdale Gdns
  RCHPK/HAM TW10 ....15 E2
Clymping Dene
  EBED/NFELT TW14 ....10 C5
Coach House La
  WIM/MER SW19 ....25 E4
Coalecroft Rd PUT/ROE SW15 .....16 D2
Cobbett Rd WHTN TW2 ....19 H1
Cobbler's Wk TEDD TW11 ....28 D2
Cobb's Rd HSLWW TW4 ....11 G2
Cobham Av NWMAL KT3 ....38 B2
Cobham Rd KUT KT1 ....3 H4
Cochrane Rd WIM/MER SW19 .....33 F2
Cockcrow Hl SURB * KT6 ....36 A5
Cocks Crs NWMAL KT3 ....38 A1
Colborne Wy WPK KT4 ....43 H2
Coldstream Gdns
  WAND/EARL SW18 ....17 G4
Cole Park Gdns TWK TW1 ....13 F4
Cole Park Rd TWK TW1 ....13 F5
Cole Rd TWK TW1 ....13 F4
Coleshill Rd TEDD TW11 ....28 D1
Colinette Rd PUT/ROE SW15 .....16 D2
Coliston Rd WAND/EARL SW18 ...17 H5
College Cl WHTN TW2 ....20 C1
College Dr THDIT KT7 ....34 D4
College Gdns NWMAL KT3 ....38 A2

College Rd ISLW TW7 ....*
Collier Cl HOR/WEW KT19 4
Collingwood Av BRYLDS KT5 3
Collingwood Cl HSLWW TW4 1
Colne Ct HOR/WEW KT19 4
Colne Rd WHTN TW2 2
Colonial Av WHTN TW2 1
Colston Rd MORT/ESHN SW14...1
Columbia Av WPK KT4 3
Colwith Rd HMSMTH W6 ....
Colwyn Crs HSLW TW3 ....
Combemartin Rd
  WAND/EARL SW18 1
Commerce Rd BTFD TW8 ....
Commondale PUT/ROE SW15 .....
Common La ESH/CLAY KT10...
Common Rd BARN SW13 1
  ESH/CLAY KT10 ....
Compass Hl RCHPK/HAM TW10...1
Compton Crs CHSGTN KT9 4
  CHSWK W4 ....
Compton Rd WIM/MER SW19 .....
Concorde Cl HSLW TW3 ....
Conifers Cl TEDD TW11 2
Coniston Cl BARN SW13 ....
  CHSWK W4 ....
  MRDN SM4 3
Coniston Rd WHTN TW2 ....
Coniston Wy CHSGTN KT9 4
Connaught Av HSLWW TW4 ....
  MORT/ESHN SW14 ....
Connaught Rd HPTN TW12 2
  NWMAL KT3 3
  RCHPK/HAM * TW10 ....
Conrad Dr WPK KT4 3
Consfield Av NWMAL KT3 3
Consort Ms ISLW TW7 1
Constable Gdns ISLW TW7 1
Constance Rd WHTN TW2 ....
Conway Rd FELT TW13 1
  HSLWW TW4 ....
  RYNPK SW20 3
Coombe Bank NWMAL KT3 3
Coombe Cl HSLW TW3 1
Coombe Crs HPTN TW12 ....
Coombe End KUTN/CMB KT2 3
Coombefield Cl NWMAL KT3 3
Coombe Gdns NWMAL KT3 3
  RYNPK SW20 ....
Coombe Hill Gld KUTN/CMB KT2 3
Coombe Hill Rd KUTN/CMB KT2 3
Coombe House Cha
  NWMAL KT3 3
Coombe La RYNPK SW20 3
Coombe La West KUTN/CMB KT2 ...3
Coombe Neville KUTN/CMB KT2 3
Coombe Pk KUTN/CMB KT2 23
Coombe Ridings KUTN/CMB KT2...23
Coombe Ri KUTN/CMB KT2 3
Coombe Rd CHSWK W4 8
  HPTN TW12 ....
  KUTN/CMB KT2 3
  NWMAL KT3 3
Coombe Vls WAND/EARL * SW18...3
Coombe Wood Rd
  KUTN/CMB KT2 23
Coppard Gdns CHSGTN KT9 4
Copperfields SUN * TW16 2
Copper Mill Dr ISLW TW7 1
Coppice Cl RYNPK SW20 3
Coppice Dr PUT/ROE SW15 16
Coppsfield E/WMO/HCT KT8 2
Copse Gld SURB KT6 3
Copse Hl RYNPK SW20 3
Copthall Gdns TWK * TW1 2
Corban Rd HSLW TW3 ....
Corkran Rd SURB KT6 3
Corney Reach Wy CHSWK W4 8
Corney Rd CHSWK W4 ....
Cornwall Av ESH/CLAY KT10...4
Cornwall Gv CHSWK W4 ....
Cornwall Rd TWK TW1 1
Corporation Av HSLWW TW4 1
Corscombe Cl KUTN/CMB KT2 2
Cortis Rd PUT/ROE SW15 16
Cortis Ter PUT/ROE SW15 ....
Cotsford Av NWMAL KT3 3
Cotswold Cl ESH/CLAY KT10...4
  KUTN/CMB KT2 3
Cotswold Rd HPTN TW12 2
Cotswold Wy WPK KT4 4
Cottage Gv SURB KT6 ....
Cottenham Dr RYNPK SW20...3
Cottenham Park Rd
  RYNPK SW20 3
Cottenham Pl RYNPK SW20 3
Cotterill Rd SURB KT6 3
Cottington Rd FELT TW13 19

...try Wy FELT TW13.....................18 D5
...ty Pde BTFD * TW8....................7 E3
...t Cl FELT TW13.........................20 A3
...t Close Av FELT TW13................20 A3
...t Crs CHSGTN KT9....................41 E5
...t Farm Av FELT TW13.................42 C4
...thope Rd WIM/MER SW19............25 F5
...thope Rd WHTN TW2..................33 F2
...tlands RCHPK/HAM TW10.............14 D3
...tlands Av HPTN TW12.................27 G1
...H/KEW TW9..................................8 A5
...tlands Dr HOR/WEW KT19............42 D5
...tlands Rd BRYLDS KT5................36 D4
...t Wy WHTN TW2...........................13 E5
...ts Av CHSGTN KT9.......................41 F4
...l Gdns MORT/ESHN SW14...........15 E2
...l La MORT/ESHN SW14.................15 E2
...l Rd MORT/ESHN SW14................15 F2
...rts Rd ESH/CLAY KT10.................44 A1
...eaze Rd KUTN/CMB KT2................2 D3
...ley Rd MORT/ESHN SW14..............15 H1
...per Rd RCHPK/HAM TW10.............22 C5
...La CHSGTN KT9...........................41 F3
...R/WEW KT19...............................42 A4
...g Rd RCHPK/HAM TW10................21 H4
...gwell Av FELT TW13....................18 B3
...brook Dr ESH/CLAY KT10.............34 B5
...HTN TW2.....................................20 A1
...brook Rd CHSWK W4.......................8 D1
...LWW TW4....................................11 G2
...M/MER SW19................................33 F2
...e Av ISLW TW7.............................13 F3
...ebank Ms TWK * TW1..................13 G3
...ebrook WHTN TW2.......................20 B2
...e Ct MORT/ESHN * SW14.............15 F2
...eford Cl WHTN TW2......................13 E5
...eford Wy WHTN TW2....................12 D5
...e Park Rd WHTN TW2...................20 A2
...e Rd WHTN TW2...........................20 D1
...es Dr BRYLDS KT5.......................36 B5
...es Pk SURB KT6...........................36 B1
...es Park Av SURB KT6....................36 B1
...es Park Crs BRYLDS KT5..............36 C1
...eswater Pk NWDGN UB2.................4 C1
...e Wy WHTN TW2..........................12 B5
...ford Cl RYNPK * SW20.................32 C3
...ford La HEST TW5..........................4 A3
...HAIR TW5.....................................10 A1
...leigh Gdns KUTN/CMB KT2............30 C1
...leigh Rd FELT TW13.....................18 A4
...M/MER SW19................................33 H5
...mer La MRDN SM4........................39 E3
...mer Ct HPTN TW12......................27 G1
...mer Rd HPTN TW12.....................20 A5
...TN/CMB KT2.................................22 B5
...ston Cl HSLW TW3.........................4 B5
...an Av FELT TW13.........................18 B2
...ord Cl KUTN/CMB KT2.....................2 E2
...ford Cl ISLW TW7...........................5 H5
...ke Hl CHSGTN KT9........................45 F1
...iton Wy ESH/CLAY KT10................40 B4
...k Cottages
...WMO/HCT * KT8..........................34 D1
...k Rd E/WMO/HCT KT8..................34 D1
...cent Gdns WIM/MER SW19...........25 H5
...cent Rd KUTN/CMB KT2................30 D2
...NPK SW20...................................33 E3
...Crescent BARN SW13.......................9 E5
...WMAL KT3....................................31 F4
...RB KT6...36 B2
...M/MER SW19................................25 H5
...swell Rd FELT TW13.....................19 F3
...VK TW1..14 A4
...sys Cnr WHTN * TW3....................12 A1
...ton Wy WPK KT4..........................39 E5
...Crest BRYLDS KT5........................36 D2
...tway PUT/ROE SW15.....................16 B4
...twood Wy HSLWW TW4.................11 G3
...keters Cl CHSGTN KT9..................41 E4
...leigh Rd FELT TW13.....................19 F4
...en Rd HMSMTH W6.........................9 H1
...kers Cl ISLW TW7.........................12 C3
...ton Av CHSWK W4...........................8 B3
...ton Ter RCH/KEW TW9..................14 C2
...Croft HEST TW5...............................4 B3
...t Wy RCHPK/HAM TW10................21 G3
...her Villas Rd
...AND/EARL SW18.............................17 G4
...nford Rd PUT/ROE SW15..............17 G3
...nford Wy NWMAL KT3...................31 G5
...nwell Av HMSMTH W6.....................9 G1
...WMAL KT3....................................38 A2
...nwell Cl CHSWK * W4......................8 A1
...nwell Pl MORT/ESHN SW14...........15 F1
...nwell Rd FELT TW13.....................18 C1
...LW TW3.......................................11 H2

KUT KT1...2 D3
TEDD TW11.....................................29 F1
WIM/MER SW19..............................39 G1
WPK KT4..42 C2
Cromwell St HSLW TW3..................11 H4
Cromwell Ter HSLW * TW3.............11 H2
Crosby Cl FELT TW13....................19 F4
Cross Deep TWK TW1.....................21 E3
Cross Deep Gdns TWK TW1............21 E2
Cross Lances Rd HSLW TW3...........12 A2
Crosslands Av NWDGN UB2...............4 C1
Crosslands Pde NWDGN * UB2..........4 D1
Crosslands Rd HOR/WEW KT19.......42 C5
Cross Rd FELT TW13......................19 F4
KUTN/CMB KT2..................................3 F1
WIM/MER SW19..............................33 H2
Cross St BARN SW13........................9 D5
HPTN TW12...................................20 B5
Crossway NWMAL KT3....................38 D1
Crossways SUN TW16.....................26 A3
The Crossways BRYLDS * KT5.........37 E5
HEST TW5...4 C3
Crown Ar KUT KT1.............................2 B1
Crown La MRDN SM4......................33 H5
Crown Rd NWMAL KT3....................31 F5
TWK TW1.......................................13 G4
WIM/MER SW19..............................39 H1
Crown Ter RCH/KEW TW9...............14 C2
Crowntree Cl ISLW TW7...................6 A2
Crown Yd HSLW TW3......................12 B1
Crowther Av BTFD TW8.....................7 F1
Crowthorne Cl
WAND/EARL SW18........................17 G5
Croylands Dr SURB KT6..................36 B4
Croysdale Av SUN TW16.................26 B5
Cuda's Cl HOR/WEW KT19..............43 E3
Cuddington Av WPK KT4.................43 E2
Cuddington Gld
HOR/WEW KT19...........................45 H5
Culsac Rd SURB KT6......................41 F1
Cumberland Cl RYNPK SW20..........33 E2
TWK TW1.......................................13 G4
Cumberland Dr CHSGTN KT9..........41 F2
ESH/CLAY KT10..............................40 B1
Cumberland Rd BARN SW13.............9 E4
RCH/KEW TW9..................................7 H4
Cumbernauld Gdns SUN TW16.......18 A5
Cumbrae Gdns SURB * KT6............36 A5
Cumnor Gdns EW KT17....................43 F5
Cunliffe Rd HOR/WEW KT19...........43 E3
Currie Hill Cl WIM/MER SW19.........25 G4
Curtis Rd HOR/WEW KT19..............42 B3
HSLWW TW4...................................11 G5
Cusack Cl TWK * TW1.....................21 E4
Cyclamen Cl HPTN TW12................27 H1
Cyclamen Wy HOR/WEW KT19........42 B4
Cygnet Av EBED/NFELT TW14.........10 D5
The Cygnets FELT TW13..................19 F4
Cypress Av WHTN TW2...................12 B5

D

Dade Wy NWDGN UB2........................4 C1
Daffodil Cl HPTN TW12....................27 H1
Dagmar Rd KUTN/CMB KT2...............3 F2
Daisy La FUL/PGN SW6...................17 H1
Dalcross Rd HEST TW5......................4 B5
Dale Av HSLWW TW4......................11 F1
Dale Rd SUN TW16..........................26 A2
Daleside Rd HOR/WEW KT19...........42 C5
Dale St CHSWK W4............................8 D1
Dalewood Gdns WPK KT4................43 C1
Dalmeny Crs HSLW TW3..................12 C2
Dalmeny Rd EW KT17.....................43 C2
Dalmore Av ESH/CLAY KT10............40 A5
Dancer Rd RCH/KEW TW9...............14 D1
Danebury PUT/ROE SW15...............16 A5
Danemere St PUT/ROE SW15..........16 D1
Danesbury Rd FELT TW13...............18 C1
Daniel Cl HSLWW TW4....................11 G5
Darby Crs SUN TW16......................26 D4
Darby Gdns SUN TW16...................26 D4
Darcy Rd ISLW TW7...........................6 A4
Darell Rd RCH/KEW TW9.................14 D1
Darfur St PUT/ROE SW15................17 E1
Darlaston Rd WIM/MER SW19..........33 E2
Darley Dr NWMAL KT3....................31 G4
Dartmouth Pl CHSWK W4..................8 D2
Darwin Rd BTFD TW8........................6 D1
Davenport Cl TEDD * TW11.............29 F1
David Twigg Cl KUTN/CMB KT2.........2 D2
Davies Wk ISLW TW7........................5 C4
Davis Rd CHSGTN KT9.....................41 H3
Dawes Av ISLW TW7........................13 F3
Dawn Cl HSLWW TW4......................11 F1
Dawson Rd KUT KT1...........................3 F6

Daylesford Av PUT/ROE SW15.........16 B2
Deacon Rd KUTN/CMB KT2...............2 E3
Deacons Wk HPTN TW12.................19 H4
Dealtry Rd PUT/ROE SW15..............16 D3
Deanhill Ct MORT/ESHN * SW14.....15 E2
Deanhill Rd MORT/ESHN SW14.......15 E2
Dean Rd HPTN TW12.......................19 H4
HSLW TW3.....................................12 A3
Deans Cl CHSWK W4.........................8 A2
Debden Cl KUTN/CMB KT2..............22 A5
Deborah Cl ISLW TW7.......................6 A4
De Broome Cl FELT TW13...............18 D1
Deepdale WIM/MER SW19...............25 F4
Deepwell Cl ISLW TW7.......................6 B4
Deerhurst Cl FELT TW13.................18 B1
Deerhurst Crs HPTN TW12...............20 B5
Dee Rd RCH/KEW TW9.....................14 C2
Deer Park Cl KUTN/CMB KT2...........31 E2
Defoe Av RCH/KEW TW9....................7 H3
Delamere Rd RYNPK SW20..............33 E3
Delcombe Av WPK KT4....................43 E3
Dellbow Rd EBED/NFELT TW14.......10 C3
Dell La EW KT17..............................43 F5
Dell Rd EW KT17.............................43 F5
The Dell BTFD TW8............................7 E6
EBED/NFELT TW14.........................10 C5
Dell Wk NWMAL KT3.......................31 H4
Delta Cl WPK KT4............................42 D2
Delta Rd WPK KT4...........................42 D2
Denbigh Gdns
RCHPK/HAM * TW10......................14 C3
Denbigh Rd HSLW TW3.....................5 E5
Dene Av HSLW TW3.........................11 G5
Dene Cl WPK KT4.............................43 E1
Dene Gdns THDIT KT7.....................40 B1
Denehurst Gdns
RCHPK/HAM TW10........................14 D2
WHTN TW2.....................................12 C5
Denham Rd EBED/NFELT TW14.......10 D5
Denison Rd FELT TW13...................18 A4
Denleigh Gdns THDIT * KT7............34 D3
Denman Dr ESH/CLAY KT10............40 B4
Denmark Av WIM/MER SW19...........33 F2
Denmark Ct MRDN SM4...................39 H2
Denmark Rd KUT KT1.........................2 D7
WHTN TW2.....................................20 B1
WIM/MER SW19..............................33 E1
Dennan Rd SURB KT6.....................36 C5
Denning Cl HPTN TW12...................27 G1
The Denningtons WPK KT4..............43 D1
Dennis Park Crs RYNPK SW20.........33 F3
Dennis Rd E/WMO/HCT KT8............34 A4
Denton Rd TWK TW1.......................14 A4
Deodar Rd PUT/ROE SW15..............17 F2
Depot Rd HSLW TW3.......................12 C1
Derby Rd BRYLDS KT5....................36 D5
HSLW TW3.....................................12 A3
MORT/ESHN SW14.........................15 F1
WIM/MER SW19..............................33 H2
Derek Av HOR/WEW KT19...............41 H5
Derek Cl HOR/WEW KT19................42 A4
Derwent Av PUT/ROE SW15............23 H4
Derwent Cl EBED/NFELT TW14........18 A1
Derwent Rd MRDN SM4...................39 E3
WHTN TW2.....................................12 A4
Devas Rd RYNPK SW20...................33 E3
Devereux La BARN SW13...................9 G3
Devey Cl KUTN/CMB KT2.................32 A2
Devon Av WHTN TW2.......................20 B1
Devon Cl HOR/WEW KT19...............45 H5
Devoncroft Gdns TWK TW1.............13 F5
Devonhurst Pl CHSWK * W4..............8 D1
Devonshire Ct FELT * TW13............18 C2
Devonshire Dr SURB KT6................36 A5
Devonshire Gdns CHSWK W4............8 B3
Devonshire Rd CHSWK W4................8 D1
FELT TW13.....................................19 F3
Devonshire St CHSWK W4..................8 D1
Devon Wy CHSGTN KT9...................40 D3
HOR/WEW KT19............................42 A4
Devon Waye HEST TW5.....................4 C3
Dewsbury Rd WPK KT4....................43 F2
Diana Gdns SURB KT6....................41 G1
Dickens Cl RCHPK/HAM TW10........22 B3
Dickenson Rd FELT TW13...............18 D5
Dickerage Hl NWMAL KT3...............31 H4
Dickerage La NWMAL KT3...............31 F5
Dickerage Rd KUT KT1....................31 F5
Dick Turpin Wy
EBED/NFELT TW14.........................10 A2
Dilton Gdns PUT/ROE SW15............24 B1
Dinton Rd KUTN/CMB KT2...............30 C1
Disraeli Rd PUT/ROE SW15.............17 F2
Distillery La HMSMTH W6..................9 H1
Distillery Rd HMSMTH W6.................9 H1
Ditton Cl THDIT KT7.........................35 H4
Ditton Grange Cl SURB KT6............36 A5
Ditton Grange Dr SURB KT6............36 A5

Ditton Hl SURB KT6........................35 H5
Ditton Hill Rd SURB KT6.................35 H5
Ditton Lawn THDIT KT7...................35 F5
Ditton Reach THDIT KT7..................35 G3
Ditton Rd NWDGN UB2......................4 C1
SURB KT6.......................................36 B5
Dock Rd BTFD * TW8.........................7 E3
Dockwell Cl EBED/NFELT TW14.......10 B2
Dollary Pde KUT * KT1......................3 J6
Dolphin Cl SURB KT6......................36 A3
Dolphin Sq CHSWK * W4....................8 C2
Dolphin St KUT KT1...........................2 C4
Dome Buildings
RCHPK/HAM * TW10......................14 A3
Donald Woods Gdns BRYLDS KT5....42 A1
Donnington Rd WPK KT4..................43 F1
Doone Cl TEDD TW11......................29 F1
Dora Rd WIM/MER SW19.................25 H5
Dorchester Gv CHSWK W4.................8 D2
Dorchester Ms TWK TW1.................13 H4
Dorchester Rd WPK KT4..................38 D5
Dorien Rd RYNPK SW20...................33 E4
Dorney Wy HSLWW TW4..................11 F3
Dorset Rd WIM/MER SW19...............33 H3
Dorset Wy WHTN TW2.....................20 B1
Dorset Waye HEST TW5.....................4 C3
Douai Gv HPTN TW12......................28 B5
Douglas Av NWMAL KT3..................38 C1
Douglas Rd HSLW TW3...................12 A1
KUT KT1..3 J5
SURB KT6.......................................41 G1
Douglas Vls KUT * KT1......................2 E5
Dover House Rd PUT/ROE SW15......16 B2
Dover Park Dr PUT/ROE SW15.........16 C5
Dover Ter RCH/KEW * TW9................7 H5
Dowdeswell Cl PUT/ROE SW15........15 H1
Downes Cl TWK TW1.......................13 G4
Downfield WPK KT4.........................38 A5
Down Hall Rd KUTN/CMB KT2...........2 B3
Down Rd TEDD TW11......................29 G1
Downside SUN TW16.......................26 B3
TWK TW1.......................................21 E3
The Downs RYNPK SW20.................33 E2
Downs Vw ISLW TW7.........................6 A4
Draco Ga PUT/ROE * SW15..............16 D1
Drake Rd CHSGTN KT9....................41 H4
Drax Av RYNPK SW20......................32 B2
Draxmont WIM/MER SW19...............33 F1
Draycot Rd SURB KT6.....................36 D5
Draymans Wy ISLW TW7.................13 E1
Drayton Cl HSLWW TW4..................11 G3
The Drive EBED/NFELT TW14..........10 D5
ESH/CLAY KT10..............................34 B5
HOR/WEW KT19............................45 G5
HSLW TW3.......................................5 G5
KUTN/CMB KT2..............................31 F2
RYNPK SW20..................................32 D2
SURB * KT6....................................36 B4
Dromore Rd PUT/ROE SW15............17 F4
Drumaline Rdg WPK KT4.................42 D1
Drummonds Pl RCH/KEW TW9........14 B2
Dryad St PUT/ROE SW15................17 E1
Dryburgh Rd PUT/ROE SW15..........16 C3
Dudley Dr MRDN SM4.....................39 F5
Dudley Rd KUT KT1...........................2 E5
RCH/KEW TW9..................................7 H5
WIM/MER SW19..............................33 H1
Duke of Cambridge Cl
WHTN TW2.....................................12 C4
Duke Rd CHSWK W4.........................8 C1
Duke's Av CHSWK W4........................8 C1
HSLWW TW4...................................11 F4
NWMAL KT3....................................31 H5
RCHPK/HAM TW10........................21 H4
Dukes Cl HPTN TW12......................19 G5
Duke St RCH/KEW TW9...................14 A2
Dumbleton Cl KUT KT1......................3 J3
Dunbar Rd NWMAL KT3...................37 F1
Duncan Rd RCH/KEW TW9..............14 B2
Dundas Gdns E/WMO/HCT KT8.......28 A5
Dundela Gdns WPK KT4...................43 G3
Dundonald Rd WIM/MER SW19........33 G2
Dungarvan Av PUT/ROE SW15........16 B2
Dunleary Cl HSLWW TW4.................11 G5
Dunmore Rd RYNPK SW20...............32 D3
Dunmow Cl FELT * TW13.................19 F4
Dunstable Rd RCH/KEW TW9...........14 B2
Dunstall Rd RYNPK SW20................32 C1
Dunstall Wy E/WMO/HCT KT8..........28 A5
Dunster Av MRDN SM4....................39 E5
Dunton Cl SURB KT6.......................36 B5
Dunvegan Cl E/WMO/HCT KT8........34 A1
Dupont Rd RYNPK SW20..................33 E4
Durbin Rd CHSGTN KT9...................41 F3
Durford Crs PUT/ROE SW15............16 D5
Durham Av HEST TW5........................4 C2
Durham Rd EBED/NFELT TW14........10 D5
RYNPK SW20..................................32 C3

Durlston Rd *KUTN/CMB* KT2............30 B1
Durnsford Av
 WAND/EARL SW18...................25 H1
Durnsford Rd
 WAND/EARL SW18...................25 H2
Durrington Av *RYNPK* SW20............32 D2
Durrington Park Rd
 RYNPK SW20........................32 D3
Dutch Gdns *KUTN/CMB* KT2............31 E1
Dutch Yd *WAND/EARL* SW18...........17 H3
Dyer's La *PUT/ROE* SW15..............16 C1
Dynevor Rd *RCHPK/HAM* TW10......14 B3
Dysart Av *KUTN/CMB* KT2..............21 H5

E

Earldom Rd *PUT/ROE* SW15............16 D2
Earle Gdns *KUTN/CMB* KT2............30 B2
Earl Rd *MORT/ESHN* SW14.............15 F2
Eastbank Rd *HPTN* TW12...............20 B5
Eastbourne Gdns
 MORT/ESHN SW14...................15 F1
Eastbourne Rd *BTFD* TW8................7 E1
 CHSWK W4............................8 B2
 FELT TW13............................19 E2
Eastbury Gv *CHSWK* W4.................8 D1
Eastbury Rd *KUTN/CMB* KT2............2 C1
Eastern Perimeter Rd
 EBED/NFELT TW14....................10 B1
East La *KUT* KT1..........................2 B6
Eastmont Rd *ESH/CLAY* KT10........40 C4
East Rd *KUTN/CMB* KT2................2 D2
East Sheen Av
 MORT/ESHN SW14...................15 G3
East St *BTFD* TW8.........................6 D3
Eastway *MRDN* SM4.....................39 E2
Eaton Dr *KUTN/CMB* KT2................3 H1
Eaton Rd *HSLW* TW3.....................12 C2
Ebbisham Rd *WPK* KT4.................43 H1
Ede Cl *HSLWW* TW4.......................11 G1
Edenfield Gdns *WPK* KT4...............43 G2
Edenhurst Av *FUL/PGN* SW6...........17 C1
Edensor Rd *CHSWK* W4..................8 D3
Eden St *KUT* KT1..........................2 C3
Edgar Rd *HSLWW* TW4..................11 G5
Edgecombe Cl *KUTN/CMB* KT2......31 G2
Edge Hi *WIM/MER* SW19...............33 E2
Edinburgh Ct *KUT* * KT1................2 A2
Edith Gdns *BRYLDS* KT5................37 E4
Edmund Gv *FELT* TW13..................19 G2
Edna Rd *RYNPK* SW20...................33 E4
Edward Cl *HPTN* TW12..................20 B5
Edward Rd *HPTN* TW12..................20 B5
Edwin Rd *WHTN* TW2....................12 D5
Effingham Rd *SURB* KT6................35 G4
Egerton Rd *NWMAL* KT3................38 A1
 WHTN TW2............................12 D5
Egliston Ms *PUT/ROE* SW15...........16 D1
Egliston Rd *PUT/ROE* SW15...........16 D1
Egmont Av *SURB* KT6....................36 C5
Egmont Rd *NWMAL* KT3................38 A1
 SURB KT6.............................36 C5
Elborough St
 WAND/EARL SW18...................25 H1
Eldon Av *HEST* TW5......................4 D3
Eldridge Cl *EBED/NFELT* TW14.......18 B1
Eleanor Gv *BARN* SW13.................15 H1
Electric Pde *SURB* KT6..................36 A3
Elfin Gv *TEDD* TW11.....................21 E5
Elgar Av *BRYLDS* KT5...................37 E5
Eliot Gdns *PUT/ROE* SW15............16 B2
Elizabeth Cottages
 RCH/KEW TW9.........................7 G4
Elizabeth Gdns *SUN* TW16............26 D5
Elizabeth Wy *FELT* TW13...............18 D4
Ellenborough Pl
 PUT/ROE SW15......................16 B2
Elleray Rd *TEDD* TW11..................29 E1
Ellerdine Rd *HSLW* TW3................12 B2
Ellerker Gdns
 RCHPK/HAM TW10..................14 B4
Ellerman Av *WHTN* TW2................19 G1
Ellerton Rd *BARN* * SW13..............9 F4
 RYNPK SW20.........................32 B2
 SURB KT6.............................41 G1
Ellesmere Rd *TWK* TW1.................13 H4
Ellingham Rd *CHSGTN* KT9...........41 E5
Ellington Rd *FELT* TW13................18 A4
 HSLW TW3..............................5 E1
Ellisfield Dr *PUT/ROE* SW15..........16 A5
Ellison Rd *BARN* SW13.................15 F5
Elm Bank Gdns *BARN* SW13...........8 D5
Elmbridge Av *BRYLDS* KT5............37 F3
Elmbrook Cl *SUN* TW16.................26 C3
Elm Cl *BRYLDS* KT5.....................37 F4
 RYNPK SW20.........................38 D1

 WHTN TW2.............................20 A2
Elm Crs *KUTN/CMB* KT2.................2 D3
Elmcroft Cl *CHSGTN* * KT9............41 F2
 EBED/NFELT TW14...................10 A4
Elmcroft Dr *CHSGTN* KT9.............41 F2
Elmdene *BRYLDS* KT5...................37 F5
Elmdon Rd *HEST* TW5....................4 A5
 HTHAIR TW6..........................10 A1
Elm Dr *SUN* TW16.......................26 D4
Elmer Gdns *ISLW* TW7..................12 C1
Elmer's Dr *TEDD* TW11..................21 G1
Elmfield Av *TEDD* TW11................21 E5
Elm Gdns *ESH/CLAY* KT10.............40 A5
Elmgate Av *FELT* TW13.................18 C3
Elm Gv *KUTN/CMB* KT2................2 D3
 WIM/MER SW19.......................33 F2
Elm Grove Rd *BARN* SW13............16 A1
Elm Rd *CHSGTN* KT9....................41 F3
 ESH/CLAY KT10......................40 A5
 EW KT17...............................43 E5
 KUTN/CMB KT2........................3 F1
 MORT/ESHN SW14...................15 F1
 NWMAL KT3...........................31 G5
Elm Rd West *MRDN* SM4..............39 G4
Elmshaw Rd *PUT/ROE* SW15.........16 B3
Elmsleigh Rd *WHTN* TW2..............20 C2
Elmstead Cl *HOR/WEW* KT19.........42 D4
Elmstead Gdns *WPK* KT4..............43 F2
The Elms *BARN* SW13..................16 A1
 ESH/CLAY * KT10...................44 A1
Elmsworth Av *HSLW* TW3................5 E5
Elm Tree Av *ESH/CLAY* KT10..........34 C4
Elmtree Rd *TEDD* TW11................20 D5
Elm Wk *RYNPK* SW20..................38 D1
Elm Wy *HOR/WEW* KT19...............42 C4
 WPK KT4...............................43 H2
Elmwood Av *FELT* TW13...............18 C3
Elmwood Rd *CHSWK* W4................8 B2
Elsenham St *WIM/MER* SW19........25 G1
Elsinore Wy *RCH/KEW* TW9...........15 E1
Elsrick Av *MRDN* SM4..................39 H2
Elsworthy *THDIT* KT7....................34 D3
Elthorne Ct *FELT* TW13.................18 D1
Elton Cl *E/WMO/HCT* KT8..............29 H2
Elton Rd *KUTN/CMB* KT2...............3 G2
Ely Cl *NWMAL* KT3......................32 A4
Ely Rd *HSLWW* TW4.....................10 D1
Embankment *PUT/ROE* SW15........17 E1
The Embankment *TWK* TW1...........21 F1
Embercourt Rd *THDIT* KT7.............34 D3
Ember Farm Av
 E/WMO/HCT KT8.....................34 C3
Ember Farm Wy
 E/WMO/HCT KT8.....................34 C2
Ember Gdns *ESH/CLAY* KT10.........34 D4
Ember La *ESH/CLAY* KT10.............34 C5
Emma Ter *RYNPK* * SW20.............32 D2
Endsleigh Gdns *SURB* KT6............35 H3
Endway *BRYLDS* KT5....................36 D4
Enfield Rd *BTFD* TW8....................7 E1
Engadine St *WAND/EARL* SW18.....25 G1
England Wy *NWMAL* KT3..............37 E1
Engleheart Dr
 EBED/NFELT TW14...................10 A4
Enmore Gdns
 MORT/ESHN SW14...................15 G3
Enmore Rd *PUT/ROE* SW15...........16 D2
Ennerdale Cl
 EBED/NFELT TW14...................18 A1
Ennerdale Rd *RCH/KEW* TW9...........7 G5
Ennismore Gdns *THDIT* KT7...........34 D3
Enterprise Wy *TEDD* TW11.............21 E5
 WAND/EARL SW18...................17 H2
Epsom Rd *MRDN* SM4..................39 G3
Epworth Rd *ISLW* TW7....................6 C3
Ericcson Cl *WAND/EARL* SW18......17 H3
Erncroft Wy *TWK* TW1..................13 E4
Ernest Gdns *CHSWK* W4.................8 A2
Ernest Rd *KUT* KT1........................3 J5
Ernest Sq *KUT* KT1........................3 J5
Ernle Rd *RYNPK* SW20.................32 C2
Ernshaw Pl *PUT/ROE* SW15..........17 F3
Erpingham Rd *PUT/ROE* SW15......16 D1
Erridge Rd *WIM/MER* SW19...........33 H4
Errol Gdns *NWMAL* KT3................38 B1
Esher Rd *E/WMO/HCT* KT8............34 C1
Esmond St *PUT/ROE* SW15...........17 F2
Essex Av *ISLW* TW7......................12 D1
Essex Cl *MRDN* SM4....................39 E4
Essex Ct *BARN* SW13....................9 E5
Estella Av *NWMAL* KT3................38 C1
Estridge Cl *HSLW* TW3.................11 H2
Ethelbert Rd *RYNPK* SW20...........33 E3
Eton Av *HEST* TW5.......................4 C1
 NWMAL KT3...........................37 G2
Eton St *RCHPK/HAM* TW10...........14 A3
Etton Rd *HSLW* TW3....................12 B3
Etwell Pl *BRYLDS* KT5..................36 C3

Eureka Rd *KUT* KT1.......................3 G5
Evans Gv *FELT* TW13...................19 H2
Evelyn Cl *WHTN* TW2...................12 A5
Evelyn Crs *SUN* TW16..................26 A5
Evelyn Gdns *RCH/KEW* TW9..........14 B2
Evelyn Rd *RCH/KEW* TW9.............14 B1
 RCHPK/HAM TW10..................21 H3
Evelyn Ter *RCH/KEW* TW9.............14 B1
Evelyn Wy *HOR/WEW* KT19...........45 H4
 SUN TW16.............................26 A5
Evenwood Cl *PUT/ROE* * SW15.....17 F3
Everatt Cl *WAND/EARL* * SW18.....17 G4
Everdon Rd *BARN* SW13................9 F2
The Everglades *HSLW* * TW3.........12 B1
Eve Rd *ISLW* TW7.........................13 F2
Eversfield Rd *RCH/KEW* TW9...........7 G5
Eversley Crs *ISLW* TW7.................5 G4
Eversley Pk *WIM/MER* SW19.........24 C5
Eversley Rd *BRYLDS* KT5..............36 C1
Evesham Ter *SURB* * KT6.............36 A3
Ewell Court Av
 HOR/WEW KT19......................42 D4
Ewell Park Wy *EW* KT17................43 F5
Ewell Rd *SURB* KT6.....................36 C3
 THDIT KT7............................35 G4
Excelsior Cl *KUT* KT1....................3 G5
Exeter Rd *FELT* TW13...................19 G3
Eyot Gdns *HMSMTH* W6.................9 E1

F

Faggs Rd *EBED/NFELT* TW14........10 A2
 EBED/NFELT TW14...................10 B2
Fairacre *ISLW* * TW7.....................5 G4
 NWMAL KT3...........................31 H5
Fairdale Gdns *PUT/ROE* SW15......16 C2
Fairfax Ms *PUT/ROE* SW15...........16 D2
Fairfax Rd *TEDD* TW11..................29 F2
Fairfield Av *WHTN* TW2................20 A1
Fairfield Cl *HOR/WEW* KT19..........42 D4
Fairfield Cnr *KUT* * KT1................2 E5
Fairfield East *KUT* KT1..................2 D4
Fairfield North *KUT* KT1.................2 D4
Fairfield Pl *KUT* KT1......................2 D5
Fairfield Rd *KUT* KT1.....................2 D4
Fairfield South *KUT* KT1................2 D6
Fairfield Wy *HOR/WEW* KT19.........42 D4
Fairfield West *KUT* KT1..................2 D5
Fairford Gdns *WPK* KT4................43 E2
Fairlawn Cl *ESH/CLAY* KT10..........40 A5
 FELT TW13............................19 G4
 KUTN/CMB KT2......................31 F1
Fairlawn Rd *WIM/MER* SW19........33 G2
Fairlawns *SUN* TW16...................26 B5
 TWK TW1..............................13 H4
Fairlight Cl *WPK* KT4...................43 H3
Fairmead *SURB* KT6....................37 E5
Fairmead Cl *HEST* TW5..................4 A3
 NWMAL KT3...........................31 G5
Fair St *HSLW* TW3.......................12 B1
Fairway *RYNPK* SW20..................32 D5
Fairway Cl *HOR/WEW* KT19..........42 B3
Fairways *ISLW* * TW7....................5 H4
 TEDD TW11...........................30 A2
The Fairway *E/WMO/HCT* KT8.......28 A5
 NWMAL KT3...........................31 G5
Falcon Cl *CHSWK* W4....................8 A2
Falcon Rd *HPTN* TW12.................27 G2
Fanshawe Rd
 RCHPK/HAM TW10..................21 H4
Fanthorpe St *PUT/ROE* SW15........16 D1
Fareham Rd *EBED/NFELT* TW14.....10 D5
Farlington Pl *PUT/ROE* SW15.........16 C5
Farlow Rd *PUT/ROE* SW15............17 E1
Farm Cottages
 E/WMO/HCT * KT8..................35 F1
Farm Rd *HSLWW* TW4..................19 F1
The Farm *WIM/MER* * SW19..........17 E5
Farm Wy *WPK* KT4......................43 H2
Farnell Rd *ISLW* TW7...................12 C1
Farnham Gdns *RYNPK* SW20........32 C4
Farquhar Rd *WIM/MER* SW19........25 H3
The Farthings *KUTN/CMB* KT2.........3 H2
Fassett Rd *KUT* KT1.....................36 B1
Fauconberg Rd *CHSWK* W4............8 B2
Fawe Park Rd *PUT/ROE* SW15......17 G2
Fearnley Crs *HPTN* TW12..............19 F5
Fee Farm Rd *ESH/CLAY* KT10........44 A1
Fellbrook *RCHPK/HAM* TW10.........21 G3
Felsham Rd *PUT/ROE* SW15..........16 D1
Feltham Av *E/WMO/HCT* KT8.........34 D1
Felthambrook Wy *FELT* TW13.......18 C3
Felthamhill Rd *FELT* TW13............18 B4
Fendall Rd *HOR/WEW* KT19..........42 B4
Ferguson Av *BRYLDS* KT5............36 C2
Ferndale Av *HSLWW* TW4.............11 F1

Ferney Meade Wy *ISLW* TW7............1
Fern Gv *EBED/NFELT* TW14............1
Fernhill Gdns *KUTN/CMB* KT2.........2
Fern La *NWDGN* UB2
Fernside Av *FELT* TW13..................1
Ferraro Cl *HEST* TW5
Ferry La *BARN* SW13
 BTFD TW8
Ferrymoor *RCHPK/HAM* TW10.......1
Ferry Rd *BARN* SW13
 E/WMO/HCT KT8..........................2
 TEDD TW11
 THDIT KT7..................................2
 TWK TW1
Ferry Sq *BTFD* TW8......................2
Festing Rd *PUT/ROE* SW15............1
Field Cl *CHSGTN* KT9.....................2
 E/WMO/HCT KT8.........................2
Fieldend *TEDD* TW11......................2
Fielding Av *WHTN* TW2..................2
Field La *BTFD* TW8
 TEDD TW11
Field Pl *NWMAL* KT3......................2
Fields Cl *EBED/NFELT* TW14...........1
Fife Rd *KUT* KT1
 MORT/ESHN SW14........................2
Fifth Cross Rd *WHTN* TW2.............2
Filby Rd *CHSGTN* KT9....................4
Finch Dr *EBED/NFELT* TW14..........1
Findon Cl *WAND/EARL* SW18..........2
Finlays Cl *CHSGTN* KT9.................4
Fircroft Rd *CHSGTN* KT9................4
Firdene *BRYLDS* KT5.....................3
Fire Bell Aly *SURB* KT6
Firebell Ms *SURB* KT6
Fir Gv *NWMAL* KT3.......................3
Fir Rd *CHEAM* SM3.......................3
 FELT TW13..............................1
Firs Av *MORT/ESHN* SW14............1
First Av *MORT/ESHN* SW14...........1
First Cl *E/WMO/HCT* KT8...............2
First Cross Rd *WHTN* TW2..............2
Firstway *RYNPK* SW20...................3
Firswood Av *HOR/WEW* KT19.........4
Fir Tree Cl *HOR/WEW* KT19...........4
Fir Tree Rd *HSLWW* TW4................1
Fisherdene *ESH/CLAY* KT10...........4
Fisherman Cl *RCHPK/HAM* TW10...2
Fitzgeorge Av *NWMAL* KT3............3
Fitzgerald Av
 MORT/ESHN SW14........................2
Fitzgerald Rd
 MORT/ESHN SW14.......................2
 THDIT KT7.................................3
Fitzroy Crs *CHSWK* * W4...............2
Fitzwilliam Av *RCH/KEW* TW9.........2
Fitz Wygram Cl *HPTN* TW12...........2
Fleece Rd *SURB* KT6
Fleetwood Cl *CHSGTN* KT9............4
Fleetwood Rd *NWMAL* KT3............3
Fleetwood Sq *NWMAL* KT3............3
Fleming Wy *ISLW* TW7...................2
Flood La *TWK* * TW1.....................2
Florence Gdns *CHSWK* W4............2
Florence Rd *FELT* TW13.................1
 KUTN/CMB KT2
Florian Rd *PUT/ROE* SW15............1
Floss St *PUT/ROE* SW15
Fontley Wy *PUT/ROE* SW15...........1
The Footpath *PUT/ROE* * SW15......1
Forest Dr *SUN* TW16.....................2
Forest Rd *CHEAM* SM3...................3
 FELT TW13..............................1
 RCH/KEW TW9...........................2
Forest Side *WPK* KT4....................3
Forge Dr *ESH/CLAY* KT10..............3
Forge La *FELT* TW13.....................1
 SUN TW16................................2
Forge Ms *SUN* * TW16..................2
Fortescue Av *WHTN* TW2..............2
The Forum *E/WMO/HCT* KT8..........3
Foster Rd *CHSWK* W4...................2
Fountains Av *FELT* TW13...............1
Fountains Cl *FELT* TW13................1
Fourth Cross Rd *WHTN* TW2..........2
Foxglove La *CHSGTN* KT9.............4
Foxwarren *ESH/CLAY* KT10...........4
Foxwood Cl *FELT* TW13.................1
Frampton Rd *HSLWW* TW4.............1
Francis Av *FELT* TW13...................1
Francis Cl *HOR/WEW* KT19............4
Francis Gv *WIM/MER* SW19...........2
Francis Rd *HSLWW* TW4................1
Franklin Cl *KUT* KT1.....................1
Franks Av *NWMAL* KT3..................3
Fraser St *CHSWK* W4
French St *SUN* TW16.....................2
Frensham Dr *PUT/ROE* SW15........1

Av PUT/ROE SW15 ....24 A3
La RCH/KEW TW9 ....14 A3
Stile Rd
PK/HAM TW10 ....14 B4
ey Cl WIM/MER SW19.....25 F2
ey Rd CHSGTN KT9 ....41 E4
m Cl NWMAL KT3 ....37 H1
nore WAND/EARL SW18....17 H3
ows Cnr CHSWK * W4 ....8 B1
Rd EBED/NFELT TW14 ....10 A5
m High St FUL/PGN SW6....17 F1
ooks Av WPK KT4 ....38 A5
s Av SURB KT5 ....41 G1
s Wy North SURB KT6 ....41 G2
s Wy South CHSGTN KT9....41 F3
ar Ct BRYLDS KT5 ....36 C3
one Cl HPTN TW12 ....19 F5
one Cl HSLWW TW4 ....11 G2
Park Av WHTN TW2 ....20 B2
ell Rd HPTN TW12 ....20 A4
ood Gdns TWK TW1 ....13 E4
ood Wk WIM/MER SW19 ....25 F1
wood SUN TW16 ....26 B3

G

el Cl FELT TW13 ....19 F4
den Rd HOR/WEW TW19 ....42 B5
borough Cl
/CLAY * KT10 ....34 C5
borough Gdns ISLW TW7 ....12 C3
borough Rd NWMAL KT3 ....37 G3
KEW TW9 ....7 G5
d Rd BARN SW13 ....9 F3
Cl HPTN TW12 ....27 F1
Cl HOR/WEW TW19 ....45 H4
te Cl WIM/MER SW19 ....25 E1
orthy Rd KUTN/CMB KT2 ....3 J2
ston Rd PUT/ROE SW15 ....17 E2
en Rd PUT/ROE SW15.....17 E2
er Green Crs HPTN TW12....27 H3
n Cl HPTN TW12 ....19 G5
/ROE SW15 ....23 G4
en Rd RCH/KEW TW9 ....14 D1
en Vls ESH/CLAY * KT10 ....44 A1
er Pl EBED/NFELT TW14 ....10 C4
eld Rd TWK TW1 ....21 F1
k Cl RCH/KEW TW9 ....14 H3
k Gdns E/WMO/HCT KT8 ....27 H5
k Rd HOR/WEW TW19.....7 H5
on Cl HSLWW TW4 ....11 H4
on La CHSGTN KT9 ....45 F1
le Cl HPTN TW12 ....28 A2
Cl KUTN/CMB KT2 ....22 C5
ON SM4 ....39 E4
d CHSWK W4 ....8 C1
N/CMB KT2 ....22 C5
ON SM4 ....39 E5
side KUTN/CMB KT2 ....22 B5
arth HPTN TW12.....28 A1
noor Gdns WIM/MER SW19 ....25 G1
n Bell Cl RCH/KEW TW9.....14 C1
ouse Cl KUTN/CMB KT2 ....31 F2
ateways RCH/KEW * TW9 ....14 A2
eld Gv FELT TW13 ....19 H2
y Av HOR/WEW KT19 ....42 A4
ck Rd WAND/EARL SW18 ....17 G5
ere Rd EW KT17 ....43 F4
va Rd KUT KT1 ....36 B1
a Rd PUT/ROE * SW15 ....16 D3
ge Rd KUTN/CMB KT2 ....31 E2
MAL KT3 ....38 A1
ge St HSLW TW3 ....4 C5
PK/HAM TW10 ....14 A3
ge Wyver Cl
/MER SW19 ....17 F5
gia Rd NWMAL KT3 ....37 F1
dine Rd CHSWK W4 ....7 H2
d Av HSLWW TW4 ....11 H5
d Rd BARN SW13 ....9 E4
en Rd KUTN/CMB KT2 ....2 D2
n Wk PUT/ROE * SW15 ....16 B2
n Cl CHSGTN * KT9 ....40 D4
TW7 ....12 C1
Hill Gdns THDIT KT7 ....35 F5
Hill Rd THDIT KT7 ....35 F4
rt St HSLW TW3 ....12 B1
s Rd CHSGTN KT9 ....41 G5
Park Rd CHEAM SM3 ....39 G5
n Ter BRYLDS KT5 ....36 C3
s Av MORT/ESHN SW14....15 G2
Crs WHTN TW2 ....12 A5
La BARN SW13 ....16 B1
ood Rd WAND/EARL SW18....17 F5
y EBED/NFELT TW14 ....10 B1

Glade Cl SURB * KT6....41 E1
The Glade EW KT17 ....43 F5
Gladioli Cl HPTN TW12....27 H1
Gladstone Av
EBED/NFELT TW14 ....10 B4
WHTN TW2 ....12 C5
Gladstone Gdns HSLW TW3 ....5 F4
Gladstone Pl E/WMO/HCT * KT8....34 D2
Gladstone Rd KUT KT1 ....3 H6
SURB KT6 ....41 E1
WIM/MER SW19 ....33 H2
Gladwyn Rd PUT/ROE SW15....17 E1
Glamorgan Rd KUT KT1....29 H2
Glasbrook Av WHTN TW2 ....19 G5
Glastonbury Rd MRDN SM4 ....39 H4
Glazebrook Rd TEDD TW11 ....29 E2
The Glebe WHTN TW2 ....38 A5
Glebe Cl CHSWK * W4 ....8 D1
Glebe Gdns NWMAL KT3 ....38 A2
Glebelands E/WMO/HCT KT8 ....34 A2
ESH/CLAY KT10 ....44 A2
Glebelands Rd
EBED/NFELT TW14 ....10 B5
Glebe Rd BARN SW13 ....9 F5
Glebe Side TWK TW1 ....13 E4
Glebe St CHSWK W4 ....8 C1
Glebe Wy FELT TW13 ....19 H3
Glegg Pl PUT/ROE * SW15....17 F2
Glen Albyn Rd WIM/MER SW19 ....25 E2
Glenavon Cl ESH/CLAY KT10....40 B5
Glenbuck Rd SURB KT6 ....36 A3
Glendarvon St PUT/ROE SW15 ....17 E1
Glendower Gdns
MORT/ESHN SW14 ....15 G1
Glendower Rd
MORT/ESHN SW14 ....15 G1
Glenhurst Rd BTFD TW8 ....6 D2
Glen Rd CHSGTN KT9 ....41 F2
Glentham Cottages
BARN * SW13 ....9 F2
Glentham Gdns BARN SW13....9 F2
Glentham Rd BARN SW13 ....9 F2
The Glen NWDGN UB2 ....4 C1
Glenthorne Cl CHEAM SM3....39 H5
Glenthorne Gdns CHEAM SM3 ....39 H5
Glenthorne Rd KUT KT1 ....3 H5
Glenthorpe Rd MRDN SM4 ....39 E2
Glenville Rd KUTN/CMB KT2 ....3 G2
Glenwood Rd EW KT17 ....43 F5
HSLW TW3 ....5 G3
Gloster Rd NWMAL KT3 ....37 H1
Gloucester Cl THDIT * KT7....35 F5
Gloucester Ct RCH/KEW * TW9 ....7 H3
Gloucester Rd FELT TW13 ....18 D1
HPTN TW12 ....28 A2
HSLWW TW4 ....11 H5
KUT KT1 ....3 H5
RCH/KEW TW9 ....7 H4
TEDD TW11 ....20 D5
WHTN TW2 ....20 B1
Goat Whf BTFD TW8 ....7 F2
Godfrey Av WHTN TW2 ....12 C5
Godfrey Wy HSLWW TW4 ....11 F5
Godstone Rd TWK TW1 ....13 F4
Godwin Cl HOR/WEW KT19 ....42 B5
Goldcliff Cl MRDN SM4 ....39 H1
Golf Club Dr KUTN/CMB KT2 ....31 G2
Golf Side WHTN TW2 ....20 B2
Golf Side Cl NWMAL KT3 ....31 H4
Gomer Gdns TEDD TW11 ....29 F1
Gomer Pl TEDD TW11 ....29 F1
Gonston Cl WIM/MER SW19 ....25 F2
Gonville St FUL/PGN SW6....17 F1
Goodenough Rd
WIM/MER SW19 ....33 H2
Gooding Cl NWMAL KT3 ....37 F1
Goodwood Cl MRDN SM4 ....39 H1
Gordon Av MORT/ESHN SW14 ....15 H2
TWK TW1 ....13 F3
Gordondale Rd WIM/MER SW19....25 H2
Gordon Rd BRYLDS KT5....36 C4
CHSWK W4 ....8 A2
HSLW TW3 ....12 B2
KUTN/CMB KT2 ....2 E3
RCH/KEW TW9 ....7 H5
Gore Rd RYNPK SW20 ....32 D4
Gosbury Hl CHSGTN KT9....41 F3
Gosling Rd WHTN TW2 ....19 H1
Gothic Rd WHTN TW2 ....20 C2
Gould Rd WHTN TW2 ....20 D1
Gower Rd ISLW TW7 ....12 A2
Graburn Wy E/WMO/HCT KT8 ....28 C5
Graemesdyke Av
MORT/ESHN SW14 ....15 E1
Grafton Cl HSLWW TW4....11 F5
WPK KT4 ....42 D2
Grafton Park Rd WPK KT4 ....42 D1
Grafton Rd NWMAL KT3 ....37 H1

WPK KT4 ....42 C2
Graham Gdns SURB KT6 ....36 B5
Graham Rd HPTN TW12 ....19 H4
WIM/MER SW19 ....33 H2
Grainger Rd ISLW TW7 ....6 A5
Granard Av PUT/ROE SW15 ....16 C3
Grand Av BRYLDS KT5 ....37 E3
Grand Dr RYNPK SW20 ....32 D5
Grandison Rd WPK KT4 ....43 E4
Grand Pde MORT/ESHN * SW14....15 F2
SURB * KT6 ....36 D5
The Grange HOR/WEW KT19 ....42 C3
NWMAL * KT3 ....38 B2
WIM/MER SW19 ....33 E1
Grange Av WHTN TW2 ....20 D2
Grange Cl E/WMO/HCT KT8 ....34 A1
NWDGN UB2 ....4 C1
Grange Park Pl RYNPK SW20 ....32 C2
Grange Rd BARN SW13 ....9 F4
CHSGTN KT9 ....41 F3
CHSWK W4 ....8 A1
E/WMO/HCT KT8 ....34 A1
KUT KT1 ....2 C6
Grantchester KUT * KT1 ....3 C5
Grantham Rd CHSWK W4 ....8 D3
Grant Wy ISLW TW7 ....6 A2
Granville Av FELT TW13 ....18 B2
HSLW TW3 ....11 H3
Granville Rd WAND/EARL SW18 ....17 G5
WIM/MER SW19 ....33 H2
Grapsome Cl CHSGTN KT9 ....44 D1
Grasmere Av WIM/MER SW19 ....33 H5
PUT/ROE SW15 ....23 G4
WIM/MER SW19 ....33 H5
Grasmere Cl EBED/NFELT TW14....18 A1
Gravel Rd WHTN TW2 ....20 D1
Grayham Crs NWMAL KT3 ....37 G1
Grayham Rd NWMAL KT3 ....37 G1
Grayswood Gdns RYNPK SW20 ....32 C4
Great Chertsey Rd CHSWK W4 ....8 B3
FELT TW13 ....19 G3
Great South-West Rd
EBED/NFELT TW14 ....10 A2
Great West Rd CHSWK W4 ....8 B2
HEST TW5 ....5 E4
Great West Rd Chiswick
CHSWK W4 ....9 E2
Great West Rd Ellesmere Rd
CHSWK W4 ....8 B2
Great West Rd Hogarth La
CHSWK W4 ....8 C2
Grebe Ter KUT * KT1 ....2 C6
Green Cl FELT TW13 ....19 F5
Greencroft Rd HEST TW5 ....4 C4
Green Dragon La BTFD TW8....7 F1
Green End CHSGTN KT9 ....41 E3
Greenfield Av BRYLDS KT5 ....37 E3
Greenlands HOR/WEW KT19 ....42 A4
Green La CHSGTN KT9 ....45 F1
E/WMO/HCT KT8 ....34 A2
FELT TW13 ....19 F5
HSLWW TW4 ....10 D2
NWMAL KT3 ....37 G2
SUN TW16 ....26 A4
WPK KT4 ....38 B5
Greenlaw Gdns NWMAL KT3....38 A4
Green Leas SUN TW16 ....26 A4
Green Leas Cl SUN TW16 ....26 A1
Green Man La
EBED/NFELT TW14 ....10 B2
Greenoak Wy WIM/MER SW19 ....25 E4
Green Pde HSLW * TW3 ....12 A4
Greenstead Gdns
PUT/ROE SW15 ....16 B3
Green St SUN TW16 ....26 B3
The Green FELT TW13 ....18 C2
HEST TW5 ....5 E3
MRDN SM4 ....39 F1
NWMAL KT3 ....31 F5
RCH/KEW TW9 ....14 A3
WHTN TW2 ....20 D1
Green Vw CHSGTN KT9 ....45 G1
Green Wk NWDGN UB2 ....4 D1
Greenway RYNPK SW20 ....38 D1
The Greenways TWK * TW1....13 F4
The Greenway HSLWW * TW4 ....11 F2
Greenwood Cl MRDN SM4 ....39 F1
THDIT KT7 ....35 F5
Greenwood La HPTN TW12 ....20 A5
Greenwood Pk KUTN/CMB KT2....31 H4
Greenwood Rd ISLW TW7 ....7 F5
THDIT KT7 ....35 F5
Grena Gdns RCH/KEW TW9....14 C2
Grena Rd RCH/KEW TW9 ....14 C2
Grenville Cl BRYLDS KT5 ....37 E4
Grenville Ms HPTN TW12....20 A5
Gresham Rd HEST TW5 ....5 F4
HPTN TW12 ....27 H1

Gresham Wy WIM/MER SW19 ....25 H3
Gressenhall Rd
WAND/EARL SW18 ....17 G4
Greville Cl TWK TW1 ....13 G5
Greville Rd RCHPK/HAM TW10....14 C4
Griffin Wy SUN TW16 ....26 B4
Griffiths Rd WIM/MER SW19 ....33 H2
Grimwood Rd TWK TW1 ....13 E5
Grosse Wy PUT/ROE SW15 ....16 C4
Grosvenor Av
MORT/ESHN SW14 ....15 H1
Grosvenor Gdns KUTN/CMB KT2 ....30 A1
MORT/ESHN SW14 ....15 H1
Grosvenor Hl WIM/MER SW19 ....33 F1
Grosvenor Rd BTFD TW8 ....7 E2
CHSWK W4 ....8 B1
HSLWW TW4 ....11 G1
RCHPK/HAM TW10 ....14 B3
TWK TW1 ....13 F5
Grotto Rd TWK TW1 ....21 E3
The Grove ISLW TW7 ....5 H4
TEDD TW11 ....21 F4
Grove Av TWK TW1 ....21 E1
Grove Cl KUT KT1 ....36 B1
Grove Cottages CHSWK * W4....8 D2
Grove Ct E/WMO/HCT KT8 ....34 C2
Grove Crs FELT TW13 ....19 F4
KUT KT1 ....2 C7
Grove End La ESH/CLAY KT10....34 C5
Grove Footpath SURB KT6 ....36 B1
Grove Gdns TEDD TW11 ....21 F4
Groveland Wy NWMAL KT3 ....37 F2
Grove La KUT KT1 ....36 B1
Groveley Rd SUN TW16 ....18 A5
Grove Park Br CHSWK W4 ....8 A3
Grove Park Gdns CHSWK W4....8 A3
Grove Park Rd CHSWK W4 ....8 A3
Grove Park Ter CHSWK W4....8 A3
Grove Rd BARN SW13 ....9 E5
BTFD TW8 ....6 D1
E/WMO/HCT KT8 ....34 C1
HSLW TW3 ....11 H2
ISLW TW7 ....5 H4
RCHPK/HAM TW10 ....14 C4
SURB KT6 ....36 A2
WHTN TW2 ....20 C3
Grove Ter TEDD TW11 ....21 F4
Grove Wy ESH/CLAY KT10....34 B4
Guernsey Cl HEST TW5 ....4 D4
Guildford Av FELT TW13 ....18 B2
Guildford Av BRYLDS KT5 ....36 C2
Gumley Gdns ISLW TW7 ....13 F1
Gunnersbury Cl CHSWK * W4....8 A1
Gunnersbury Ct CHSWK W4 ....8 A1
Gwalior Rd PUT/ROE SW15 ....17 E3
Gwendolen Av PUT/ROE SW15 ....17 E3
Gwynne Whf CHSWK W4 ....9 E2

H

Haddon Cl NWMAL KT3 ....38 A2
Hadleigh Cl RYNPK SW20 ....33 G4
Hadley Gdns CHSWK W4 ....8 C1
NWDGN UB2 ....4 C1
Haggard Rd TWK TW1 ....13 G5
Hailsham Cl SURB KT6 ....36 A4
Haining Cl CHSWK W4 ....7 H1
Haldon Rd WAND/EARL SW18 ....17 G4
Half Acre BTFD TW8 ....7 E2
Half Acre Ms BTFD TW8 ....7 E3
Halford Rd RCHPK/HAM TW10....14 B3
Haliburton Rd TWK TW1 ....13 F3
Halifax Cl TEDD TW11 ....28 C1
Hall Ct TEDD TW11 ....21 E5
Hall Farm Dr WHTN TW2 ....12 C5
Hall Rd ISLW TW7 ....12 C3
The Ham BTFD TW8 ....6 D3
Hambledon Rd
WAND/EARL SW18 ....17 G5
Hambleton Cl WPK KT4 ....43 H1
Ham Common
RCHPK/HAM TW10 ....22 A3
Ham Farm Rd
RCHPK/HAM TW10 ....22 A4
Ham Gate Av
RCHPK/HAM TW10 ....22 B4
Hamilton Av SURB KT6 ....41 H1
Hamilton Cl FELT TW13 ....18 A5
Hamilton Crs HSLW TW3 ....12 A3
Hamilton Pde FELT * TW13....18 B4
Hamilton Pl SUN TW16 ....26 C2
Hamilton Rd BTFD TW8 ....7 E2
WHTN * TW2 ....20 D1
Hammersmith Br HMSMTH W6....9 G1
Hammersmith Bridge Rd
BARN SW13 ....9 G2

Hammersmith Emb
 BARN * SW13 ....9 H1
Hammersmith F/O
 HMSMTH W6 ....9 H1
Hammersmith Ter
 HMSMTH * W6......................9 F1
Hammond Cl HPTN TW12......27 H3
Hampden Rd KUT KT1............3 H6
Hampton Cl RYNPK * SW20 ......32 D2
Hampton Court Av
 E/WMO/HCT KT8......................34 C3
Hampton Court Crs
 E/WMO/HCT * KT8 ....28 C5
Hampton Court Est THDIT * KT7 ...34 D2
Hampton Court Rd HPTN TW12 ...28 C4
Hampton Court Wy THDIT KT7 ...34 D4
Hampton La FELT TW13 ......19 F4
Hampton Rd WHTN TW2......20 C3
 WPK TW4......................43 F1
Hampton Rd East FELT TW13 ...19 G3
Hampton Rd West FELT TW13 ...19 F2
Ham Ridings RCHPK/HAM TW10 ...22 C5
Ham St RCHPK/HAM TW10......21 H2
Handside Cl WPK KT4......39 E5
Hanford Cl WAND/EARL SW18 ...25 H1
Hanover Av FELT TW13 ......18 B1
Hanover Rd RCH/KEW TW9......7 H1
Hansler Gv E/WMO/HCT KT8 ...34 C2
Hanson Cl MORT/ESHN SW14......15 F1
Hanworth Rd FELT TW13 ......18 C1
 HPTN TW12......................19 G4
 HSLW TW3......................12 A1
 HSLWW TW4......................11 C5
 SUN TW16......................26 B2
Hanworth Ter HSLW TW3......12 A2
Harbridge Av PUT/ROE SW15 ...16 A5
Harcourt Cl ISLW TW7......13 F1
Harcourt Rd WIM/MER SW19 ...33 H2
Harding Cl KUTN/CMB KT2......2 C1
Hardman Rd KUTN/CMB KT2......2 D4
Hardwicke Av HEST * TW5......4 D4
Hardwicke Rd
 RCHPK/HAM TW10......21 H4
Hardwick's Wy
 WAND/EARL SW18......17 H3
Harewood Rd ISLW TW7......6 A3
Harfield Rd SUN TW16......27 E4
Harlequin Av BTFD TW8......6 B2
Harlequin Cl ISLW TW7......12 D3
Harlequin Rd TEDD * TW11......29 G2
Harlington Rd East
 EBED/NFELT TW14......10 C5
Harlington Rd West
 EBED/NFELT TW14......10 C4
Harpers Yd ISLW * TW7......6 A5
Harris Cl HEST TW5......4 D4
Harrow Cl CHSGTN KT9......45 E1
Harrowdene Gdns TEDD TW11 ...29 F2
Harte Rd HSLW TW3......4 C5
Hartfield Crs WIM/MER SW19 ...33 G2
Hartfield Rd CHSGTN KT9......41 E4
 WIM/MER SW19......................33 G1
Hartford Rd HOR/WEW KT19 ...41 H5
Hartham Cl ISLW TW7......6 B4
Hartham Rd ISLW TW7......6 A4
Hartington Rd CHSWK W4......8 A3
 TWK TW1......................13 C5
Hartland Rd HPTN TW12......20 A4
 ISLW TW7......................13 F1
 MRDN SM4......................39 G4
Hartland Wy MRDN SM4......39 G4
Harvard Hl CHSWK W4......8 A1
Harvard Rd CHSWK W4......8 A1
 ISLW TW7......................5 H4
Harvesters Cl ISLW TW7......12 C3
Harvest La THDIT TW5......35 F3
Harvest Rd FELT TW13......18 B4
Harvey Dr HPTN TW12......28 A3
Harvey Rd HSLWW TW4......11 G5
Haslam Av CHEAM SM3......39 F5
Haslemere Cl HPTN TW12......19 G5
Hastings Dr SURB KT6......35 H3
Hatch Pl RCHPK/HAM TW10 ...22 C5
Hatherleigh Cl CHSGTN KT9 ...41 E4
 MRDN SM4......................39 H1
Hatherley Rd RCH/KEW TW9......7 G4
Hatherop Rd HPTN TW12......27 G2
Hatton Cross Est HTHAIR * TW6 ...10 A2
Hatton Gn EBED/NFELT TW14 ...10 B2
Hatton Rd HTHAIR TW6......10 A2
Havana Rd WIM/MER SW19 ...25 H2
Haven Cl WIM/MER SW19......25 H3
Haven Ct BRYLDS * KT5......36 C1
The Haven RCH/KEW TW9......14 D1
 SUN TW16......................26 B2
Haverfield Gdns RCH/KEW TW9 ...7 H3
Haversham Cl TWK TW1......14 A5
Hawkesbury Rd PUT/ROE SW15 ...16 C3

Hawkesley Cl TWK TW1......21 F4
Hawkes Rd EBED/NFELT TW14 ...10 B5
Hawkewood Rd SUN TW16......26 C5
Hawkhurst Wy NWMAL KT3......37 G2
Hawkins Rd TEDD TW11......29 G1
Hawks Rd KUT KT1......3 F5
Hawthorn Cl HPTN TW12......19 H5
Hawthorn Hatch BTFD TW8......6 C3
Hawthorn Rd BTFD TW8......6 C3
The Hawthorns EW KT17......43 E5
Haycroft Rd SURB KT6......41 E1
Haydon Park Rd
 WIM/MER SW19......................25 H5
Haygarth Pl WIM/MER SW19 ...25 E5
Haygreen Cl KUTN/CMB KT2 ...31 E1
Haylett Gdns KUT * KT1......36 A1
Hayling Av FELT TW13......18 C4
Haymer Gdns WPK KT4......43 F2
Haynt Wk RYNPK SW20......33 F5
Hayward Gdns PUT/ROE SW15 ...16 D4
Hayward Rd THDIT KT7......35 E5
Hazel Bank BRYLDS KT5......37 F5
Hazelbury Cl WIM/MER SW19 ...33 H4
Hazel Cl BTFD * TW8......6 C3
 WHTN TW2......................12 B5
Hazelwood Ct SURB KT6......36 B3
Hazledene Rd CHSWK W4......8 B2
Hazlemere Gdns WPK KT4......38 B5
Hazlewell Rd PUT/ROE SW15 ...16 D3
Hazlitt Cl FELT TW13......19 F4
Headley Cl CHSGTN KT9......41 H5
Headway Cl RCHPK/HAM TW10 ...21 H4
Hearne Rd CHSWK W4......7 H1
Heatham Pk WHTN TW2......13 E5
Heathcote Rd TWK TW1......13 C4
Heathcroft Av SUN TW16......26 A2
Heathdale Av HSLWW TW4......11 F1
Heath Dr RYNPK SW20......38 D1
Heather Cl HPTN TW12......27 G3
 ISLW TW7......................12 C3
Heatherdale Cl KUTN/CMB KT2 ...30 D1
Heatherlands SUN TW16......26 B1
Heathfield Gdns CHSWK W4......8 B1
Heathfield North WHTN TW2......12 D5
Heathfield South WHTN TW2 ...13 E5
Heathfield Ter CHSWK W4......8 B1
Heath Gdns TWK TW1......21 E1
Heath Gv SUN TW16......26 A2
Heathlands Cl SUN TW16......26 A4
 TWK TW1......................21 E2
Heathlands Ct HSLWW TW4......11 F3
Heathlands Wy HSLWW TW4......11 F3
Heath Md WIM/MER SW19......25 E3
Heath Ri PUT/ROE SW15......17 E4
Heath Rd HSLW TW3......12 B2
 TWK TW1......................21 E1
Heathside HSLWW TW4......11 G5
Heathview Gdns
 PUT/ROE SW15......................16 D5
Heddon Cl ISLW TW7......13 F2
Hedley Rd HSLWW TW4......11 H5
Heidegger Crs BARN SW13......9 G3
Heights Cl RYNPK SW20......32 C2
Heldmann Cl ISLW TW7......12 C2
Helen Av EBED/NFELT TW14......10 C5
Helen Cl E/WMO/HCT KT8......34 A1
Helm Cl HOR/WEW KT19......45 H1
Helme Cl WIM/MER SW19......25 E5
Hemingford Rd CHEAM SM3 ...43 H3
Hemming Cl HPTN TW12......27 H3
Hemsby Rd CHSGTN KT9......41 G5
Hendon Gv HOR/WEW KT19 ...45 H2
Henfield Rd WIM/MER SW19 ...33 G3
Henley Cl ISLW TW7......6 A3
Henley Dr KUTN/CMB KT2......32 A2
Henley Wy FELT TW13......19 E5
Henry Jackson Rd
 PUT/ROE SW15......................17 E1
Henry Macaulay Av
 KUTN/CMB KT2......................2 C5
Henry Peters Dr TEDD TW11 ...20 D5
Henty Wk PUT/ROE SW15......16 C3
Hepple Cl ISLW TW7......6 C5
Herbert Gdns CHSWK W4......8 A2
Herbert Rd KUT KT1......2 E7
 WIM/MER SW19......................33 G2
Hereford Gdns WHTN * TW2 ...20 B1
Hereford Rd FELT TW13......18 D3
Hereford Wy CHSGTN KT9......40 D4
Herm Cl ISLW TW7......5 H4
Hermitage Cl ESH/CLAY KT10 ...40 B5
 RCHPK/HAM * TW10......14 A3
The Hermitage BARN * SW13 ...9 E4
 FELT * TW13......................18 A3
 KUT * KT1......................36 A1
 RCHPK/HAM TW10......14 B3
Herne Rd SURB KT6......41 E1

Heron Ct KUT * KT1......2 C7
Heron Rd TWK TW1......13 F2
Herons Pl ISLW TW7......13 G1
Hersham Cl PUT/ROE SW15 ...16 B5
Hershell Ct MORT/ESHN * SW14 ...15 E2
Hertford Av MORT/ESHN SW14 ...15 G3
Hester Ter RCH/KEW TW9......14 D1
Heston Av HEST TW5......4 B3
Heston Grange La HEST TW5......4 C2
Heston Rd HEST TW5......4 D3
Hexham Gdns ISLW TW7......6 B3
Heyford Av RYNPK SW20......33 G5
Heythorp St WAND/EARL SW18 ...25 G1
Hibernia Gdns HSLW TW3......11 H3
Hibernia Rd HSLW TW3......11 H2
Hidcote Gdns RYNPK SW20......32 C5
Highbury Cl NWMAL KT3......37 F1
Highbury Rd WIM/MER SW19 ...25 F5
High Cedar Dr RYNPK SW20 ...25 C2
Highclere Rd NWMAL KT3......31 G5
Highcliffe Dr PUT/ROE SW15 ...16 A4
High Coombe Pl KUTN/CMB KT2 ...31 G2
Highdown WPK KT4......42 D1
Highdown Rd PUT/ROE SW15 ...16 C4
High Dr NWMAL KT3......31 F3
Highfield Cl SURB KT6......35 H5
Highfield Rd BRYLDS KT5......37 F5
 FELT TW13......................18 B1
 ISLW TW7......................6 A4
High Foleys ESH/CLAY KT10 ...44 C1
Highland Pk FELT TW13......18 A4
Highlands Cl HSLW TW3......5 E4
High Park Rd RCH/KEW TW9......7 H4
High St BTFD TW8......6 B3
 ESH/CLAY KT10......................40 A5
 FELT TW13......................18 A3
 HPTN TW12......................28 A3
 HSLW TW3......................12 A1
 KUT KT1......................2 B5
 NWMAL KT3......................37 H1
 TEDD TW11......................21 F5
 THDIT KT7......................35 E3
 WHTN TW2......................12 B5
 WIM/MER SW19......................25 F5
High Street Ms WIM/MER SW19 ...25 F5
Hillary Dr ISLW TW7......13 E2
Hillbrow NWMAL KT3......32 A5
Hill Crs BRYLDS KT5......36 C2
 WPK KT4......................43 H1
Hill Crest SURB * KT6......36 B4
Hillcrest Gdns ESH/CLAY KT10 ...40 A2
Hillcross Av MRDN SM4......39 F3
Hillersdon Av BARN SW13......9 F5
Hill Field Rd HPTN TW12......27 G3
Hill Gv FELT TW13......19 C2
Hill House Dr HPTN TW12......27 H3
Hillier Pl CHSGTN KT9......41 E5
Hill Ri ESH/CLAY KT10......40 C1
 RCHPK/HAM * TW10......14 A3
Hillside WIM/MER SW19......33 E1
Hillside Cl MRDN SM4......39 F1
Hill Top MRDN SM4......39 G4
Hillview RYNPK SW20......32 C2
Hill View Rd ESH/CLAY KT10......44 B1
 TWK TW1......................13 F4
Hinchley Cl ESH/CLAY KT10......40 A2
Hinchley Dr ESH/CLAY KT10......40 A2
Hinchley Wy ESH/CLAY KT10 ...40 B2
Hinton Av HSLWW TW4......11 E2
Hobart Pl RCHPK/HAM TW10 ...14 C5
Hobart Rd WPK KT4......43 G2
Hobbes Wk PUT/ROE SW15 ...16 C3
Hogarth Gdns HEST TW5......4 D2
Hogarth Ter CHSWK * W4......8 B2
Hogarth Wy HPTN TW12......28 B3
Hogsmill Wy HOR/WEW KT19 ...42 B4
Holcombe St HMSMTH W6......9 G1
Holdernesse Rd ISLW TW7......6 B3
Holland Av RYNPK SW20......32 A3
The Hollands WPK KT4......38 A5
Holles Cl HPTN TW12......27 H1
Hollies Cl TWK TW1......21 E2
Hollington Crs NWMAL KT3......38 A3
Holloway St HSLW TW3......12 A1
Hollybank Cl HPTN TW12......19 H5
Holly Bush La HPTN TW12......27 G3
Hollybush Rd KUTN/CMB KT2 ...2 D2
Holly Cl FELT TW13......19 F5
Holly Farm Rd NWDGN UB2 ...4 A3
Hollyfield Rd BRYLDS KT5......36 C4
Hollygrove Cl HSLWW TW4......11 G2
Holly Rd HPTN TW12......28 B1
 HSLW TW3......................12 A1
 TWK TW1......................21 F1
Hollytree Cl WIM/MER SW19 ...25 E1
Holman Rd HOR/WEW KT19 ...42 B4
Holmbush Rd PUT/ROE SW15 ...17 F4

Holmesdale Av
 MORT/ESHN SW14......................14 D4
Holmesdale Rd RCH/KEW TW9 ...7 G3
 TEDD TW11......................21 H5
Holmes Rd TWK TW1......21 E1
Holm Oak Cl WAND/EARL SW18 ...18 A4
Holmsley Cl NWMAL KT3......38 A3
Holmwood Rd CHSGTN KT9......40 C4
Holne Cha MRDN SM4......39 E3
Holroyd Rd ESH/CLAY KT10......40 B5
 PUT/ROE SW15......................16 D2
Holsworthy Wy CHSGTN KT9......40 C4
The Holt MRDN * SM4......39 F2
Holybourne Av PUT/ROE SW15 ...16 C5
Holyport Rd FUL/PGN SW6......9 E5
Home Ct FELT * TW13......18 A2
 SURB * KT6......................36 A4
Home Farm Cl THDIT KT7......35 E5
Homefield Rd WIM/MER SW19 ...33 E5
The Homefield MRDN * SM4......39 E2
Home Park Ct KUT * KT1......2 B7
Home Park Rd WIM/MER SW19 ...25 G3
Home Park Ter KUT KT1......2 B5
Home Park Wk SURB KT6......36 A5
Homersham Rd KUT KT1......3 J4
Homewaters Av SUN TW16......26 B3
Homewood Cl HPTN TW12......19 G5
Honeywood Rd ISLW * TW7......13 G1
Honnor Gdns ISLW TW7......5 H5
Hood Av MORT/ESHN SW14......14 D4
Hood Rd RYNPK SW20......32 A3
Hook Ri North SURB KT6......42 C1
Hook Ri South CHSGTN KT9......42 C1
Hook Rd CHSGTN KT9......41 E5
Hook Underpass
 (Kingston By-Pass)
 SURB KT6......................42 C1
Hope Cl BTFD TW8......6 C2
Hopes Cl HEST TW5......4 D2
Hoppingwood Av NWMAL KT3 ...38 A1
Hopton Gdns NWMAL KT3......38 A3
Horace Rd KUT KT1......3 H6
Hornbeam Crs BTFD TW8......6 A4
Hornchurch Cl KUTN/CMB KT2 ...30 D1
Horndean Cl PUT/ROE SW15 ...16 B5
Horne Wy PUT/ROE SW15......16 D1
Horse Fair KUT KT1......2 C4
Horsley Dr KUTN/CMB KT2......30 D1
Horticultural Pl CHSWK W4......8 A1
Horton La HOR/WEW KT19......45 E5
Hospital Bridge Rd WHTN TW2 ...12 B3
Hospital Rd HSLW TW3......12 A1
Hotham Cl E/WMO/HCT KT8......34 A1
Hotham Rd PUT/ROE SW15 ...16 D1
Houblon Rd RCHPK/HAM TW10 ...14 C4
Houghton Cl HPTN TW12......19 F2
Hounslow Av HSLW TW3......12 A3
Hounslow Gdns HSLW TW3......12 A3
Hounslow Rd
 EBED/NFELT TW14......................18 C1
 FELT TW13......................18 C3
 HSLW TW3......................11 H1
Houston Rd SURB KT6......35 G5
Howard Cl HPTN TW12......28 B2
 SUN TW16......................26 A2
Howard Rd BRYLDS KT5......36 C2
 ISLW TW7......................13 E1
 NWMAL KT3......................37 H1
Howard's La PUT/ROE SW15 ...16 D2
Howard St THDIT KT7......35 G4
Howgate Rd MORT/ESHN SW14 ...15 F2
Howsman Rd BARN SW13......9 F2
Howson Ter RCHPK/HAM * TW10 ...14 C5
Hubbard Dr CHSGTN KT9......40 C5
Hughenden Rd WPK KT4......38 B4
Hunter Rd RYNPK SW20......32 D3
Hunters Ct RCH/KEW TW9......14 A2
Hunters Rd CHSGTN KT9......41 E3
Huntingdon Gdns CHSWK * W4 ...8 A3
 WPK KT4......................43 H1
Huntingfield Rd PUT/ROE SW15 ...16 B3
Hunting Gate Dr CHSGTN KT9 ...45 E5
Hunting Gate Ms WHTN * TW2 ...13 E5
Huntley Wy RYNPK * SW20......32 B4
Huntsman Cl FELT TW13......18 B4
Huntsmoor Rd HOR/WEW KT19 ...42 C5
Hurlingham Gdns FUL/PGN SW6 ...9 H1
Hurlingham Pk FUL/PGN * SW6 ...9 H1
Hurlingham Sq FUL/PGN * SW6 ...9 H1
Hurn Court Rd HEST TW5......4 B3
Hurst Cl CHSGTN KT9......45 H4
Hurstfield Rd E/WMO/HCT KT8 ...28 A5
Hurst La E/WMO/HCT KT8......34 A1
Hurst Rd E/WMO/HCT KT8......34 A1
Hussars Cl HSLWW TW4......11 E1
Hyacinth Cl HPTN TW12......27 H3
Hyacinth Rd PUT/ROE SW15 ...16 B5
Hyde Rd RCHPK/HAM TW10 ...14 D5

Wk MRDN SM4 ......39 H4

I

. CHSWK W4 ......8 B4
.Gdns PUT/ROE SW15 ......24 B1
.ton Rd WPK KT4 ......38 A4
.ton Sq WPK KT4 ......38 A4
.SUN TW16 ......26 D4
.Cross THDIT * KT7 ......35 E4
.Gv ESH/CLAY KT10 ......34 C4
.Park Rd ESH/CLAY KT10 ......34 C5
.s St CHSWK W4 ......8 D1
.Park Rd WIM/MER SW19 ......25 E2
.Cl RYNPK SW20 ......33 F4
.sl/ROE SW15 ......16 C4
.esk Gdns WPK KT4 ......43 E2
.ness Rd HSLW TW3 ......11 G2
.k KT4 ......39 E5
.a PI EBED/NFELT TW14 ......18 A1
.od Av HSLW TW3 ......12 B1
.od Rd HSLW TW3 ......12 B1
.SURB * KT6 ......36 C4
.r KT19 ......42 A4
.la Ct RCHPK/HAM * TW10 ......14 C4
.Gdns HSLWW TW4 ......11 E1
.oe Rd HSLWW TW4 ......11 E1
.r FELT TW13 ......18 B2
.dge Cl TWK TW1 ......13 F4
.SUN TW16 ......26 D4
.HSLWW TW4 ......11 G2
.B * KT6 ......41 H1

J

.anda Cl NWMAL KT3 ......31 H5
.ood Child Wy KUT KT1 ......3 J6
.s St HSLW TW3 ......12 C1
.n Rd HOR/WEW KT19 ......42 A5
.ett Cl HPTN * TW12 ......28 A1
.ha Rd KUTN/CMB KT2 ......3 J3
.ngs Cl SURB KT6 ......35 H4
.ha Rd WAND/EARL SW18 ......17 H4
.y Rd HEST TW5 ......5 E4
.Cl HPTN * TW12 ......27 H2
.yn Rd RCH/KEW TW9 ......14 B1
.ll Cl ISLW TW7 ......6 B4
.Austin Cl KUTN/CMB KT2 ......2 C3
.sons Dr HPTN * TW12 ......28 B3
.St HSLW TW3 ......12 B1
.ns Ms WHTN TW2 ......20 D2
.e Av WHTN TW2 ......20 D2
.e Cl KUT KT1 ......29 H3
.e Vis ESH/CLAY * KT10 ......34 D5
.e Wy CHSGTN KT9 ......42 A2
.er/NFELT TW14 ......18 B1
.er Gdns SUN TW16 ......26 A1
.Cl BTFD TW8 ......7 E3

K

.Cl WPK KT4 ......38 A5
.Rd BARN SW13 ......9 G2
.ers Ms TEDD TW11 ......29 H1
.eep KUTN/CMB KT2 ......30 C1
.l Dr WIM/MER SW19 ......17 E5
.n Vis KUT * KT1 ......3 F5
.don Cl KUTN/CMB KT2 ......30 D1
.nbrook E/WMO/HCT KT8 ......28 A5
.n Cl HOR/WEW KT19 ......41 H5
.n Dr TWK TW1 ......13 G4
.n Rd SURB KT6 ......41 F2
.ton Av SUN TW16 ......26 C3
.ton Cl SUN TW16 ......26 C3
.ton Pk SUN * TW16 ......26 D3
.ton Rd HPTN TW12 ......27 G4
.al Cl EBED/NFELT TW14 ......18 A1
.all Rd ISLW TW7 ......6 B5
.al PI PUT/ROE SW15 ......17 G5
.rey Gdns WHTN TW2 ......12 D4
.worth Av WIM/MER SW19 ......25 H5
.worth Rd EW KT17 ......43 F5
.ey Rd KUT KT1 ......3 K4
.K TW1 ......13 F4
.M/MER SW19 ......33 H4
.et Rd ISLW TW7 ......13 E1
.ington Gdns KUT KT1 ......2 B6
.Dr TEDD TW11 ......20 D5
.on Av SUN TW16 ......27 E4
.Rd E/WMO/HCT KT8 ......34 B1

KUT KT1 ......2 B6
Kent Wy SURB KT6 ......41 F2
Kentwode Gn BARN SW13 ......9 F3
Kenwyn Rd RYNPK SW20 ......32 D3
Kenyngton Dr SUN TW16 ......18 B5
Kersfield Rd PUT/ROE SW15 ......17 E4
Kestrel Cl HOR/WEW KT19 ......45 H4
KUTN/CMB KT2 ......22 A4
Keswick Av KUTN/CMB KT2 ......23 H5
WIM/MER SW19 ......33 H4
Keswick Rd PUT/ROE SW15 ......17 F3
WHTN TW2 ......12 B4
Kevin Cl HSLWW TW4 ......4 A5
Kew Br RCH/KEW TW9 ......7 H2
Kew Bridge Arches CHSWK * W4 ......7 H2
Kew Bridge Rd BTFD TW8 ......7 G2
Kew Foot Rd RCH/KEW TW9 ......14 B2
Kew Gardens Rd RCH/KEW TW9 ......7 G3
Kew Gn RCH/KEW TW9 ......7 G2
Kew Meadow Pth RCH/KEW TW9 ......8 A4
Kew Rd RCH/KEW TW9 ......7 G2
RCH/KEW TW9 ......14 B2
Keywood Dr SUN TW16 ......26 B1
Kilberry Cl ISLW TW7 ......5 G4
Killester Gdns EW KT17 ......43 G5
Kilmington Rd BARN SW13 ......9 F2
Kilmorey Gdns TWK TW1 ......13 G3
Kilmorey Rd TWK TW1 ......13 G2
Kilnside ESH/CLAY KT10 ......34 D5
Kimber Rd WAND/EARL SW18 ......17 H5
King Charles Crs BRYLDS KT5 ......36 C4
King Charles' Rd BRYLDS KT5 ......36 C3
King Charles Wk
WIM/MER * SW19 ......25 F1
King Edward Dr SURB KT6 ......41 F2
King Edward's Gv TEDD TW11 ......29 G1
Kingfisher Dr
RCHPK/HAM TW10 ......21 H4
King George Sq
RCHPK/HAM TW10 ......14 C4
King Henry's Rd KUT KT1 ......3 K6
Kings Arbour NWDGN UB2 ......4 B1
King's Av HEST TW5 ......5 F1
NWMAL KT3 ......38 A1
SUN TW16 ......18 A5
Kingsbridge Rd MRDN SM4 ......39 E4
Kings Cha E/WMO/HCT KT8 ......28 B5
Kingsclere Cl PUT/ROE SW15 ......16 B5
Kingscliffe Gdns
WIM/MER SW19 ......25 G1
Kings Cl THDIT KT7 ......35 F3
Kingscote Rd NWMAL KT3 ......31 G5
Kingsdowne Rd SURB KT6 ......36 B4
Kings Dr BRYLDS KT5 ......36 D4
THDIT KT7 ......35 G3
Kings Farm Av
RCHPK/HAM TW10 ......14 D2
Kingsgate Rd KUT KT1 ......2 C2
Kingshill Av WPK KT4 ......38 B4
Kings Keep SURB * KT6 ......36 B1
Kingslawn Cl PUT/ROE SW15 ......16 C3
Kingsley Av HSLW TW3 ......5 F5
Kingsley Dr WPK KT4 ......43 E1
Kingsley Rd HSLW TW3 ......5 F5
Kingsmead RCHPK/HAM TW10 ......14 C5
Kingsmead Av SUN TW16 ......26 D5
SURB KT6 ......41 H1
WPK KT4 ......43 G2
Kingsmead Cl TEDD TW11 ......29 G1
Kingsmere Cl PUT/ROE SW15 ......17 E1
Kingsmere Rd WIM/MER SW19 ......25 E2
Kingsnympton Pk
KUTN/CMB KT2 ......31 E2
King's Paddock HPTN TW12 ......28 B3
King's Pas KUTN/CMB KT2 ......2 B2
Kings Pl CHSWK W4 ......8 B1
Kings Rd FELT TW13 ......18 D1
KUTN/CMB KT2 ......2 C2
MORT/ESHN SW14 ......15 G1
RCHPK/HAM TW10 ......14 C3
SURB KT6 ......35 H5
TEDD TW11 ......20 D5
TWK TW1 ......13 G4
WIM/MER SW19 ......33 H1
Kingston Br KUT KT1 ......2 A4
Kingston By-Pass BRYLDS KT5 ......37 F4
CHSGTN KT9 ......42 A1
Kingston Cl TEDD TW11 ......29 G1
Kingston Hall Rd KUT KT1 ......2 B4
Kingston Hl KUTN/CMB KT2 ......3 H2
Kingston Hill Pl KUTN/CMB KT2 ......23 F4
Kingston House Est SURB * KT6 ......35 G3
Kingston La TEDD TW11 ......21 F5
Kingston Ldg NWMAL KT3 ......37 H1
Kingston Rd BRYLDS KT5 ......42 A1
NWMAL KT3 ......37 G1
PUT/ROE SW15 ......24 C1

RYNPK SW20 ......33 F4
TEDD TW11 ......29 G1
Kingston V PUT/ROE SW15 ......23 G4
King St RCH/KEW TW9 ......14 A3
TWK TW1 ......21 F1
King Street Pde TWK * TW1 ......21 F1
Kingsway MORT/ESHN SW14 ......15 E1
NWMAL KT3 ......38 D1
Kingswood Av HEST TW5 ......4 C5
HPTN TW12 ......28 A1
Kingswood Cl NWMAL KT3 ......38 A3
SURB KT6 ......36 B4
Kingswood Rd WIM/MER SW19 ......33 G3
Kingsworthy Cl KUT KT1 ......3 F6
Kings Yd PUT/ROE * SW15 ......17 E1
Kinnaird Av CHSWK W4 ......8 B3
Kinross Av WPK KT4 ......43 F1
Kinross Cl SUN TW16 ......18 A5
Kinross Dr SUN TW16 ......18 A5
Kirby Cl HOR/WEW KT19 ......43 E4
Kirkleas Rd SURB KT6 ......36 B5
Kirkley Rd WIM/MER SW19 ......33 H3
Kirrane Cl NWMAL KT3 ......38 D1
Kitson Rd BARN SW13 ......9 F4
Kneller Gdns ISLW TW7 ......12 C4
Kneller Rd NWMAL KT3 ......37 H4
WHTN TW2 ......12 B4
Knight's Pk KUT KT1 ......2 D6
Knightwood Crs NWMAL KT3 ......37 H5
Knollmead BRYLDS KT5 ......37 F5
Knolls Cl WPK KT4 ......43 G2
Knowle Rd WHTN TW2 ......20 D1

L

Laburnum Crs SUN TW16 ......26 C3
Laburnum Gv HSLW TW3 ......11 G2
NWMAL KT3 ......31 G4
Lacey Dr HPTN TW12 ......27 G3
Lacy Rd PUT/ROE SW15 ......17 E2
Ladderstile Ride
RCHPK/HAM TW10 ......23 E5
Lady Booth Rd KUT KT1 ......2 C5
Lady Forsdyke Wy
HOR/WEW KT19 ......45 H2
Lady Harewood Wy
HOR/WEW KT19 ......45 H2
Lady Hay WPK KT4 ......43 E1
Ladywood Rd SURB KT6 ......41 H1
Lafone Av FELT TW13 ......18 D2
Lainlock Pl HSLW TW3 ......5 E4
Lainson St WAND/EARL SW18 ......17 H4
Lake Gdns RCHPK/HAM TW10 ......21 G1
Lakehurst Rd HOR/WEW KT19 ......42 D4
Lake Rd WIM/MER SW19 ......25 G5
Lakeside HOR/WEW KT19 ......42 D5
Lambert Av RCH/KEW TW9 ......14 D1
Lambert's Rd SURB KT6 ......36 B2
Lambourne Av WIM/MER SW19 ......25 G4
Lambourne Gv KUT KT1 ......3 J4
Lambton Rd RYNPK SW20 ......32 D3
Lammas Rd RCHPK/HAM TW10 ......21 H4
Lampton Av HEST TW5 ......4 D4
Lampton House Cl
WIM/MER SW19 ......25 E5
Lampton Park Rd HSLW TW3 ......5 E5
Lampton Rd HSLW TW3 ......5 E5
Lancaster Av WIM/MER SW19 ......25 E5
Lancaster Gdn KUTN/CMB KT2 ......22 A5
Lancaster Gdns WIM/MER SW19 ......25 F5
Lancaster Ms RCHPK/HAM TW10 ......14 B3
Lancaster Pk RCHPK/HAM TW10 ......14 B3
Lancaster Pl TWK TW1 ......21 E1
WIM/MER SW19 ......25 E5
Lancaster Rd WIM/MER SW19 ......25 E5
Lancing Rd FELT TW13 ......18 A2
Landford Rd PUT/ROE SW15 ......16 D1
Landgrove Rd WIM/MER SW19 ......25 H5
Landseer Rd NWMAL KT3 ......37 G4
Laneway PUT/ROE SW15 ......16 C3
Langbourne Wy ESH/CLAY KT10 ......40 A5
Langdale Cl MORT/ESHN SW14 ......15 E3
Langdon Pl MORT/ESHN SW14 ......15 F1
Langham Gdns
RCHPK/HAM TW10 ......21 H4
Langham House Cl
RCHPK/HAM TW10 ......22 A4
Langham Pl CHSWK W4 ......8 B2
Langham Rd RYNPK SW20 ......32 D3
TEDD TW11 ......21 G5
Langhorn Dr WHTN TW2 ......12 D5
Langley Av SURB KT6 ......36 A5
Langley Gv NWMAL KT3 ......31 G4
Langley Rd ISLW TW7 ......5 H5
SURB KT6 ......36 B4
WIM/MER SW19 ......33 G3

Langridge Ms HPTN TW12 ......27 G1
Langside Av PUT/ROE SW15 ......16 B2
Langton Rd E/WMO/HCT KT8 ......34 B2
Langwood Cha TEDD TW11 ......29 H1
Lanigan Dr HSLW TW3 ......5 G3
Lansbury Av EBED/NFELT TW14 ......10 C4
Lansdowne Cl BRYLDS KT5 ......42 A1
RYNPK SW20 ......33 E2
TWK TW1 ......21 E1
Lansdowne Copse WPK * KT4 ......43 F1
Lansdowne Ct WPK KT4 ......43 F1
Lansdowne Rd HSLW TW3 ......12 A1
RYNPK SW20 ......32 D2
Lantern Cl PUT/ROE SW15 ......16 B2
Lara Cl CHSGTN KT9 ......45 F1
Larch Crs HOR/WEW KT19 ......42 A5
Larch Dr CHSWK * W4 ......7 H1
Larches Av MORT/ESHN SW14 ......15 G2
Largewood Av SURB KT6 ......41 H1
Larkfield Rd RCH/KEW TW9 ......14 B2
Larkspur Wy HOR/WEW KT19 ......42 B4
Larpent Av PUT/ROE SW15 ......16 D3
Latchmere Cl RCHPK/HAM TW10 ......22 B5
Latchmere La KUTN/CMB KT2 ......30 C1
Latchmere Rd KUTN/CMB KT2 ......30 B1
Lateward Rd BTFD TW8 ......7 E2
Latham Rd TWK TW1 ......13 E5
Latimer Cl WPK KT4 ......43 G3
Latimer Rd TEDD TW11 ......21 E5
Lattimer Pl CHSWK W4 ......8 D3
Lauderdale Dr
RCHPK/HAM TW10 ......22 A3
Laurel Av TWK TW1 ......21 E1
Laurel Gdns HSLWW TW4 ......11 F2
Laurel Rd BARN SW13 ......9 F5
HPTN TW12 ......27 G2
RYNPK SW20 ......32 C3
Lauriston Rd WIM/MER SW19 ......33 E1
Lavender Av WPK KT4 ......43 H2
Lavender Ct E/WMO/HCT KT8 ......28 A5
Lavender Rd HOR/WEW KT19 ......42 A4
Lavenham Rd
WAND/EARL SW18 ......25 C2
Laverstoke Gdns
PUT/ROE SW15 ......16 A5
Lawford Rd CHSWK W4 ......8 B3
The Lawn NWDGN UB2 ......4 D1
Lawn Cl NWMAL KT3 ......31 H4
Lawn Crs RCH/KEW TW9 ......7 H5
Lawrence Av NWMAL KT3 ......37 G3
Lawrence Pde ISLW * TW7 ......13 G1
Lawrence Rd HPTN TW12 ......27 G2
HSLWW TW4 ......10 D2
RCHPK/HAM TW10 ......21 H4
Lawson Cl WIM/MER SW19 ......25 E3
Layton Pl RCH/KEW TW9 ......7 H4
Layton Rd BTFD TW8 ......7 E1
HSLW TW3 ......12 A3
Layton's La SUN TW16 ......26 B4
Leaf Cl THDIT KT7 ......34 D2
Leafield Rd RYNPK SW20 ......33 G5
Leamington Av MRDN SM4 ......39 G1
Leamington Cl HSLW TW3 ......12 B3
Leas Cl CHSGTN KT9 ......45 G1
Lebanon Av FELT TW13 ......19 E5
Lebanon Gdns
WAND/EARL SW18 ......17 H4
Lebanon Pk TWK TW1 ......13 G5
Lebanon Rd WAND/EARL SW18 ......17 H3
Leconfield Av BARN SW13 ......16 A1
Leeward Gdns WIM/MER SW19 ......33 F1
Legrace Av HSLWW TW4 ......4 A5
Leicester Cl WPK KT4 ......43 H5
Leigham Dr ISLW TW7 ......5 H3
Leigh Cl NWMAL KT3 ......37 G1
Leigh Rd HSLW TW3 ......12 C2
Leinster Av MORT/ESHN SW14 ......15 F1
Lenelby Rd SURB KT6 ......36 D5
Lenton Ri RCH/KEW TW9 ......14 B1
Leopold Av WIM/MER SW19 ......25 G5
Leopold Rd WIM/MER SW19 ......25 G4
Letchworth Av
EBED/NFELT TW14 ......10 A5
Levana Cl WIM/MER SW19 ......25 F1
Lewesdon Cl WIM/MER SW19 ......25 E1
Lewin Rd MORT/ESHN SW14 ......15 G1
Lewis Rd RCHPK/HAM * TW10 ......14 A3
Leyborne Pk RCH/KEW TW9 ......7 H4
Leyfield WPK KT4 ......42 D1
Lichfield Gdns RCH/KEW * TW9 ......14 B3
Lichfield Rd HSLWW TW4 ......10 D1
RCH/KEW TW9 ......7 G4
Lichfield Ter
RCHPK/HAM * TW10 ......14 B3
Lifford St PUT/ROE SW15 ......17 E2
Lillian Rd BARN SW13 ......9 F2
Lime Crs SUN TW16 ......26 D4
Lime Gv NWMAL KT3 ......31 G5

TWK TW1 ....13 E4
The Limes *WAND/EARL* * SW18 ....17 H4
Limes Av *BARN* SW13 ....9 E5
Limes Field Rd *BARN* SW13 ......15 H1
Limes Gdns *WAND/EARL* SW18....17 H4
Lime Tree Av *THDIT* KT7 ....34 D5
Lime Tree Rd *HEST* TW5 ....5 E4
Limpsfield Av
  WIM/MER SW19 ....25 E2
Lincoln Av *WHTN* TW2 ....20 B2
  WIM/MER SW19 ....25 E3
Lincoln Rd *FELT* TW13 ....19 G3
  NWMAL KT3 ....31 F5
  WPK KT4 ....38 C5
Linden Av *WHTN* TW3.............12 A3
Linden Cl *THDIT* KT7............35 F4
Linden Cottages
  WIM/MER * SW19 ....33 F1
Linden Crs *KUT* KT1 ....3 F5
Linden Gdns *CHSWK* W4 ....8 C1
Linden Gv *NWMAL* KT3 ....31 H5
Linden Rd *HPTN* TW12............27 H3
The Lindens *CHSWK* W4 ....8 B4
Lindisfarne Rd *RYNPK* SW20 ....32 B2
Lindley Pl *RCH/KEW* TW9 ....7 H4
Lindsay Cl *CHSGTN* KT9 ....45 F1
Lindsay Rd *HPTN* TW12 ....20 A4
  WPK KT4 ....43 C1
Lindum Rd *TEDD* TW11 ....29 H2
Lingfield Av *BRYLDS* KT5........36 B1
Lingfield Rd *WIM/MER* SW19 ....33 E1
  WPK KT4 ....43 H2
Lingwood Gdns *ISLW* TW7 ....5 H3
The Link *TEDD* TW11 ....29 E1
Linkfield *E/WMO/HCT* KT8 ......27 H5
Linkfield Rd *ISLW* TW7 ....6 A5
Link Rd *EBED/NFELT* TW14 .....10 A5
Links Av *MRDN* SM4 ....39 H1
Linkside *NWMAL* KT3 ....31 H4
Linksview Ct *HPTN* * TW12 .....20 C4
Links View Rd *HPTN* TW12 ......20 B5
Link Wy *RCHPK/HAM* TW10 .....21 G2
Linkway *RYNPK* SW20 ....32 C5
Linslade Cl *HSLWW* TW4 ....11 F3
Linstead Wy *WAND/EARL* SW18...17 F5
Lion Av *TWK* TW1 ....21 E1
Lionel Rd South *BTFD* TW8.......7 G1
Lion Gate Gdns *RCH/KEW* TW9 ....14 C1
Lion Park Av *CHSGTN* KT9 ......41 H3
Lion Rd *WHTN* TW2 ....21 E1
Lion Wy *BTFD* TW8 ....7 E3
Lion Wharf Rd *ISLW* TW7 ....6 C4
Lisbon Av *WHTN* TW2 ....20 B2
Lismore *WIM/MER* * SW19 ....25 C5
Lismore Cl *ISLW* TW7 ....6 B5
Lissant Cl *SURB* KT6 ....35 H4
Litchfield Av *MRDN* SM4 ....39 G4
Littlecombe Cl *PUT/ROE* * SW15 ...17 E4
Littlecote Cl *WIM/MER* SW19 ....17 E5
Little Ferry Rd *TWK* * TW1 ......21 G1
Littlefield Cl *KUT1* KT1 ....2 D5
Little Park Dr *FELT* TW13 ....19 E2
Little Queens Rd *TEDD* TW11 ....29 E1
Little St Leonards
  MORT/ESHN SW14 ....15 F1
Liverpool Rd *KUTN/CMB* KT2 ....30 D2
Livesey Cl *KUT* KT1 ....2 E6
Livingstone Rd *HSLW* TW3 ....12 B3
Lloyd Rd *WPK* KT4 ....43 H2
Lochaline St *HMSMTH* W6 ....9 H2
Locksley Sq *SURB* * KT6 ....36 A3
Lock Rd *RCHPK/HAM* TW10 .....21 H4
Locksmeade Rd
  RCHPK/HAM TW10 ....21 G4
Lockwood Wy *CHSGTN* KT9 .....41 H4
Locomotive Dr
  EBED/NFELT TW14 ....18 B1
Lodge Cl *ISLW* TW7 ....6 C4
Lofthouse Pl *CHSGTN* KT9....40 D5
Logan Rd *HSLWW* TW4 ....11 G1
London Rd *EW* KT17 ....43 H6
  ISLW TW7 ....5 C5
  KUTN/CMB KT2 ....2 D1
  MRDN SM4 ....39 H2
  TWK TW1 ....13 F3
London Stile *CHSWK* W4 ....7 H1
Longfellow Rd *WPK* KT4 ....38 B5
Longfield Av *MORT/ESHN* SW14 ...15 E3
Longfield Dr *MORT/ESHN* SW14 ...15 E3
Longfield St *WAND/EARL* SW18 ...17 H5
Longford Cl *FELT* TW13 ....19 G2
Longford Gv *HOR/WEW* KT19 ....42 B3
Longford Rd *WHTN* TW2 ....20 A2
Longmead Rd *THDIT* KT7 ....34 D4
Longstaff Crs *WAND/EARL* SW18 ...17 H4
Longstaff Rd *WAND/EARL* SW18 ...17 H4
Long Wk *NWMAL* KT3 ....31 F5
Longwood Ct *WPK* KT4 ....43 F1
Longwood Dr *PUT/ROE* SW15 ...16 B4

Lonsdale Ms *RCH/KEW* * TW9 ....7 H4
Lonsdale Rd *BARN* SW13 ....9 E3
Loraine Rd *CHSWK* W4 ....8 A2
Lord Chancellor Wk
  KUTN/CMB KT2 ....31 F3
Lord Napier Pl *HMSMTH* W6 ......9 F1
Lords Cl *FELT* TW13 ....19 F2
Loring Rd *ISLW* TW7 ....6 A5
Lorne Rd *RCHPK/HAM* TW10 .....14 C3
Lovekyn Cl *KUTN/CMB* KT2.......2 D4
Lovelace Gdns *SURB* KT6 ....36 A4
Lovelace Rd *SURB* KT6 ....35 H4
Lovelace Vls *THDIT* * KT7 ....35 G4
Love La *MRDN* SM4 ....39 H4
  SURB KT6 ....41 E1
Lovell Rd *RCHPK/HAM* TW10 .....21 H3
Lower Common South
  PUT/ROE SW15 ....16 C1
Lower Downs Rd *RYNPK* SW20 ....33 E3
Lower Green Gdns *WPK* KT4 ......38 B5
Lower Grove Rd
  RCHPK/HAM TW10 ....14 C4
Lower Hampton Rd *SUN* TW16 ....27 E4
Lower Ham Rd *KUTN/CMB* KT2 ....30 A1
Lower Marsh La *KUT* KT1 ....36 D1
Lower Morden La *MRDN* SM4 ....38 D3
Lower Mortlake Rd
  RCH/KEW TW9 ....14 B2
Lower Richmond Rd
  PUT/ROE SW15 ....16 D1
  RCH/KEW TW9 ....14 D1
Lower Sand Hills *SURB* KT6 ......35 H4
Lower Sunbury Rd *HPTN* TW12...27 G4
Lower Teddington Rd *KUT* KT1 ....2 A3
Lower Wood Rd *ESH/CLAY* KT10...40 B5
Lowther Man *BARN* * SW13 ....9 F4
Lowther Rd *BARN* SW13 ....9 E4
  KUTN/CMB KT2 ....3 F2
Loxley Rd *HPTN* TW12 ....19 G4
Ludlow Rd *FELT* TW13 ....18 B3
Ludovick Wk *PUT/ROE* SW15 .....15 H2
Lulworth Av *HEST* TW5 ....5 H4
Luttrell Av *PUT/ROE* SW15 ......16 C3
Lydney Cl *WIM/MER* SW19 ....25 F2
Lymington Gdns
  HOR/WEW KT19 ....43 E4
Lyncroft Gdns *HSLW* TW3 ....12 B3
Lyndale *ESH/CLAY* * KT10 ....34 D4
Lyndale Hampton Court Wy
  ESH/CLAY KT10 ....34 D4
Lyndhurst Av *BRYLDS* KT5 ....37 E5
  SUN TW16 ....26 B5
  WHTN TW2 ....19 G1
Lyndhurst Dr *NWMAL* KT3 ....37 H3
Lynmouth Av *MRDN* SM4 ....39 E4
Lynmouth Gdns *HEST* TW5 ....4 A4
Lynton Cl *CHSGTN* KT9 ....41 F3
  ISLW TW7 ....13 E2
Lynton Rd *NWMAL* KT3 ....37 G2
Lynwood Dr *WPK* KT4 ....43 F1
Lynwood Rd *ESH/CLAY* KT10 .....40 A1
Lynwood Ter *WIM/MER* * SW19...33 G3
Lyric Rd *BARN* SW13 ....9 F4
Lysander Gdns *SURB* KT6 ....36 C3
Lysons Wk *PUT/ROE* * SW15 .....16 B3
Lytcott Dr *E/WMO/HCT* KT8 .....27 G5
Lytton Gv *PUT/ROE* SW15.........17 E3

M

Macbeth St *HMSMTH* W6 ....9 G1
Macfarlane La *ISLW* TW7 ....6 A2
Maddison Cl *TEDD* TW11...........29 E1
Madrid Rd *BARN* SW13 ....9 F4
Mafeking Av *BTFD* TW8 ....7 F2
Magdala Rd *ISLW* TW7 ....13 F1
Magnolia Cl *KUTN/CMB* KT2 .....31 E1
Magnolia Rd *CHSWK* W4 ....8 A2
Magnolia Wy *HOR/WEW* KT19 ....42 B4
Magnolia Whf *CHSWK* * W4 ....8 A2
Maguire Dr *RCHPK/HAM* TW10 ....21 H4
Main St *FELT* TW13 ....19 E5
Maitland Cl *HSLWW* TW4..........11 G1
Malbrook Rd *PUT/ROE* SW15...16 C2
Malcolm Dr *SURB* KT6 ....36 A5
Malcolm Rd *WIM/MER* SW19 .....33 F1
Malden Green Av *WPK* KT4.......38 C5
Malden Hl *NWMAL* KT3 ....38 A1
Malden Hill Gdns *NWMAL* KT3 ....32 A5
Malden Pk *NWMAL* KT3 ....38 A3
Malden Rd *NWMAL* KT3 ....38 A4
Malden Wy *NWMAL* KT3 ....37 G3
Malden Wy (Kingston By-Pass)
  NWMAL KT3 ....37 H3
The Mall *BTFD* * TW8 ....7 E2
  MORT/ESHN SW14 ....15 F3

SURB KT6 ....36 A2
Mallard Cl *HSLWW* TW4 ....11 H5
Mallard Pl *TWK* TW1...............21 F3
Mall Rd *HMSMTH* W6................9 G1
Mall Vls *HMSMTH* * W6 ....9 G1
Maltby Rd *CHSGTN* KT9 ....41 H5
Malthouse Dr *FELT* TW13 ....19 F3
Malting Wy *ISLW* TW7 ....13 E1
Malvern Cl *SURB* KT6 ....36 B5
Malvern Dr *FELT* TW13 ....19 E5
Malvern Rd *HPTN* TW12 ....27 H3
  SURB KT6 ....41 F1
Manbre Rd *HMSMTH* W6 ....9 H2
Mandeville Cl *WIM/MER* SW19 ....33 F2
Mandeville Dr *SURB* KT6 ....36 A5
Mandeville Rd *ISLW* TW7 ....6 B5
Manfred Rd *PUT/ROE* SW15 .....17 G3
Manning Pl *RCHPK/HAM* TW10 ....14 C4
Manningtree Cl *WIM/MER* SW19...25 F1
Mann's Cl *ISLW* TW7 ....13 E3
Manoel Rd *WHTN* TW2 ....20 B2
Manor Av *HSLWW* TW4 ....11 E1
Manor Cl *WPK* KT4 ....37 H5
Manor Ct *KUTN/CMB* * KT2 ....3 G3
Manor Crs *BRYLDS* KT5 ....36 D3
  HOR/WEW KT19 ....45 H5
Manordene Cl *THDIT* KT7 ....35 F5
Manor Dr *BRYLDS* KT5 ....36 D3
  ESH/CLAY KT10 ....40 A2
  FELT TW13 ....19 E5
  HOR/WEW KT19 ....42 D5
  SUN TW16 ....26 B4
The Manor Dr *WPK* KT4 ....37 H5
Manor Dr North *NWMAL* KT3 ....37 G4
Manor Gdns *HPTN* TW12 ....28 A2
  RCH/KEW TW9 ....14 C2
  RYNPK SW20 ....33 G4
  SUN TW16 ....26 B4
Manorgate Rd *KUTN/CMB* KT2 ....3 G3
Manor Gv *RCH/KEW* TW9 ....14 D2
Manor House Wy *ISLW* TW7 ......13 H1
Manor La *FELT* TW13 ....18 B2
  SUN TW16 ....26 B4
Manor Pk *RCH/KEW* TW9 ....14 C2
Manor Pl *EBED/NFELT* TW14 .....18 B1
Manor Rd *E/WMO/HCT* KT8 ....34 C1
  RCH/KEW TW9 ....14 C1
  RYNPK SW20 ....33 G4
  TEDD TW11 ....21 F5
  WHTN TW2 ....19 H1
Manor Rd North *ESH/CLAY* KT10...40 A2
Manor V *BTFD* TW8 ....7 H4
Manor Wy *WPK* KT4 ....37 H5
Mansel Rd *WIM/MER* SW19 ......33 F1
Mansfield Rd *CHSGTN* KT9 ....40 D4
Manston Gv *KUTN/CMB* KT2....22 A5
Maple Cl *HPTN* TW12 ....27 G1
Maple Ct *NWMAL* KT3 ....31 G5
Maple Gv *BTFD* TW8 ....6 C3
Maplehurst Cl *KUT* KT1 ....36 B1
Maple Rd *SURB* KT6 ....36 A1
The Maples *E/WMO/HCT* * KT8 ....29 H2
  ESH/CLAY * KT10 ....40 A4
Mapleton Rd *WAND/EARL* SW18...17 H4
Maple Wy *FELT* TW13 ....18 B3
Marble Hill Cl *TWK* TW1 ....13 G5
Marble Hill Gdns *TWK* TW1 ....13 G5
Marchmont Rd
  RCHPK/HAM TW10 ....14 C3
March Rd *TWK* TW1 ....13 E5
Marchside Cl *HEST* TW5 ....4 A4
Margaret Lockwood Cl
  KUT * KT1 ....36 C1
Margin Dr *WIM/MER* SW19 ....25 E5
Marguerite Vls *RYNPK* * SW20 ....32 C2
Maria Theresa Cl *NWMAL* KT3 ....37 G3
Marina Av *NWMAL* KT3 ....38 C3
Marina Wy *TEDD* TW11 ....30 A2
Mariner Gdns
  RCHPK/HAM TW10 ....21 G3
Market Pde *FELT* * TW13 ....19 F2
Market Pl *BTFD* * TW8 ....6 D3
  KUT KT1 ....2 B5
Market Rd *RCH/KEW* TW9 ....14 D1
Market Ter *BTFD* * TW8 ....7 F2
The Market *RCH/KEW* * TW9 .....14 A3
Markhole Cl *HPTN* TW12 ....27 G3
Marksbury Av *RCH/KEW* TW9 ....14 D1
Mark Ter *RYNPK* * SW20 ....32 C2
The Markway *SUN* TW16 ....26 D4
Marlborough Rd *CHSWK* W4 .....8 B1
  FELT TW13 ....19 E2
  HPTN TW12 ....27 H1
  RCHPK/HAM TW10 ....14 B4
Marlingdene Cl *HPTN* TW12 ......27 H1
Marlow Crs *TWK* TW1 ....13 E4
Marmot Rd *HSLWW* TW4 ....11 E1

Marnell Wy *HSLWW* TW4............
Marrick Cl *PUT/ROE* SW15 ....
Marryat Pl *WIM/MER* SW19 ....
Marryat Rd *WIM/MER* SW19 ......
Marshall Cl *HSLWW* TW4 ....
Marsh Farm Rd *WHTN* TW2 ......
Marston Av *CHSGTN* KT9..........
Marston Rd *TEDD* TW11 ....
Martindale *MORT/ESHN* SW14 ....
Martindale Rd *HSLWW* TW4 ......
Martingales Cl
  RCHPK/HAM TW10 ....
Martin Gv *WIM/MER* SW19 ....
Martin Wy *RYNPK* SW20 ....
Mary Adelaide Cl
  PUT/ROE SW15 ....
Maryland Wy *SUN* TW16 ....
Mary Rose Cl *HPTN* TW12 ....
Mary's Ter *TWK* TW1 ....
Masefield Rd *FELT* TW13 ....
Mason Cl *HPTN* TW12 ....
  RYNPK SW20 ....
Maswell Park Crs *HSLW* TW3 .....
Maswell Park Rd *HSLW* TW3 .....
Matham Rd *E/WMO/HCT* KT8 ....
Matlock Wy *NWMAL* KT3 ....
Mavis Av *HOR/WEW* KT19 ....
Mavis Cl *HOR/WEW* KT19 ....
Mawson Cl *RYNPK* SW20..........
Mawson La *CHSWK* W4 ....
May Bate Av *KUTN/CMB* KT2 .....
Mayberry Pl *BRYLDS* KT5 ....
May Cl *CHSGTN* KT9 ....
Maycross Av *MRDN* SM4 ....
Mayfair Av *WHTN* TW2 ....
  WPK KT4 ....
Mayfair Cl *SURB* KT6 ....
Mayfield Cl *THDIT* KT7 ....
Mayfield Rd *WIM/MER* SW19 .....
May Rd *WHTN* TW2 ....
Mayroyd Av *SURB* KT6 ....
Mays Rd *HPTN* TW12 ....
Maze Rd *RCH/KEW* TW9 ....
McCarthy Rd *FELT* TW13 ....
McDonough Cl *CHSGTN* KT9 .....
McDougall Ct *RCH/KEW* TW9 .....
McKay Rd *RYNPK* SW20...........
McKenzie Wy *HOR/WEW* KT19 ....
Meade Cl *CHSWK* W4 ....
Meadlands Dr
  RCHPK/HAM TW10 ....
Meadowbank *BRYLDS* KT5 ....
Meadowbank Cl *FUL/PGN* SW6 ....
Meadow Cl *ESH/CLAY* KT10 ......
  HSLWW TW4 ....
  RCHPK/HAM TW10 ....
  RYNPK SW20 ....
Meadow Hl *NWMAL* KT3 ....
Meadow Pl *CHSWK* * W4 ....
Meadow Rd *FELT* TW13 ....
Meadows End *SUN* TW16 ....
Meadowside *TWK* TW1 ....
Meadowsweet Cl *NWMAL* KT3 ....
Meadow Vw *HOR/WEW* KT19 .....
Meadow Wy *CHSGTN* KT9 ....
Meadow Waye *HEST* TW5 ....
Mead Rd *RCHPK/HAM* TW10......
Meadway *BRYLDS* KT5 ....
  RYNPK SW20 ....
  WHTN TW2 ....
Medcroft Gdns
  MORT/ESHN SW14 ....
Medfield St *PUT/ROE* SW15 ......
Melbourne Rd *TEDD* TW11 ....
  WIM/MER SW19 ....
Melbury Cl *ESH/CLAY* KT10 ......
Melbury Gdns *RYNPK* SW20 ......
Meldone Cl *BRYLDS* KT5 ....
Melford Cl *CHSGTN* KT9 ....
Melrose Av *WHTN* TW2 ....
  WIM/MER SW19 ....
Melrose Gdns *NWMAL* KT3 ....
  WAND/EARL SW18............
  WIM/MER SW19 ....
Melville Av *RYNPK* SW20..........
Melville Rd *BARN* SW13 ....
Memorial Cl *HEST* TW5 ....
Mendip Cl *WPK* KT4 ....
Mercer Cl *THDIT* KT7 ....
Mercier Rd *PUT/ROE* SW15.......
Mercury Rd *BTFD* TW8 ....
Mere Cl *WIM/MER* SW19 ....
Meredyth Rd *BARN* SW13 ....
Mereway Rd *WHTN* TW2...........
Merivale Rd *PUT/ROE* SW15......
Merrilands Rd *WPK* KT4 ....
Merrilyn Cl *ESH/CLAY* KT10......

t Gdns *CHSGTN* KT9..............40 D5
weather Ct *NWMAL* * KT3 ....37 H2
n Hall Gdns *RYNPK* SW20....33 F3
n Hall Rd *WIM/MER* SW19 ...33 F3
n Rd *WAND/EARL* SW18 .....17 H5
n Wy *E/WMO/HCT* KT8........34 B1
ews *TWK* * TW1 ....13 G4
d Rd *PUT/ROE* SW15............17 G2
elmas Cl *RYNPK* SW20.........32 D5
lham Gdns *TWK* TW1............21 E3
e Green Cl *BRYLDS* KT5 ......36 C3
e La *TEDD* TW11 ....29 E1
eton Rd *NWMAL* KT3 ....31 F5
oor Rd *WIM/MER* SW19 ....33 E3
mmer Av *HSLWW* TW4 ....11 G2
ay *CHEAM* SM3......................39 G4
PI *BRYLDS* * KT5 ....36 C1
Rd *NWMAL* KT3 ....37 H4
Wy *HOR/WEW* KT19.............42 B3
urne Rd *FELT* TW13.............19 F4
s Ct *CHSWK* W4 ....9 E1
arm Crs *HSLWW* TW4...........19 F1
Id Rd *HSLWW* TW4...............19 F1
BARN* SW13............................16 B1
II Rd *BARN* SW13...................16 C1
KUT* KT1 ....2 E6
at *ISLW* TW7 ....6 B5
at Wy *ISLW* TW7.....................6 B5
ot Cl *FUL/PGN* SW6...............9 H4
e PI *ISLW* TW7 ....6 C5
KUT* KT1 ....2 D6
y *EBED/NFELT* TW14 ....10 C3
ood Rd *HSLW* TW3 ....12 B3
r Dr *WHTN* TW2......................12 C5
r Rd *KUT* KT1 ....2 B7
norpe Rd *CHSWK* W4 ....8 C2
n Rd *HPTN* TW12....................27 H2
RT/ESHN* SW14 ....15 G1
Rd *WIM/MER* SW19...............33 H3
va Rd *KUT* KT1 ....1 E2
ax Cl *EBED/NFELT* TW14.....10 H3
edale *BRYLDS* KT5 ....36 C3
ead Gdns *PUT/ROE* SW15 ...16 A5
el Gdns *BRYLDS* KT5.............36 C1
on Cl *EBED/NFELT* TW14....18 A1
oat *NWMAL* KT3 ....31 H3
Side *FELT* TW13 ....18 B4
en La *ISLW* TW7 ....13 E3

Abbey Gdns
HO/HCT* KT8............................27 H5
Ct *HOR/WEW* KT19................17 H5
nber Rd *E/WMO/HCT* KT8....34 D2
ey Park Av
MO/HCT KT8..........................34 A2
ey Park Cl
MO/HCT KT8..........................34 B2
ey Park Rd
HO/HCT* KT8............................34 A2
ham Cl *E/WMO/HCT* KT8....28 A5
ham Wy *E/WMO/HCT* KT8 ....34 A1
ween Gdns
HO/HCT* KT8............................28 A5
k's Rw *WAND/EARL* SW18 ...17 G4
leigh Rd *MRDN* SM4 ....33 F5
nouth Av *KUT* KT1.................29 H2
be Dr *MORT/ESHN* SW14.....15 E3
p PI *HOR/WEW* KT19.............45 H2
IPK/HAM* TW10 ....14 B4
ana Rd *RYNPK* SW20 ....32 D3
em Rd *NWMAL* KT3...............37 H1
fort PI *WIM/MER* SW19 ....33 H3
olieu Gdns *PUT/ROE* SW15 ...16 C3
pelier Rw *TWK* TW1 ....13 G3
rose Av *WHTN* TW2...............12 A5
rose Vls *HSMSTH* * W6 ....9 F1
serrat Rd *PUT/ROE* SW15 .....17 F2
Cl *MORT/ESHN* SW14...........15 F3
field Rd *CHSGTN* KT9 ....41 F4
loorings *CHSWK* * W4 ....7 H2
La *CHSGTN* KT9.....................41 F3
mead Dr *HOR/WEW* KT19....42 D4
Mead Rd *TWK* TW1 ....13 F4
Park Gdns *KUTN/CMB* KT2 ...31 H2
en Wy *CHEAM* SM3...............39 H4
coombe Cl *KUTN/CMB* KT2 ...31 E2
sby Av *BRYLDS* KT5...............37 E4
on Av *ISLW* TW7 ....5 G4
ton Rd *WPK* KT4......................43 F1
ol Rd *HPTN* TW12 ....19 G5
y Rd *CHEAM* SM3 ....39 G5
La *NWMAL* KT3 ....14 A4
ngside Rd *WPK* KT4..............43 G1

Mornington Wk
RCHPK/HAM TW10 ....21 H4
Morris Gdns *WAND/EARL* SW18 ....17 H5
Morris Rd *ISLW* TW7 ....13 E1
Mortimer Crs *WPK* KT4.............42 C2
Mortlake High St
MORT/ESHN SW14 ....15 G1
Mortlake Rd *MORT/ESHN* SW14 ...15 E1
RCH/KEW TW9..........................7 H3
Mossville Gdns *MRDN* SM4........33 G5
Mostyn Rd *WIM/MER* SW19 ....33 G4
Motspur Pk *NWMAL* KT3 ....38 A3
Moulton Av *HEST* TW5 ....4 B5
The Mount *NWMAL* KT3.............32 A5
WPK KT4....................................43 G3
Mount Angelus Rd
PUT/ROE SW15 ....16 A5
Mount Ararat Rd
RCHPK/HAM TW10 ....14 B3
Mountcombe Cl *SURB* KT6..........36 B4
Mount Pleasant Rd *NWMAL* KT3 ...31 F5
Mount Rd *CHSGTN* KT9..............41 G3
FELT TW13 ....19 F3
NWMAL KT3 ....31 G5
WAND/EARL SW18...................31 E1
Mount View Rd *ESH/CLAY* KT10....44 C1
Mountwood *E/WMO/HCT* KT8.....28 A5
Mowbray Rd *RCHPK/HAM* TW10 ...21 H3
Muirdown Av
MORT/ESHN SW14 ....15 F2
Mulberry Crs *BTFD* TW8 ....6 C3
Mulberry PI *HSMSTH* W6.............9 F1
Mullins Pth *MORT/ESHN* SW14 ...15 G1
Munnings Gdns *ISLW* TW7 ....12 C3
Munster Av *HSLWW* TW4 ....11 F2
Munster Rd *TEDD* TW11 ....29 H1
Murfett Cl *WIM/MER* SW19 ....25 F2
Murray Av *HSLW* TW3 ....12 A3
Murray Rd *RCHPK/HAM* TW10 .....21 G2
WIM/MER SW19 ....33 E1
Musgrave Rd *ISLW* TW7 ....6 A4
Muybridge Rd *NWMAL* KT3 ....31 F4
Mylne Cl *HSMSTH* * W6 ....9 F1
Myrtle Gv *NWMAL* KT3...............31 G4
Myrtle Rd *HPTN* TW12 ....28 B1
HSLW TW3 ....5 F5

N

Nallhead Rd *FELT* TW13...............18 D5
Napier Av *FUL/PGN* SW6............17 H5
Napier Rd *ISLW* TW7 ....13 F2
Napoleon Rd *TWK* * TW1 ....13 C5
Naseby Cl *ISLW* TW7 ....5 H4
Nassau Rd *BARN* SW13 ....9 E4
Nell Gwynne Cl *HOR/WEW* KT19 ...45 H4
Nelson Cl *EBED/NFELT* * TW14......18 A1
Nelson Gdns *HSLWW* TW4...........11 H4
Nelson Rd *HSLWW* TW4...............11 H4
NWMAL KT3 ....37 G2
Nelson Wk *HOR/WEW* KT19 ....45 H4
Nene Gdns *FELT* TW13 ....19 H3
Nepean St *PUT/ROE* SW15 ....16 B4
Netheravon Rd *CHSWK* W4...........9 E1
Netheravon Rd South
CHSWK W4.................................9 E2
Netherton Rd *TWK* TW1 ....13 F3
Netley Rd *BTFD* TW8 ....7 F2
Nevada Cl *NWMAL* KT3 ....37 F3
Neville Av *NWMAL* KT3 ....31 G3
Neville Cl *HSLW* TW3 ....4 D5
Neville Gill Cl *WAND/EARL* SW18 ...17 H4
Neville Rd *KUT* KT1 ....3 H4
RCHPK/HAM TW10 ....21 H3
Newbolt Av *CHEAM* SM3.............43 H4
Newborough Gn *NWMAL* KT3......37 G1
Newbury Gdns
HOR/WEW KT19.......................43 E3
New Cl *FELT* TW13 ....19 F5
Newfield Cl *HPTN* TW12 ....27 H5
Newgate Cl *FELT* TW13 ....19 H4
New Heston Rd *HEST* TW5 ....4 C3
Newhouse Cl *NWMAL* KT3...........37 H4
New Kelvin Av *TEDD* TW11..........28 D1
Newlands Cl *THDIT* KT7..............34 D5
Newlands Cl *NWDGN* UB2............4 B1
Newlands Wy *CHSGTN* KT9.........40 D4
Newport Rd *BARN* SW13...............9 F4
New Rd *BTFD* * TW8 ....6 D2
E/WMO/HCT KT8......................27 H5
EBED/NFELT TW14 ....14 D3
FELT TW13 ....19 F5
HSLW TW3 ....12 A2
KUTN/CMB KT2 ....30 D2
RCHPK/HAM TW10 ....21 H4
Newry Rd *TWK* TW1 ....13 F2

Newstead Wy *WIM/MER* SW19 ....25 E4
Newton Rd *ISLW* TW7 ....6 A5
WIM/MER SW19 ....33 F2
Newton's Yd *WAND/EARL* SW18 ...17 H3
Nicholes Rd *HSLW* TW3 ....11 H2
Nicholson Ms *KUT* KT1...............36 B1
Nigel Fisher Wy *CHSGTN* KT9 ......44 D1
Nigel Playfair Av *HMSMTH* W6 ......9 G1
Nightingale Cl *CHSWK* W4 ....8 B2
HOR/WEW KT19......................45 H5
Nightingale Dr *HOR/WEW* KT19...42 A5
Nightingale La
RCHPK/HAM TW10 ....14 D5
Nightingale Ms *KUT* * KT1.............2 B6
Nightingale Rd
E/WMO/HCT KT8.....................34 A2
HPTN TW12 ....28 A1
Nine Elms Cl *EBED/NFELT* TW14 ...18 A1
Niton Rd *RCH/KEW* * TW9............14 D1
Noble Cnr *HEST* * TW5...................4 D4
Norbiton Av *KUT* KT1 ....3 H4
Norbiton Common Rd
NWMAL KT3 ....3 K6
Norbury Av *HSLW* TW3 ....12 C3
Norbury Vls *KUT* * KT1 ....3 G3
Norcutt Rd *WHTN* TW2................20 D1
Norfolk Cl *TWK* * TW1 ....13 G4
Norfolk Rd *FELT* TW13................18 D1
Norley V *PUT/ROE* SW15.............24 B1
Norman Av *FELT* TW13 ....19 F2
TWK TW1 ....13 G5
Normanby Cl *PUT/ROE* SW15......17 G3
Norman Crs *HEST* TW5.................4 A3
Normanhurst Dr *TWK* TW1 ....13 G3
Normansfield Av
E/WMO/HCT KT8.....................29 H2
Normanton Av *WIM/MER* SW19 ...25 H2
Norroy Rd *PUT/ROE* SW15 ....17 E2
Norstead PI *PUT/ROE* SW15........24 B2
North Av *RCH/KEW* TW9...............7 H4
Northcliffe Cl *WPK* KT4...............42 D2
North Cl *MRDN* SM4...................39 F1
ISLW TW7 ....13 F3
Northcote Av *BRYLDS* KT5...........36 D4
ISLW TW7 ....13 F3
Northcote Rd *NWMAL* KT3..........31 F5
TWK TW1 ....13 F3
North Dene *HEST* TW5 ....5 E4
North Dr *HSLW* TW3.....................5 F4
Northernhay Wk *MRDN* SM4 ....39 F1
North Eyot Gdns *HMSMTH* * W6 ....9 F1
North Field Rd *HEST* TW5..............4 A2
Northfields *WAND/EARL* SW18......17 H2
North Hyde La *NWDGN* UB2...........4 B1
North La *TEDD* TW11 ....29 E1
North Lodge Cl
PUT/ROE * SW15......................17 E3
North Pde *CHSGTN* KT9...............41 G4
North Pas *WAND/EARL* SW18.......17 H3
North PI *TEDD* TW11 ....29 E1
North Rd *BTFD* TW8 ....7 F2
RCH/KEW TW9..........................7 H5
SURB KT6 ....36 A3
North St *ISLW* TW7 ....13 F1
Northumberland Av *ISLW* TW7 ....6 A4
North Verbena Gdns
HMSMTH * W6..........................9 F1
North Vw *WIM/MER* SW19 ....24 C5
Northway *RYNPK* SW20 ....33 F5
North Weald La *KUTN/CMB* KT2 ...21 H5
North Worple Wy
MORT/ESHN SW14 ....15 G1
Norton Av *BRYLDS* KT5...............37 E4
Norwood Cl *WHTN* TW2..............20 C2
Nottingham Rd *ISLW* TW7 ....6 A5
Nova Ms *MRDN* SM4...................39 F4
Nowell Rd *BARN* SW13.................9 F2
Nursery Cl *EBED/NFELT* TW14 ....10 H5
Nursery Gdns *CHEAM* SM3..........39 H5
HSLWW TW4.............................11 G3
SUN TW16 ....26 A4
Nursery Rd *SUN* TW16................26 B3
WIM/MER SW19 ....33 F2
Nylands Av *RCH/KEW* TW9............7 H5
Nymans Gdns *RYNPK* SW20 ....32 C5

O

Oak Av *HEST* TW5.........................4 A3
HPTN TW12 ....19 F5
Oakcombe Cl *NWMAL* KT3...........31 H3
Oakcroft Rd *CHSGTN* KT9............41 G3
Oakcroft Vls *CHSGTN* KT9............41 G3
Oakdene Av *THDIT* KT7 ....35 F5
Oakdene Dr *BRYLDS* KT5..............37 F5
Oakdene Ms *CHEAM* SM3.............39 G5
Oaken Dr *ESH/CLAY* KT10 ....40 A5

Oakenshaw Cl *SURB* KT6 ....36 B4
Oakfield Cl *NWMAL* KT3..............38 A2
Oakfield Rd *WIM/MER* SW19 ....25 E3
Oak Gv *SUN* TW16 ....26 C2
Oakhall Dr *SUN* TW16 ....18 A5
Oakhill *ESH/CLAY* KT10 ....40 B5
Oak HI *SURB* KT6 ....36 B4
Oak Hill Crs *SURB* KT6 ....36 B4
Oak Hill Gv *SURB* KT6 ....36 B3
Oakhill PI *PUT/ROE* SW15 ....17 H3
Oakhill Rd *PUT/ROE* SW15 ....17 G3
Oak Hill Rd *SURB* * KT6 ....36 B3
Oakhurst Cl *TEDD* TW11 ....20 D5
Oakhurst Rd *HOR/WEW* KT19 .....42 B5
Oakington Dr *SUN* TW16.............26 D4
Oaklands Av *ESH/CLAY* KT10 ....34 C5
ISLW TW7 ....6 A2
Oaklands Cl *CHSGTN* KT9............40 D3
Oaklands Rd *MORT/ESHN* SW14 ...15 G1
Oakland Wy *HOR/WEW* KT19.......42 C5
Oak La *ISLW* TW7 ....12 D2
TWK TW1 ....13 F5
Oakleigh Av *SURB* KT6 ....36 D5
Oakleigh Rd *SURB* KT6 ....36 D5
Oakley Cl *ISLW* TW7 ....5 G4
Oak Park Gdns *WIM/MER* SW19 ...25 E1
Oak Rd *NWMAL* KT3 ....31 G4
The Oaks *FELT* * TW13 ....19 F2
MRDN * SM4 ....39 F1
SURB KT6 ....40 D2
Oaks Av *FELT* TW13 ....19 F2
WPK KT4..................................43 G3
Oaks Wy *SURB* KT6 ....41 E1
Oakway *RYNPK* SW20 ....38 D1
Oakwood Cl *HOR/WEW* KT19 ....45 H2
Oakwood Rd *RYNPK* SW20...........32 B5
Oarsman PI *E/WMO/HCT* KT8.......34 D1
Observatory Rd
MORT/ESHN SW14 ....15 F2
Octavia Rd *ISLW* TW7 ....13 E1
Odeon Pde *ISLW* * TW7 ....5 H5
Oil Mill La *HMSMTH* W6 ....9 F1
Old Bridge St *KUT* KT1..................2 A4
Old Claygate La *ESH/CLAY* KT10 ...40 B5
Old Cote Dr *HEST* TW5..................4 D2
Old Deer Pk *RCH/KEW* * TW9 ......14 C1
Old Deer Park Gdns
RCH/KEW TW9..........................14 B1
Old Dock Cl *RCH/KEW* TW9...........7 H2
Old Farm Cl *HSLWW* TW4 ....11 G2
Old Farm Rd *HPTN* TW12 ....27 H4
Oldfield Rd *HPTN* TW12..............27 H3
WIM/MER SW19 ....33 F1
Old House Cl *WIM/MER* SW19 .....25 F5
Old House Gdns *TWK* * TW1 ....13 H4
Old Kingston Rd *WPK* KT4 ....42 B2
Old Malden La *WPK* KT4..............42 D1
Old Manor Dr *ISLW* TW7 ....12 B4
Old Mill Rd *KUT* KT1 ....3 F7
Old Orch *SUN* TW16 ....26 D4
Old Palace Yd *RCH/KEW* TW9 ......13 H3
Old Park Ms *HEST* TW5.................4 C3
Old Pound Cl *ISLW* TW7 ....6 B4
Old School Sq *THDIT* KT7 ....35 E3
Old Station Gdns *TEDD* * TW11 ...29 F1
Oliver Cl *CHSWK* W4.....................8 A2
Oliver Rd *NWMAL* KT3 ....31 H4
Onslow Av *RCHPK/HAM* TW10 .....14 B3
Onslow Gdns *THDIT* KT7..............34 D5
Onslow Rd *NWMAL* KT3..............38 B1
RCHPK/HAM TW10 ....14 B4
Onslow Wy *THDIT* KT7................34 C5
Opossum Wy *HSLWW* TW4 ....10 D5
The Orangery *RCHPK/HAM* TW10...21 H2
Orchard Av *HEST* TW5..................4 B3
NWMAL KT3 ....31 H4
THDIT KT7 ....35 F5
Orchard Cl *HOR/WEW* * KT19 ......42 A5
RYNPK SW20 ....38 D1
Orchard Cottages
KUTN/CMB * KT2.......................3 G3
Orchard Ct *WPK* * KT4.................38 B5
Orchard Gdns *CHSGTN* KT9.........41 F3
Orchard Ga *ESH/CLAY* KT10 ....34 C5
Orchard La *E/WMO/HCT* KT8 ....34 C3
RYNPK SW20 ....32 C3
Orchard Ri *KUTN/CMB* KT2 ....31 F3
RCHPK/HAM TW10 ....15 E2
Orchard Rd *BTFD* TW8..................6 D2
CHSGTN KT9............................41 F3
HPTN TW12 ....27 G2
HSLWW TW4.............................11 G3
KUT KT1 ....2 C5
RCH/KEW TW9..........................14 D1
SUN TW16 ....26 B2
TWK TW1 ....13 F3
Orchard St *THDIT* KT7 ....35 G5
Orchid Cl *CHSGTN* KT9...............44 D1

Ordnance Cl *FELT* TW13 ....18 B2
Oregon Cl *NWMAL* KT3 ....37 F1
Orford Gdns *TWK* TW1 ....21 E2
Oriel Dr *BARN* SW13 ....9 H2
Orleans Rd *TWK* TW1 ....13 G5
Orme Rd *KUT* KT1 ....3 K4
Ormond Av *HPTN* TW12 ....28 A3
Ormond Crs *HPTN* TW12 ....28 A2
Ormond Dr *HPTN* TW12 ....28 A2
Ormonde Rd
  MORT/ESHN SW14 ....15 C1
Ormond Rd *RCHPK/HAM* TW10 ......14 A3
Orpwood Cl *HPTN* TW12 ....27 C1
Osborne Cl *FELT* TW13 ....19 E5
Osborne Rd *HSLWW* TW4 ....11 C1
  KUTN/CMB KT2 ....30 B2
Osiers Rd *WAND/EARL* SW18 ....17 H2
Osterley Av *ISLW* TW7 ....5 G3
Osterley Crs *ISLW* TW7 ....5 H4
Osterley La *ISLW* TW7 ....5 H1
  NWDGN UB2 ....5 E1
Osterley Rd *ISLW* TW7 ....5 H3
Otterburn Gdns *ISLW* TW7 ....6 B3
Overdale Av *NWMAL* KT3 ....31 F4
Overton Rd *ISLW* TW7 ....6 A4
Oxford Av *HEST* TW5 ....4 D1
  RYNPK SW20 ....33 F4
Oxford Crs *NWMAL* KT3....................37 G3
Oxford Gdns *CHSWK* W4 ....7 H1
Oxford Rd *HPTN* TW12 ....20 C5
  PUT/ROE SW15 ....17 F2
Oxford Rd North *CHSWK* W4 ....8 A1
Oxford Rd South *CHSWK* W4 ....7 H1
Oxford Rw *SUN* TW16.......................26 D5
Oxleigh Cl *NWMAL* KT3 ....37 H2

P

Pacific Cl *EBED/NFELT* TW14 ....18 A1
Paddock Cl *WPK* KT4 ....37 H5
Padstow Wk *EBED/NFELT* TW14 .....18 A2
Page Cl *FELT* TW13 ....27 F1
Pages Yd *CHSWK* * W4 ....8 D2
Paget Cl *HPTN* TW12 ....20 C4
Paget La *ISLW* TW7 ....12 C1
Paget Pl *KUTN/CMB* * KT2 ....31 F1
  THDIT KT7 ....35 E5
Pagoda Av *RCH/KEW* TW9 ....14 C1
Palace Rd *E/WMO/HCT* KT8 ....28 B5
  KUT KT1 ....36 A1
Palewell Common Dr
  MORT/ESHN SW14 ....15 C2
Palewell Pk *MORT/ESHN* SW14 ......15 C3
Palmer Av *CHEAM* SM3 ....43 H3
Palmer Cl *HEST* TW5 ....4 D4
Palmer Crs *KUT* KT1 ....2 C6
Palmers Rd *MORT/ESHN* SW14 ......15 F1
Palmerston Gv
  WIM/MER SW19 ....33 H2
Palmerston Rd *HSLW* TW3 ....12 F4
  MORT/ESHN SW14 ....15 F2
  WHTN TW2 ....12 D4
  WIM/MER SW19 ....33 H2
Palmers Whf *KUT* * KT1 ....2 A5
Pams Wy *HOR/WEW* KT19 ....42 C4
Pankhurst Cl *ISLW* TW7 ....13 E1
Panmuir Rd *RYNPK* SW20 ....32 C3
The Parade *KUT* * KT1 ....2 A7
  RCH/KEW * TW9 ....14 D1
  SUN TW16 ....26 A2
Paradise Rd *RCHPK/HAM* TW10 ......14 B3
Paragon Cl *BRYLDS* KT5 ....36 C3
Parbury Ri *CHSGTN* KT9 ....41 F5
Parfrey St *HMSMTH* W6 ....9 H2
Park Av *HSLW* TW3 ....12 A4
  MORT/ESHN SW14 ....15 C2
Park Av East *EW* KT17 ....43 F5
Park Av West *EW* KT17 ....43 F5
Park Cl *HPTN* TW12 ....28 B3
  HSLW TW3 ....12 B3
  KUTN/CMB KT2 ....3 G1
Park Ct *NWMAL* KT3..........................37 G1
Park Crs *WHTN* TW2 ....20 C1
Park Dr *MORT/ESHN* SW14 ....15 C3
Parke Rd *BARN* SW13 ....9 F4
Park Farm Rd *KUTN/CMB* KT2 ....30 B2
Parkfield Av *FELT* TW13 ....18 B3
  MORT/ESHN SW14 ....15 H2
Parkfield Crs *FELT* TW13 ....18 B3
Parkfield Pde *FELT* * TW13 ....18 B3
Parkfield Rd *FELT* TW13 ....18 B3
Parkfields *PUT/ROE* SW15 ....16 E2
Parkfields Av *RYNPK* SW20 ....32 D3
Parkfields Rd *KUTN/CMB* KT2 ....22 C5

Park Gdns *KUTN/CMB* KT2 ....22 C5
Parkgate Cl *KUTN/CMB* KT2 ....31 E1
Park Gate Ct *HPTN* * TW12 ....20 B5
Parkgate Gdns
  MORT/ESHN SW14 ....15 G3
Park Hl *RCHPK/HAM* TW10 ....14 C4
Park House Gdns *TWK* TW1 ....13 H3
Parklands *KUTN/CMB* KT2 ....36 C2
Parklands Cl *MORT/ESHN* SW14 ....15 F3
Parklands Pde *HEST* * TW5 ....4 A5
Park La *RCH/KEW* * TW9 ....14 A2
  TEDD TW11 ....29 E1
Parkleys *KUTN/CMB* KT2..................22 A4
Parkleys Pde *KUTN/CMB* * KT2 ....22 A4
Parkmead *PUT/ROE* SW15 ....16 C4
Park Pl *HPTN* TW12 ....28 B1
Park Rd *BRYLDS* KT5 ....8 A3
  CHSWK W4 ....8 C2
  E/WMO/HCT KT8 ....29 H3
  E/WMO/HCT KT8 ....34 B1
  FELT TW13 ....18 D3
  HPTN TW12 ....20 B5
  HSLW TW3 ....12 B3
  ISLW TW7 ....6 C4
  KUTN/CMB KT2 ....22 C5
  NWMAL KT3 ....37 G1
  RCHPK/HAM TW10 ....14 B3
  SUN TW16 ....26 C2
  TEDD TW11 ....29 E2
  TWK TW1 ....13 H4
Park Rd North *CHSWK* W4 ....8 A1
Parkshot *RCH/KEW* TW9 ....14 A2
Parkside *HPTN* TW12 ....20 C5
  WIM/MER SW19 ....25 E4
Parkside Av *WIM/MER* SW19 ....25 E4
Parkside Crs *BRYLDS* KT5 ....37 F3
Parkside Gdns *WIM/MER* SW19 .....25 E4
Parkside Rd *HSLW* TW3 ....12 A3
Parkstead Rd *PUT/ROE* SW15 ....16 B3
Park St *TEDD* TW11 ....28 D1
Park Ter *WPK* KT4 ....37 H5
Park Vw *NWMAL* KT3 ....32 A5
Park Wy *E/WMO/HCT* KT8 ....28 A5
  EBED/NFELT TW14 ....10 C5
Parkway *RYNPK* SW20 ....39 E1
Parkwood Av *ESH/CLAY* KT10 ....34 B5
Parkwood Gv *SUN* TW16 ....26 B5
Parkwood Rd *ISLW* TW7 ....6 A4
  WIM/MER SW19 ....25 F5
Parr's Pl *HPTN* TW12 ....27 H2
Parsons Md *E/WMO/HCT* KT8 ....28 B5
Partridge Rd *HPTN* TW12 ....27 C1
Pauline Crs *WHTN* TW2 ....20 B1
The Pavement *TEDD* * TW11 ....29 C2
  WIM/MER * SW19 ....33 C1
Paxton Cl *RCH/KEW* TW9 ....7 G5
Paxton Rd *CHSWK* W4 ....8 D2
Paynesfield Av
  MORT/ESHN SW14 ....15 C1
Peabody Est *HMSMTH* * W6 ....9 H1
Pears Rd *HSLW* TW3 ....12 B1
Peek Crs *WIM/MER* SW19 ....25 E5
Pegasus Ct *BTFD* TW8 ....7 G1
Pegg Rd *HEST* TW5 ....4 A3
Pelham Av *WIM/MER* SW19 ....33 H2
Pemberley Cha
  HOR/WEW KT19 ....42 A4
Pemberley Cl *HOR/WEW* KT19 ....42 A4
Pemberton Rd *E/WMO/HCT* KT8 .....34 B1
Pembridge Av *HSLWW* TW4 ....11 C2
Pembroke Av *BRYLDS* KT5 ....37 E2
Pembroke Cl *ISLW* TW7.....................11 H5
Pembury Av *WPK* KT4 ....38 A4
Penbury Rd *NWDGN* UB2 ....4 A1
Pendarves Rd *RYNPK* SW20 ....32 D3
Penderel Rd *HSLW* TW3 ....12 A3
The Pennards *SUN* TW16 ....26 D5
Penner Cl *WIM/MER* SW19 ....25 F2
Penners Gdns *SURB* KT6 ....36 B4
Penrhyn Crs
  MORT/ESHN * SW14 ....15 F2
Penrhyn Gdns *KUT* * KT1 ....36 A1
Penrhyn Rd *KUT* KT1 ....36 B1
Penrith Cl *PUT/ROE* SW15 ....17 F3
Penrith Rd *NWMAL* KT3 ....37 G1
Pensford Av *RCH/KEW* TW9 ....7 H5
Pentelow Gdns
  EBED/NFELT TW14 ....10 B4
Pentlow St *PUT/ROE* SW15 ....9 H1
Pentney Rd *RYNPK* SW20 ....33 F3
Penwerris Av *ISLW* TW7 ....5 F3
Pepys Rd *RYNPK* SW20 ....32 D3
Percival Rd *FELT* TW13 ....18 A2
  MORT/ESHN SW14 ....15 F1
Percival Wy *HOR/WEW* KT19 ....42 B3
Percy Gdns *WPK* KT4 ....37 G5
Percy Rd *HPTN* TW12 ....27 H2

ISLW TW7 ....13 F2
  WHTN TW2 ....20 A1
Percy Wy *WHTN* TW2 ....20 A1
Peregrine Wy *WIM/MER* SW19 ....32 D2
Perryfield Wy
  RCHPK/HAM TW10 ....21 G2
Perry How *WPK* KT4 ....38 A5
Perth Cl *RYNPK* SW20 ....32 A4
Petauel Rd *TEDD* TW11 ....20 D5
Petavel Rd *TEDD* TW11 ....28 D1
Petersfield Ri *PUT/ROE* SW15 ....24 C1
Petersham Cl
  RCHPK/HAM TW10 ....22 A2
Petersham Rd
  RCHPK/HAM TW10 ....14 B4
  RCHPK/HAM TW10 ....22 A3
Peterstow Cl *WIM/MER* SW19 ....25 F2
Petley Rd *HMSMTH* W6 ....9 H2
Pettiward Cl *PUT/ROE* SW15 ....16 D2
Petworth Gdns *RYNPK* SW20 ....32 C5
Pevensey Cl *ISLW* TW7 ....5 F3
Pevensey Rd *FELT* TW13 ....19 F1
Peveril Dr *TEDD* TW11 ....20 D5
Phoenix Ct *BTFD* TW8 ....7 F1
Phoenix Pk *BTFD* * TW8 ....7 E1
Phoenix Wy *HEST* TW5 ....4 A2
Phyllis Av *NWMAL* KT3 ....38 C2
Pickwick Cl *HSLWW* TW4 ....11 B3
Pier Rd *EBED/NFELT* TW14 ....10 C3
Pigeon La *HPTN* TW12 ....19 H4
Pilsden Cl *WIM/MER* * SW19 ....25 E1
Pine Gdns *BRYLDS* KT5 ....36 D3
Pine Gv *WIM/MER* SW19 ....25 C5
Pinelees Ct *MORT/ESHN* * SW14 ....15 F2
The Pines *SUN* TW16 ....26 B5
Pine Wk *BRYLDS* KT5 ....36 D3
Pine Wd *SUN* TW16 ....26 B3
Pinewood Rd *FELT* TW13 ....18 C3
Pinkcoat Cl *FELT* TW13 ....18 C3
Piper Rd *KUT* KT1 ....36 C1
Pirbright Rd *WAND/EARL* SW18 .....25 C1
Plane Tree Crs *FELT* TW13 ....18 C3
Plantagenet Cl *HOR/WEW* KT19 .....42 C3
Playfair St *HMSMTH* * W6 ....9 H1
Pleasance Rd *PUT/ROE* SW15 ....16 C3
The Pleasance *PUT/ROE* SW15 ....16 C2
Plevna Rd *HPTN* TW12 ....28 A3
Plough La *TEDD* * TW11 ....21 F5
Ploughmans End *ISLW* TW7 ....12 C5
Point Pleasant
  WAND/EARL SW18 ....17 H2
Polesden Gdns *RYNPK* SW20 ....32 C5
Pond Wy *TEDD* TW11 ....29 H1
Ponsonby Rd *PUT/ROE* SW15 ....16 C5
Poole Court Pde *HEST* TW5 ....4 B5
Poole Rd *HOR/WEW* KT19 ....42 C5
Pope Cl *EBED/NFELT* TW14 ....18 A1
Pope's Av *WHTN* TW2 ....20 D2
Pope's Gv *WHTN* TW2 ....20 D2
Popham Cl *FELT* TW13 ....19 F3
Popham Gdns *RCH/KEW* * TW9 ....15 E1
Poplar Court Pde *TWK* * TW1 ....13 H4
Poplar Crs *HOR/WEW* KT19 ....42 B5
Poplar Farm Cl *HOR/WEW* KT19 .....42 B5
Poplar Gdns *NWMAL* KT3 ....31 C4
Poplar Gv *NWMAL* KT3 ....31 C5
Poplar Rd *CHEAM* SM3 ....39 C5
  WIM/MER SW19 ....33 H4
Poplar Rd South
  WIM/MER SW19 ....33 H5
Poplar Wy *FELT* TW13 ....18 B3
Porchester Rd *KUT* KT1 ....3 J4
Portinscale Rd *PUT/ROE* SW15 ....17 F3
Portland Av *NWMAL* KT3 ....38 A4
Portland Rd *KUT* KT1 ....2 D7
Portland Ter *RCH/KEW* * TW9 ....14 A2
Portman Av *MORT/ESHN* SW14 ......15 C1
Portman Rd *KUT* KT1 ....3 F5
Portsmouth Av *THDIT* KT7 ....35 F4
Portsmouth Rd *PUT/ROE* SW15 ......16 C5
Portugal Gdns *WHTN* * TW2 ....20 B2
Post La *WHTN* TW2 ....20 C5
Potterne Cl *WIM/MER* SW19 ....17 E5
Potters Gv *NWMAL* KT3....................37 F1
Pottery Rd *BTFD* TW8 ....7 F2
Poulett Gdns *TWK* TW1 ....21 E2
Pound Cl *SURB* KT6 ....35 H5
Powder Mill La *WHTN* TW2 ....19 C1
Powers Ct *TWK* TW1 ....14 A5
Pownall Gdns *HSLW* TW3 ....12 A2
Pownall Rd *HSLW* TW3 ....12 A2
Presburg Rd *NWMAL* KT3 ....37 H2
Preston Cl *WHTN* TW2 ....20 D3
Preston Dr *HOR/WEW* KT19 ....42 B4
Preston Pl *RCHPK/HAM* TW10 ....14 B3
Preston Rd *RYNPK* SW20 ....32 B2
Preston Vls *KUT* * KT1 ....3 F5
Prestwick Cl *NWDGN* UB2 ....4 B1

Priests Br *MORT/ESHN* SW14 ....
Prince George's Av
  RYNPK SW20 ....
Prince of Wales Ter *CHSWK* W4 ....
Prince Regent Rd *HSLW* TW3 ....
Princes Av *SURB* KT6 ....
Prince's Cl *HPTN* TW12 ....
Princes Ms *HMSMTH* * W6 ....
Princes Rd *FELT* TW13 ....
  HPTN TW12 ....
  KUTN/CMB KT2 ....
  MORT/ESHN SW14 ....
  RCH/KEW TW9 ....
  RCHPK/HAM TW10 ....
  WIM/MER SW19 ....
Prince's St *RCH/KEW* TW9 ....
Princes Wy *WIM/MER* SW19 ....
Priory Cl *HPTN* TW12 ....
  SUN TW16 ....
Priory Gdns *BARN* SW13 ....
  HPTN TW12 ....
Priory La *PUT/ROE* SW15 ....
Priory Rd *CHSGTN* KT9 ....
  HPTN TW12 ....
  HSLW TW3 ....
  RCH/KEW TW9 ....
Proctors Cl *EBED/NFELT* TW14......
Promenade Approach Rd
  CHSWK W4 ....
The Promenade *CHSWK* W4...........
Prospect Cl *HEST* TW5 ....
Prospect Cottages
  WAND/EARL SW18 ....
Prospect Crs *WHTN* TW2 ....
Prospect Pl *CHSWK* W4 ....
  RYNPK SW20 ....
Prospect Rd *SURB* KT6 ....
Pulborough Rd
  WAND/EARL SW18 ....
Pulborough Wy *HSLWW* TW4 ....
Pullman Gdns *PUT/ROE* SW15 ......
Pump Aly *BTFD* TW8 ....
Pumping Station Rd *CHSWK* W4 ....
Purbeck Av *NWMAL* KT3 ....
Putney Br *PUT/ROE* SW15 ....
Putney Bridge Ap
  PUT/ROE SW15 ....
Putney Bridge Rd
  PUT/ROE SW15 ....
Putney Common
  PUT/ROE SW15 ....
Putney Ex *PUT/ROE* * SW15............
Putney Heath *PUT/ROE* SW15 ....
Putney Heath La
  PUT/ROE SW15 ....
Putney High St *PUT/ROE* SW15 .....
Putney Hl *PUT/ROE* SW15 ....
Putney Park Av *PUT/ROE* SW15 ....
Putney Park La *PUT/ROE* SW15 .....
Pyne Rd *SURB* KT6 ....
Pyrland Rd *RCHPK/HAM* TW10 ......
Pyrmont Rd *CHSWK* W4 ....

Q

The Quadrant *RCH/KEW* TW9 ....
  RYNPK SW20 ....
Quadrant Rd *RCH/KEW* TW9 ....
Queen Annes Cl *WHTN* TW2 ....
Queen Caroline Est *HMSMTH* W6 ...
Queen Caroline St *HMSMTH* W6 .....
Queen Elizabeth Gdns
  MRDN SM4 ....
Queen Elizabeth Rd
  KUTN/CMB KT2 ....
Queen Elizabeth Wk *BARN* SW13 ...
Queen Mary Av *MRDN* SM4 ....
Queen Mary Cl *CHSGTN* KT9 ....
Queens Av *FELT* TW13 ....
Queensbridge Pk *ISLW* TW7 ....
Queens Crs *RCHPK/HAM* TW10 .....
Queens Dr *BRYLDS* KT5 ....
  THDIT KT7 ....
Queen's Gdns *HEST* TW5.................
Queensgate Gdns
  PUT/ROE SW15 ....
Queens Keep *TWK* * TW1 ....
Queensmere Cl
  WIM/MER SW19 ....
Queensmere Rd
  WIM/MER SW19 ....
Queens Park Gdns *FELT* * TW13......
Queen's Pl *MRDN* SM4 ....
Queen's Ride *BARN* SW13 ....
Queen's Ri *RCHPK/HAM* TW10 ....
Queen's Rd *FELT* TW13 ....

V TW12 ...20 A4
V TW3 ...12 A1
T ...3 H1
T/ESHN SW14 ...15 C1
N SM4 ...39 H1
MAL SM4 ...38 A1
PK/HAM TW10 ...22 C4
T TW11 ...29 E1
T KT7 ...35 E2
TW1 ...21 E1
s Ter ISLW TW7 ...13 F2
s T* KT7 ...35 F3
s Wy FELT TW13 ...18 D4
sway SUN TW16 ...26 C4
swood Av HEST TW5 ...4 A5
TW12 ...28 A1
d CHSWK W4 ...8 D1
n Av RYNPK SW20 ...33 F3
on Rd THDIT KT7 ...35 F5

R

Rd NWMAL KT3 ...37 G1
s Pk EBED/NFELT * TW14 ...10 A2
y CI EBED/NFELT TW14 ...18 A1
r Gdns TWK TW1 ...21 E2
r Rd TWK TW1 ...21 E1
n Av BRYLDS KT5 ...37 E3
rn CI KUT KT1 ...2 A1
n CI HSLWW TW4 ...11 F3
ead Rd ISLW TW7 ...13 G2
y Ap TWK TW1 ...21 E1
y Rd TEDD TW11 ...20 D4
y Side BARN SW13 ...15 H1
y Ter FELT TW13 ...18 B1
lle Rd HMSMTH W6 ...9 H2
h Dr BRYLDS KT5 ...37 F5
h Rd FELT TW13 ...18 A2
GN UB2 ...4 B1
/KEW TW9 ...14 C1
h Wy FELT TW13 ...18 D5
e Rd RCHPK/HAM TW10 ...21 H4
lph CI KUTN/CMB * KT2 ...23 F5
agh Av BARN SW13 ...9 F5
PGN SW6 ...17 G1
agh Dr TWK TW1 ...13 G2
agh Gdns CHSWK W4 ...8 B3
PGN SW6 ...17 F1
rd CI CHSGTN KT9 ...41 G2
el Dr THDIT KT7 ...35 E4
dale Rd SUN TW16 ...26 A4
na Rd PUT/ROE SW15 ...17 E3
s Ait SURB * KT6 ...36 A2
sbourne Rd TWK TW1 ...13 H4
scar Rd SURB KT6 ...41 G1
scourt SUN TW16 ...26 A3
sdale Rd HSLWW TW4 ...11 F1
sfield Gdns
/WEW KT19 ...42 D4
swood Av SURB KT6 ...41 G1
swood Ct
N/CMB KT2 ...31 E1
swood Gdns ISLW TW7 ...5 H4
gh Av TEDD TW11 ...28 D1
gh Ct KUT KT1 ...3 G4
gh Rd WIM/MER SW19 ...33 G3
ond Rd WIM/MER SW19 ...33 F1
ond Wy ESH/CLAY * KT10 ...40 B5
r's Rd PUT/ROE SW15 ...17 F3
/WMO/HCT KT8 ...34 A2
rs Wy TWK TW1 ...12 C3
nd CHSWK W4 ...8 D1
ry CI RYNPK SW20 ...32 D4
B KT6 ...35 H5
ry Gv FELT TW13 ...19 G4
ry La SURB KT6 ...35 H5
ry Orch WIM/MER SW19 ...25 H5
gh BARN SW13 ...9 H5
se Av MRDN SM4 ...39 H2
dale Gdns ISLW TW7 ...6 B3
n Av HSLWW TW4 ...11 H5
rd CI CHSWK W4 ...8 A3
te Ter PUT/ROE SW15 ...17 E4
ave Rd PUT/ROE SW15 ...17 E4
ESH/CLAY KT10 ...40 B5
on ISLW TW7 ...13 F2
on Ct HSLW* TW3 ...12 A1
on Rd SURB KT6 ...41 G1
on Sq WAND/EARL * SW18 ...17 H3
on St RCHPK/HAM TW10 ...14 A3
y Dr WHTN TW2 ...12 B5

Regency CI HPTN TW12 ...19 G5
Regent Rd BRYLDS KT5 ...36 C2
Regent St CHSWK W4 ...3 H1
Rembrandt Ct HOR/WEW KT19 ...43 E5
Renfrew Rd HEST TW5 ...4 A5
    KUTN/CMB KT2 ...31 F2
Replingham Rd
    WAND/EARL SW18 ...25 G1
Retreat Rd RCH/KEW TW9 ...14 A3
The Retreat BARN SW13 ...15 H1
    BRYLDS KT5 ...36 C3
    WPK KT4 ...43 G2
Revell Rd KUT KT1 ...3 K3
Revelstoke Rd WIM/MER SW19 ...25 H4
Reynolds Av CHSGTN KT9 ...45 F1
Reynolds PI RCHPK/HAM TW10 ...14 C4
Reynolds Rd NWMAL KT3 ...37 G4
Rhodrons Av CHSGTN KT9 ...41 F4
Ricards CI SURB KT6 ...41 F1
Richens CI HSLW TW3 ...5 G5
Richlands Av EW KT17 ...43 F5
Richmond Av RYNPK SW20 ...33 F3
Richmond HI RCHPK/HAM TW10 ...14 B4
Richmond Pde TWK * TW1 ...13 H4
Richmond Park Rd
    KUTN/CMB KT2 ...2 D2
    MORT/ESHN SW14 ...15 F3
Richmond Rd ISLW TW7 ...13 F1
    KUTN/CMB KT2 ...22 A5
    RYNPK SW20 ...32 C3
    TWK TW1 ...13 G5
Rickards CI SURB KT6 ...41 F1
The Ride BTFD TW8 ...6 C1
Ridge Rd CHEAM SM3 ...39 G5
The Ridge BRYLDS KT5 ...36 D2
    WHTN TW2 ...12 C5
Ridge Wy FELT TW13 ...19 F3
Ridgeway Rd ISLW TW7 ...5 H3
Ridgeway Rd North ISLW TW7 ...5 H3
Ridgway RCHPK/HAM * TW10 ...14 B4
    WIM/MER SW19 ...32 D2
Ridgway Gdns WIM/MER SW19 ...33 E2
Ridgway PI WIM/MER SW19 ...33 F1
The Ridings BRYLDS KT5 ...36 D2
    SUN TW16 ...26 B3
Ringford Rd WAND/EARL SW18 ...17 G2
Ringway NWDGN UB2 ...4 B1
Ringwood Gdns PUT/ROE SW15 ...24 B2
Ringwood Wy HPTN TW12 ...19 H4
Ripley Gdns MORT/ESHN SW14 ...15 G1
Ripley Rd HOR/WEW KT19 ...45 H4
Ripon Gdns CHSGTN KT9 ...41 E4
Risborough Dr WPK KT4 ...38 B4
River Av THDIT KT7 ...35 F4
Riverbank E/WMO/HCT KT8 ...28 D5
River Bank KUT KT1 ...35 E2
Riverbank Wy BTFD TW8 ...6 D2
Riverdale Gdns TWK TW1 ...13 H3
Riverdale Rd FELT TW13 ...19 G4
    TWK TW1 ...13 H4
River Gdns EBED/NFELT TW14 ...10 C3
River La RCHPK/HAM TW10 ...22 A1
Rivermead E/WMO/HCT KT8 ...28 B5
    SURB * KT6 ...36 A2
Rivermead Ct TEDD TW11 ...21 C5
River Meads Av WHTN TW2 ...20 A3
River Reach TEDD TW11 ...29 H1
Riversdale Rd THDIT KT7 ...35 F2
The Riverside
    E/WMO/HCT * KT8 ...28 C5
    SUN * TW16 ...27 E4
    TWK * TW1 ...21 G1
Riverside Av E/WMO/HCT KT8 ...34 C2
Riverside CI KUT KT1 ...36 A1
Riverside Dr CHSWK W4 ...8 C3
    RCHPK/HAM TW10 ...21 G3
Riverside Gdns HMSMTH W6 ...9 G1
Riverside Vls SURB * KT6 ...35 H3
Riverside Wk ISLW TW7 ...12 D1
    KUT KT1 ...2 A4
River Ter HMSMTH W6 ...9 H1
Riverview Gdns BARN SW13 ...9 H3
River View Gdns TWK TW1 ...21 E2
Riverview Rd CHSWK W4 ...8 A3
    HOR/WEW KT19 ...42 B3
River Wk SUN TW16 ...27 E4
River Wy FELT TW13 ...20 A2
    HOR/WEW KT19 ...42 C4
Roberts Ct CHSGTN * KT9 ...41 E4
Robin CI HPTN TW12 ...19 F5
Robin Gv BTFD TW8 ...6 D3
Robin Hood La PUT/ROE SW15 ...23 H2
Robin Hood Rd PUT/ROE SW15 ...23 H4
Robin Hood Wy
    (Kingston By-Pass)
    PUT/ROE SW15 ...23 H4

Robinwood PI RCHPK/HAM TW10..23 G4
Rochester Av FELT TW13 ...18 A2
Rochester Pde FELT * TW13 ...18 B3
Rock Av MORT/ESHN SW14 ...15 G1
Rockingham CI PUT/ROE SW15 ...16 A2
Rockland Rd PUT/ROE SW15 ...17 F2
Rocks La BARN SW13 ...16 B1
Rodney CI NWMAL KT3 ...37 H2
Rodney Rd HSLWW TW4 ...11 H4
    NWMAL KT3 ...37 H2
Rodway Rd PUT/ROE SW15 ...16 B5
Roebuck CI FELT TW13 ...18 C4
Roebuck Rd CHSGTN KT9 ...41 H4
Roedean Crs PUT/ROE SW15 ...15 H4
Roehampton CI PUT/ROE SW15 ...16 B2
Roehampton Ga PUT/ROE SW15..15 H4
Roehampton High St
    PUT/ROE SW15 ...16 B5
Roehampton La PUT/ROE SW15 ...16 B2
Roehampton V PUT/ROE SW15 ...24 A3
Rokeby PI RYNPK SW20 ...32 C2
Roland Wy WPK KT4 ...43 E1
Rollesby Rd CHSGTN KT9 ...41 H5
Rollit Crs HSLW TW3 ...11 H3
Roman CI EBED/NFELT TW14 ...10 D3
Romany Gdns CHEAM SM3 ...39 H4
Romney CI CHSGTN KT9 ...41 F3
Romney Rd NWMAL KT3 ...37 G3
Ronelean Rd SURB KT6 ...41 G1
Rookeries CI FELT TW13 ...18 C3
Rooksmead Rd SUN TW16 ...26 A4
Rookwood Av NWMAL KT3 ...38 B1
Rosamond Vls
    MORT/ESHN * SW14 ...15 G3
Rosary CI HSLW TW3 ...4 B5
Rosebank CI TEDD TW11 ...29 F1
Rosebery Av NWMAL KT3 ...32 A4
Rosebery CI MRDN SM4 ...39 E3
Rosebery Rd ISLW TW7 ...12 B3
    KUT KT1 ...3 J5
Rosebery Sq KUT KT1 ...3 J5
Rosebine Av WHTN TW2 ...12 C5
Rosecroft Gdns WHTN TW2 ...20 A1
Rosedale Rd EW KT17 ...43 F4
    RCH/KEW TW9 ...14 B2
Rosedene Av MRDN SM4 ...39 H2
Rose End WPK KT4 ...38 C5
Rose Gdns FELT TW13 ...18 B2
Roseheath Rd HSLWW TW4 ...11 G3
Rosehill RCHPK/HAM KT10 ...40 B5
    HPTN TW12 ...27 H3
Roseleigh CI TWK TW1 ...14 A5
Rosemary Av E/WMO/HCT KT8 ...27 H5
    HSLWW TW4 ...4 B5
Rosemary Gdns CHSGTN KT9 ...41 F3
Rosemary La
    MORT/ESHN SW14 ...15 F1
Rosemead Av FELT TW13 ...18 A2
Rosemont Rd NWMAL KT3 ...31 F5
    RCHPK/HAM TW10 ...14 B4
Roseville Av HSLWW TW4 ...11 H5
Rosevine Rd RYNPK SW20 ...32 D3
Rose Wk BRYLDS KT5 ...37 E2
Rosewood Ct KUTN/CMB KT2 ...2 E1
Roskell Rd PUT/ROE SW15 ...17 E1
Rossdale Rd PUT/ROE SW15 ...16 D2
Rossindel Rd HSLW TW3 ...11 H3
Rosslyn Av BARN SW13 ...15 H1
    EBED/NFELT TW14 ...10 B4
Rosslyn Rd TWK TW1 ...13 H4
Ross Rd WHTN TW2 ...20 B1
Rostrevor Gdns NWDGN UB2 ...4 B1
Rostrevor Rd WIM/MER SW19 ...25 H5
Rothbury Gdns ISLW TW7 ...6 B3
Rotherwood CI WIM/MER SW19 ...33 G3
Rotherwood Rd PUT/ROE SW15 ...17 E1
Rothesay Av RCHPK/HAM TW10 ...15 E2
    RYNPK SW20 ...33 F4
Rougemont Av MRDN SM4 ...39 H4
The Roundway ESH/CLAY KT10...40 B5
Rowan CI NWMAL KT3 ...31 H4
Rowan Rd BTFD TW8 ...6 C3
The Rowans SUN TW16 ...18 A5
Rowan Ter WIM/MER * SW19 ...33 F2
Rowden Rd HOR/WEW KT19 ...42 B3
Rowlls Rd KUT KT1 ...3 F6
Rowntree Rd WHTN TW2 ...20 D1
Roxborough Av ISLW TW7 ...6 A3
Royal Av WPK KT4 ...42 D1
Royal CI WPK KT4 ...42 D1
Royal Orchard CI
    WAND/EARL SW18 ...17 F5
Royal Rd TEDD TW11 ...20 C5
Roy Gv HPTN TW12 ...28 A1
Royston Rd RCHPK/HAM TW10 ...14 B3
The Roystons BRYLDS KT5 ...37 E2
Rugby Rd WHTN TW2 ...12 A5
Rumsey CI HPTN TW12 ...27 G1

Runnymede CI WHTN TW2 ...12 A4
Runnymede Gdns WHTN TW2 ...12 A4
Runnymede Rd WHTN TW2 ...12 A4
Ruscombe Wy
    EBED/NFELT TW14 ...10 A5
Rushett CI THDIT KT7 ...35 G5
Rushett La CHSGTN KT9 ...45 E5
Rushett Rd THDIT KT7 ...35 G4
Rushey CI NWMAL KT3 ...37 G1
Rushmead RCHPK/HAM TW10 ...21 G3
Rushmere Ct WPK KT4 ...43 F1
Rushmere PI WIM/MER SW19 ...25 E5
Rushmon Vls NWMAL * KT3 ...38 A1
Rusholme Rd PUT/ROE SW15 ...17 E4
Ruskin Av EBED/NFELT TW14 ...10 A5
    RCH/KEW TW9 ...7 H3
Ruskin Dr WPK KT4 ...43 G1
Ruskin Rd ISLW TW7 ...13 E1
Russell Gdns RCHPK/HAM TW10 ...21 H2
Russell Kerr CI CHSWK * W4 ...8 B3
Russell Rd BTFD TW8 ...13 E4
    WIM/MER SW19 ...33 H2
Rustington Wk MRDN SM4 ...39 G4
Ruston Av BRYLDS KT5 ...37 E4
Rutherwyke CI EW KT17 ...43 F5
Rutland CI MORT/ESHN SW14 ...15 E1
Rutland Dr MRDN SM4 ...39 H4
    RCHPK/HAM TW10 ...22 A1
Rutland Gv HMSMTH W6 ...9 G1
Rutland Rd WHTN TW2 ...20 C2
Rutlish Rd WIM/MER SW19 ...33 H3
Ruvigny Gdns PUT/ROE SW15 ...17 E1
Ruxley CI HOR/WEW KT19 ...42 A4
Ruxley Crs ESH/CLAY KT10 ...44 C1
Ruxley La HOR/WEW KT19 ...42 A5
Ruxley Ms HOR/WEW KT19 ...42 A4
Ruxley Rdg ESH/CLAY KT10 ...44 B1
Ruxley Towers
    ESH/CLAY * KT10 ...44 B1
Ryan Dr BTFD TW8 ...6 B2
Rydal Gdns HSLW TW3 ...12 A4
    PUT/ROE SW15 ...23 H5
Ryde PI TWK TW1 ...13 H4
Ryecroft Av WHTN TW2 ...20 A1
Rye Wk PUT/ROE SW15 ...17 E3
Ryfold Rd WIM/MER SW19 ...25 H3
Ryland CI FELT TW13 ...18 A4
Rythe Ct THDIT KT7 ...35 F4

S

Sable CI HSLWW TW4 ...10 D1
Saddlers Ms KUT * KT1 ...29 H3
Sadlers Ride E/WMO/HCT KT8 ...28 B4
Saffron Wy SURB KT6 ...36 A5
Sage Yd SURB * KT6 ...36 C5
St Agatha's Dr KUTN/CMB KT2 ...30 C1
St Albans Av FELT TW13 ...19 E5
St Albans Farm HSLWW * TW4 ...10 D3
St Alban's Gdns TEDD TW11 ...21 F5
St Albans Rd KUTN/CMB KT2 ...30 B1
St Andrews CI THDIT KT7 ...35 G5
St Andrew's Rd SURB KT6 ...36 A3
St Andrew's Sq SURB KT6 ...36 A3
St Anns Rd BARN * SW13 ...9 E5
St Anthony's Wy
    EBED/NFELT TW14 ...10 A2
St Aubyn's Av HSLWW TW4 ...11 H3
    WIM/MER SW19 ...25 G5
St Catherines CI CHSGTN KT9 ...41 E5
St Catherines Ct FELT TW13 ...18 B1
St Chads CI SURB KT6 ...35 H4
St Christopher's CI ISLW TW7 ...5 H4
St Clair Dr WPK KT4 ...43 G2
St Dunstan's Rd FELT TW13 ...18 A3
St Edmund's La WHTN TW2 ...12 A5
St Edmunds Sq BARN SW13 ...9 H1
St George's Gdns SURB KT6 ...42 A1
St Georges Ms CHSWK * W4 ...8 B2
St George's Rd FELT TW13 ...19 E4
    KUTN/CMB KT2 ...3 G1
    RCH/KEW TW9 ...14 C1
    TWK TW1 ...13 G3
    WIM/MER SW19 ...33 G1
St Georges Sq NWMAL * KT3 ...31 H5
St Helena Ter RCH/KEW * TW9 ...14 A3
St Helens THDIT * KT7 ...34 D4
St Heliers Av HSLWW TW4 ...11 H3
St Hilda's Rd BARN SW13 ...9 G2
St James' CI NWMAL KT3 ...38 A2
St James' Rd SURB KT6 ...36 A3
St James's Av HPTN TW12 ...20 B5
St James's Cottages
    RCHPK/HAM * TW10 ...14 A3
St James's Ct KUT * KT1 ...2 C7
St James Sq SURB KT6 ...35 H4

St James's Rd *HPTN* TW12 ....20 A5
  KUT KT1 ....2 B5
St James's Rw *CHSGTN* * KT9 .....41 E5
St James St *HMSMTH* W6 ....9 H1
St John's Av *PUT/ROE* SW15 ....17 E3
St John's Ct *ISLW* TW7 ....6 A5
St John's Gv *BARN* * SW13 ....9 E5
  RCH/KEW * TW9 ....14 B3
St John's Rd *E/WMO/HCT* KT8 .....34 C1
  FELT TW13 ....19 G4
  ISLW TW7 ....6 A5
  KUT KT1 ....29 H4
  NWMAL KT3 ....31 F5
  RCH/KEW TW9 ....14 B2
  WIM/MER SW19 ....33 F2
St Leonard's Gdns *HEST* TW5 ....4 B3
St Leonard's Rd
  ESH/CLAY KT10 ....40 A5
  MORT/ESHN SW14 ....15 F1
  SURB KT6 ....36 A2
  THDIT KT7 ....35 F3
St Margarets
  RCHPK/HAM * TW10 ....23 F5
St Margarets Ct
  PUT/ROE * SW15 ....16 C2
St Margaret's Crs
  PUT/ROE * SW15 ....16 C3
St Margaret's Dr *TWK* TW1 ....13 G3
St Margaret's Gv *TWK* TW1 ....13 F4
St Margarets Ms
  RCHPK/HAM * TW10 ....23 F5
St Margaret's Rd *TWK* TW1 ....13 G2
St Mark's Hl *SURB* KT6 ....36 B3
St Mark's Pl *WIM/MER* * SW19 .....33 C1
St Mark's Rd *TEDD* TW11 ....29 G2
St Mary's Av *TEDD* * TW11 ....29 E1
St Mary's Cl *CHSGTN* KT9 ....45 C1
St Mary's Crs *ISLW* TW7 ....5 G3
St Mary's Gv *BARN* SW13 ....16 C1
  CHSWK W4 ....8 A2
  RCH/KEW TW9 ....14 C2
  SURB KT6 ....35 H4
  WIM/MER SW19 ....25 F5
  WPK KT4 ....42 D1
St Matthew's Av *SURB* KT6 ....36 B5
St Michaels Cl *WPK* KT4 ....43 E1
St Nicholas Rd *THDIT* KT7 ....35 E3
St Paul's Cl *CHSGTN* KT9 ....41 E3
  HSLW TW3 ....4 B5
St Paul's Rd *BTFD* TW8 ....7 E2
  RCH/KEW TW9 ....14 C1
St Peter's Rd *HMSMTH* * W6 ....9 H1
  KUT KT1 ....3 G5
  TWK TW1 ....13 G3
St Peter's Sq *HMSMTH* W6 ....9 H1
St Philip's Av *WPK* KT4 ....43 E1
St Philip's Rd *SURB* KT6 ....36 A3
St Simon's Av *PUT/ROE* SW15 ......16 D3
St Stephen's Gdns *TWK* TW1 ....13 H4
St Stephen's Rd *HSLW* TW3 ....11 H4
St Theresa's Rd
  EBED/NFELT TW14 ....10 A2
St Thomas Cl *SURB* KT6 ....36 C5
St Thomas' Rd *CHSWK* W4 ....8 B3
St Vincent Rd *WHTN* TW2 ....12 B4
St Winifred's Rd *TEDD* TW11 ....29 G1
Salamander Cl *KUTN/CMB* KT2 ....21 H5
Salamander Quay *KUT* KT1 ....2 A3
Salcombe Dr *MRDN* SM4 ....39 E5
Salisbury Cl *WPK* KT4 ....43 E2
Salisbury Gdns *WIM/MER* * SW19 ..33 F2
Salisbury Rd *FELT* TW13 ....19 E1
  HOR/WEW KT19 ....42 C3
  HSLWW TW4 ....10 D1
  NWMAL KT3 ....31 G5
  RCH/KEW TW9 ....14 B2
  WIM/MER SW19 ....33 F2
Salix Cl *SUN* TW16 ....26 C2
Salmons Rd *CHSGTN* KT9 ....41 F5
Salvin Rd *PUT/ROE* SW15 ....17 E1
Samels Ct *HMSMTH* W6 ....9 F1
Samuel Gray Gdns *KUTN/CMB* KT2 ..2 B3
Sandal Rd *NWMAL* KT3 ....37 H1
Sandalwood Rd *FELT* TW13 ....18 C3
Sanders Cl *HPTN* TW12 ....20 B5
Sandhurst Av *BRYLDS* KT5 ....37 E4
Sandon Cl *ESH/CLAY* KT10 ....34 C4
Sandpits Rd *RCHPK/HAM* TW10 ....22 A2
Sandra Cl *HSLW* TW3 ....12 A3
Sandringham Av *RYNPK* SW20 .....33 F3
Sandringham Cl
  WIM/MER * SW19 ....25 F1
Sandringham Rd *WPK* KT4 ....43 F2
Sandycombe Rd
  EBED/NFELT TW14 ....18 B1
  RCH/KEW TW9 ....7 H5
Sandycoombe Rd *TWK* TW1 ....13 H4

Sandy La *RCHPK/HAM* TW10 ....21 H2
  TEDD TW11 ....29 F2
Sandy Md *HOR/WEW* KT19 ....45 H3
Sanger Av *CHSGTN* KT9 ....41 G4
Santos Rd *PUT/ROE* SW15 ....17 H3
Sark Cl *HEST* TW5 ....4 D3
Sarsen Av *HSLW* TW3 ....3 A5
Savery Dr *SURB* KT6 ....35 G4
Savile Cl *NWMAL* KT3 ....37 H2
  THDIT KT7 ....35 E5
Savile Rd *TWK* TW1 ....21 E1
Savill Gdns *RYNPK* SW20 ....32 B5
Savona Cl *WIM/MER* SW19 ....33 E2
Sawkins Cl *WIM/MER* SW19 ....25 E2
Sawyer's Hl *RCHPK/HAM* TW10 ....14 C5
Saxon Av *FELT* TW13 ....19 H1
Saxonbury Av *SUN* TW16 ....26 C5
Saxonbury Gdns *SURB* KT6 ....35 H5
Saxon Cl *SURB* KT6 ....36 A3
Scarth Rd *BARN* SW13 ....16 A1
School House La *TEDD* TW11 ....29 G2
School La *KUT* KT1 ....29 H3
  SURB KT6 ....36 C5
School Pas *KUT* KT1 ....3 F5
School Rd *E/WMO/HCT* KT8 ....34 C1
  HPTN TW12 ....28 B1
  HSLW TW3 ....12 B1
  KUT * KT1 ....2 A6
School Road Av *HPTN* TW12 ....28 B1
Schubert Rd *PUT/ROE* SW15 ....17 G3
Scope Wy *KUT* KT1 ....36 B1
Scott Cl *HOR/WEW* KT19 ....42 B4
Scott Farm Cl *THDIT* KT7 ....35 G5
Scott Gdns *HEST* TW5 ....4 B3
Scotts Dr *HPTN* TW12 ....28 A2
Scotts Farm Rd *HOR/WEW* KT19 ..42 B5
Scott Trimmer Wy *HEST* TW5 ....4 B3
Seaforth Av *NWMAL* KT3 ....38 C2
Seaforth Gdns *HOR/WEW* KT19 ....43 E3
Seaton Cl *PUT/ROE* SW15 ....16 C5
  WHTN TW2 ....12 C4
Seaton Rd *WHTN* TW2 ....12 C4
Second Av *MORT/ESHN* SW14 ......15 H1
Second Cl *E/WMO/HCT* KT8 ....34 A1
Second Cross Rd *WHTN* TW2 ....20 C2
Sedleigh Rd *WAND/EARL* SW18 ....17 G4
Seething Wells La *SURB* KT6 ....35 H3
Sefton St *PUT/ROE* SW15 ....9 H5
Sekhon Ter *FELT* TW13 ....19 H3
Selborne Rd *NWMAL* KT3 ....31 H4
Selbourne Av *SURB* KT6 ....41 G1
Selby Cl *CHSGTN* KT9 ....45 F1
Selhurst Cl *WIM/MER* SW19 ....25 E1
Selkirk Rd *WHTN* TW2 ....20 B2
Selsdon Cl *SURB* KT6 ....36 B2
Selwood Rd *CHEAM* SM3 ....32 D5
  CHSGTN KT9 ....41 E3
Selwyn Av *RCH/KEW* TW9 ....14 C1
Selwyn Cl *HSLWW* TW4 ....11 F2
Selwyn Rd *NWMAL* KT3 ....37 H2
Severn Dr *ESH/CLAY* KT10 ....40 B1
Seymour Av *MRDN* SM4 ....39 E4
Seymour Cl *E/WMO/HCT* KT8 ....34 B2
Seymour Gdns *BRYLDS* KT5 ....36 C2
  FELT TW13 ....18 C4
  TWK TW1 ....13 G5
Seymour Rd *E/WMO/HCT* KT8 ......34 B2
  HPTN TW12 ....20 B5
  KUT KT1 ....2 A2
  WAND/EARL SW18 ....17 G5
  WIM/MER SW19 ....25 E3
Shacklegate La *TEDD* TW11 ....20 D4
Shadbolt Cl *WPK* KT4 ....43 E1
Shaef Wy *TEDD* TW11 ....29 F2
Shaftesbury Av
  EBED/NFELT TW14 ....10 B4
Shaftesbury Rd *RCH/KEW* TW9 ....14 B1
Shaftesbury Wy *WHTN* TW2 ....20 C3
Shakespeare Av
  EBED/NFELT TW14 ....10 B4
Shakespeare Ter
  RCH/KEW * TW9 ....14 D1
Shakespeare Wy *FELT* TW13 ....18 D4
Shaldon Dr *MRDN* SM4 ....39 D4
Shalstone Rd
  MORT/ESHN SW14 ....15 E1
Shalston Vls *SURB* KT6 ....36 C4
Shannon Cl *HEST* TW5 ....4 A1
Sharon Cl *SURB* KT6 ....35 H5
Sharon Rd *CHSWK* W4 ....8 C1
Shawford Rd *HOR/WEW* KT19 ......42 C5
Sheaf Cottages *THDIT* * KT7 ....34 D5
Sheaths Cottages *THDIT* * KT7 .....35 G4
Sheen Common Dr
  RCHPK/HAM TW10 ....14 D2
Sheen Court Rd
  RCHPK/HAM TW10 ....14 D2
Sheendale Rd *RCH/KEW* TW9 ....14 C2

Sheen Gate Gdns
  MORT/ESHN SW14 ....15 F2
Sheen La *MORT/ESHN* SW14 ....15 F2
Sheen Pk *RCH/KEW* TW9 ....14 B2
Sheen Rd *RCHPK/HAM* TW10 ....14 B2
Sheephouse Wy *NWMAL* KT3 ....37 G5
Sheep Walk Ms *WIM/MER* SW19 ...33 E1
Shelburne Dr *HSLWW* TW4 ....11 H4
Shelley Crs *HEST* TW5 ....4 A4
Shelson Av *FELT* TW13 ....18 A3
Shelson Pde *FELT* * TW13 ....18 A3
Shelton Rd *WIM/MER* SW19 ....33 H3
Shenley Rd *HEST* TW5 ....4 B4
Sheppard Cl *SURB* KT6 ....36 B1
Sherborne Rd *CHSGTN* KT9 ....41 F4
Shere Cl *CHSGTN* KT9 ....41 E4
Sherfield Cl *KUT* KT1 ....37 E1
Sherfield Gdns *PUT/ROE* SW15 .....16 A4
Sheridan Ct *HSLWW* TW4 ....11 F3
Sheridan Pl *HPTN* TW12 ....28 A3
Sheridan Rd *RCHPK/HAM* TW10 ...21 H3
  WIM/MER SW19 ....33 G3
Sheringham Av *WHTN* TW2 ....19 G1
Sherland Rd *TWK* TW1 ....21 E1
Sherringham Av *FELT* TW13 ....18 B3
Sherwood *SURB* KT6 ....41 E1
Sherwood Rd *HPTN* TW12 ....20 B5
  WIM/MER SW19 ....33 G2
Shield Dr *BTFD* TW8 ....6 C2
Ship La *MORT/ESHN* SW14 ....15 F1
Shire Horse Wy *ISLW* TW7 ....13 F3
The Shires *RCHPK/HAM* TW10 ......22 B4
Shirley Cl *HSLW* TW3 ....12 B3
Shirley Dr *HSLW* TW3 ....12 B3
Shore Cl *EBED/NFELT* TW14 ....10 B5
  HPTN TW12 ....19 F5
Shore Gv *FELT* TW13 ....19 H3
Shortlands Rd *KUTN/CMB* KT2 ....3 F1
Short Rd *CHSWK* W4 ....8 D2
Short Wy *WHTN* TW2 ....12 B5
Shottfield Av *MORT/ESHN* SW14 ...15 H2
Shrewsbury Av
  MORT/ESHN SW14 ....15 F2
Shrewsbury Cl *SURB* KT6 ....41 F1
The Shrubbery *SURB* * KT6 ....36 B5
Shrubland Gv *WPK* KT4 ....43 H2
Siddeley Dr *HSLWW* TW4 ....11 F1
Sidmouth Av *ISLW* TW7 ....5 H5
Sidney Gdns *BTFD* TW8 ....6 D2
Sidney Rd *TWK* TW1 ....13 F4
Sigrist Sq *KUTN/CMB* KT2 ....2 D3
Silverdale Dr *SUN* TW16 ....26 C4
Silver Dene *PUT/ROE* * SW15 ....16 D2
Silverglade *CHSGTN* KT9 ....44 D5
Silverhall St *ISLW* TW7 ....13 F1
Simpson Rd *HSLWW* TW4 ....11 G4
  RCHPK/HAM TW10 ....21 H4
Simpson Wy *SURB* KT6 ....35 H3
Sion Rd *TWK* TW1 ....21 G1
Sir Abraham Dawes Cottages
  PUT/ROE * SW15 ....17 F2
Sir Cyril Black Wy
  WIM/MER SW19 ....33 G2
Sispara Gdns *WAND/EARL* SW18 ...17 G4
Sixth Cross Rd *WHTN* TW2 ....20 B3
Skeena Hl *WIM/MER* SW19 ....17 F5
Skelgill Rd *PUT/ROE* SW15 ....17 F2
Skelwith Rd *HMSMTH* W6 ....9 H2
Skerne Rd *KUTN/CMB* KT2 ....2 B3
Skinners La *HEST* TW5 ....5 E4
Slattery Rd *FELT* TW13 ....18 D1
Smallberry Av *ISLW* TW7 ....6 A5
Smeaton Rd *WAND/EARL* SW18 ....17 G5
Smith St *BRYLDS* KT5 ....36 C3
Smithwood Cl *WIM/MER* SW19 .....25 F1
Snowdrop Cl *HPTN* TW12 ....27 H1
Snowy Fielder Waye *ISLW* TW7 ....6 C5
Soames Wk *NWMAL* KT3 ....31 H3
Solna Av *PUT/ROE* SW15 ....16 D3
Solway Cl *HSLWW* TW4 ....11 F1
Somerset Av *CHSGTN* KT9 ....41 E3
  RYNPK SW20 ....32 C4
Somerset Cl *NWMAL* KT3 ....37 H3
Somerset Gdns *TEDD* TW11 ....20 D5
Somerset Rd *BTFD* TW8 ....6 D2
  KUT KT1 ....2 A5
  TEDD TW11 ....20 D5
  WIM/MER SW19 ....25 E3
Somerset Waye *HEST* TW5 ....4 B2
Somerton Av *RCH/KEW* TW9 ....15 E1
Somerville Av *BARN* SW13 ....9 H2
Sonia Gdns *HEST* TW5 ....4 B2
Sonning Gdns *HPTN* TW12 ....27 F1
Sopwith Av *CHSGTN* KT9 ....41 E4
Sopwith Cl *RCHPK/HAM* TW10 .....22 C5
Sopwith Wy *KUTN/CMB* KT2 ....2 C3
South Av *RCH/KEW* * TW9 ....7 H5

South Bank *SURB* KT6 ....36 C4
Southbank *THDIT* KT7 ....35 F4
South Bank Ter *SURB* * KT6 ....36 C4
South Black Lion La
  HMSMTH W6 ....8 D1
Southborough Cl *SURB* KT6 ....36 A4
Southborough Rd *SURB* KT6 ....36 B4
Southborough Rd (The Lane)
  SURB * KT6 ....36 B4
South Cl *FELT* TW13 ....18 D3
Southcote Av *BRYLDS* KT5 ....37 E3
  FELT TW13 ....18 D3
Southdean Gdns
  WIM/MER SW19 ....17 E5
Southdown Dr *RYNPK* SW20 ....33 E4
Southdown Rd *RYNPK* SW20 ....33 E5
Southern Av *EBED/NFELT* TW14 ...10 B3
Southern Down *FELT* * TW13 ....18 B3
Southey Rd *WIM/MER* SW19 ....33 H3
Southfield Gdns *TWK* TW1 ....21 E4
Southfields *E/WMO/HCT* KT8 ....34 B3
Southfields Ms
  WAND/EARL SW18 ....17 H4
Southfields Rd
  WAND/EARL SW18 ....17 H4
Southlands Dr *WIM/MER* SW19 ....25 E2
Southland Wy *ISLW* TW7 ....13 H1
South La *KUT* KT1 ....2 C5
  NWMAL KT3 ....37 H2
South La West *NWMAL* KT3 ....37 H2
Southmead Rd *WIM/MER* SW19 ....17 E5
South Park Gv *NWMAL* KT3 ....37 G2
South Park Rd *WIM/MER* SW19 .....33 H2
South Pl *BRYLDS* KT5 ....36 D4
Southridge Pl *RYNPK* SW20 ....33 E3
South Rd *FELT* TW13 ....19 E4
  HPTN TW12 ....27 F2
  WHTN TW2 ....20 C2
Southsea Rd *KUT* KT1 ....2 C6
Southside Common
  WIM/MER SW19 ....33 E2
South St *ISLW* TW7 ....6 B5
South Ter *SURB* KT6 ....36 B4
South Vale Rd *SURB* KT6 ....36 B5
Southville Rd *THDIT* KT7 ....35 F4
Southway *RYNPK* SW20 ....33 G2
South Western Rd *TWK* TW1 ....13 G4
Southwood Av *KUTN/CMB* KT2 ......3 H5
Southwood Cl *WPK* KT4 ....43 H1
Southwood Dr *BRYLDS* KT5 ....37 G3
Southwood Gdns
  ESH/CLAY KT10 ....40 D1
South Worple Wy
  MORT/ESHN SW14 ....15 G1
Space Waye *EBED/NFELT* TW14 ....10 C1
Sparks Cl *HPTN* TW12 ....27 F1
Sparrow Cl *HPTN* TW12 ....27 F1
Sparrow Farm Dr
  EBED/NFELT TW14 ....10 D4
Sparrow Farm Rd *EW* KT17 ....42 D5
Speart La *HEST* TW5 ....4 C2
Speer Rd *THDIT* KT7 ....35 E4
Speirs Cl *NWMAL* KT3 ....38 B2
Spelthorne Gv *SUN* TW16 ....26 A1
Spencer Gdns *MORT/ESHN* SW14 ..15 F3
Spencer Hl *WIM/MER* SW19 ....33 G3
Spencer Hill Rd *WIM/MER* SW19 ...33 G3
Spencer House *SURB* * KT6 ....36 B4
Spencer Rd *CHSWK* W4 ....8 B2
  E/WMO/HCT KT8 ....34 A3
  ISLW TW7 ....6 A4
  RYNPK SW20 ....33 E3
  WHTN TW2 ....20 B2
Spencer Wk *PUT/ROE* SW15 ....17 E2
The Spinney *BARN* * SW13 ....9 F2
  CHEAM SM3 ....39 H5
  SUN TW16 ....26 B4
Spinney Cl *NWMAL* KT3 ....37 H3
  WPK KT4 ....43 E5
Spreighton Rd *E/WMO/HCT* KT8 ...34 B2
Spring Cnr *FELT* * TW13 ....18 C4
Spring Cottages *SURB* * KT6 ....35 H3
Springfield Av *HPTN* TW12 ....27 H1
  RYNPK SW20 ....33 F5
Springfield Gv *SUN* TW16 ....26 A3
Springfield Pl *NWMAL* KT3 ....37 G1
Springfield Rd *KUT* KT1 ....2 B6
  TEDD TW11 ....21 E5
  WHTN TW2 ....20 D2
  WIM/MER SW19 ....33 H3
Spring Gdns *E/WMO/HCT* KT8 ......34 A3
Spring Gv *CHSWK* W4 ....8 A1
  HPTN TW12 ....28 A2
Spring Grove Crs *HEST* TW5 ....5 E4
Spring Grove Rd *HSLW* TW3 ....5 F5
  RCHPK/HAM TW10 ....14 C3
Spring Rd *FELT* TW13 ....18 C3
Springvale Av *BTFD* TW8 ....7 E4

gwell Rd HEST TW5 .....4 A4
ield E/WMO/HCT KT8 ....28 A5
DED/NFELT TW14 .....10 C3
W TW7 .....6 B3
quare HMSMTH W6 .....9 H1
HPK/HAM TW10 .....14 B3
es Ct WIM/MER SW19 .....25 H4
rel Cl HSLWW TW4 .....10 D1
rels Gn WPK KT4 .....43 E1
ord Pl RCHPK/HAM TW10 .....14 C5
ord Rd NWMAL KT3 .....31 F5
La PUT/ROE SW15 .....24 A3
Wy ISLW TW7 .....6 A2
es Rd EBED/NFELT TW14 .....10 A4
WW TW4 .....11 E3
TN TW2 .....20 B3
es Rd East SUN TW16 .....26 B2
es Rd West SUN TW16 .....26 A2
orough Rd HSLW TW12 .....27 G1
orough Rd HSLW TW3 .....12 C1
oridge Rd PUT/ROE SW15 .....16 D1
ard Rd HSLWW TW4 .....11 F1
len Rd WAND/EARL SW18 .....17 H5
ord Cl HPTN TW12 .....27 G1
ope Ter TWK * TW1 .....13 E5
ey Av NWMAL KT3 .....38 B2
eycroft Cl ISLW TW7 .....5 H4
ey Gardens Rd TEDD TW11 .....20 D5
ey Rd HSLW TW3 .....12 B2
RT/ESHN SW14 .....15 E2
DN SM4 .....39 H1
TN TW2 .....20 C3
/MER SW19 .....33 H2
more Gdns RCH/KEW TW9 .....14 C1
more Rd RCH/KEW TW9 .....14 C1
on Av TEDD TW11 .....28 D1
on Rd HOR/WEW KT19 .....42 A4
on WPK KT4 .....43 E5
on Rd BARN SW13 .....9 E5
eford Cl KUT KT1 .....1 H5
/MER SW19 .....17 F5
& Garter Hl
HPK/HAM TW10 .....22 B1
Rd ISLW TW7 .....5 G5
n Gdns TWK * TW1 .....21 E5
on Ap ESH/CLAY KT10 .....40 A2
/PGN * SW6 .....17 F1
R/WEW KT19 .....43 E4
TN TW12 .....27 H3
/HAM TW9 .....14 C1
TW16 .....26 B3
n Approach Rd
SWK W4 .....8 B3
on NWMAL KT3 .....31 H5
on Cl HPTN TW12 .....28 A3
on Estate Rd
ED/NFELT TW14 .....18 C1
on Gdns CHSWK W4 .....8 B3
on Pde CHSWK * W4 .....8 B3
ED/NFELT * TW14 .....10 C5
/KEW TW9 .....7 H4
n Rd BARN SW13 .....9 E5
GTN KT9 .....41 F4
/CLAY KT10 .....34 C5
TN TW12 .....28 A3
.W TW3 .....12 A2
TN/CMB KT2 .....3 G3
MAL KT3 .....38 C2
TW16 .....26 A4
D TW11 .....29 F1
DIT KT7 .....35 F1
KW TW1 .....21 E1
n Yd TWK * TW1 .....13 F5
aton Rd KUTN/CMB KT2 .....30 C2
ley Gdns CHSWK W4 .....8 C4
ley Rd CHSWK W4 .....8 B3
fast Rd KUT KT1 .....2 B3
n Farm La
ED/NFELT TW14 .....10 A2
e Rd ISLW TW7 .....13 F2
le Cl FUL/PGN SW6 .....17 F1
enson Rd HSLWW TW4 .....11 H5
y Dr HOR/WEW KT19 .....42 D3
DIT KT7 .....34 D3
Biko Wy HSLW TW3 .....11 H1
ns Cl HPTN TW12 .....27 G1
ns' La ESH/CLAY KT10 .....44 B1
art Cl HPTN TW12 .....27 F1
DIT KT7 .....34 D3
gfleet Rd BARN SW13 .....9 F3
g Gv HSLW TW3 .....5 F5
Rd WHTN TW2 .....11 H5

Stirling Wk BRYLDS KT5 .....37 E3
Stockhurst Cl PUT/ROE SW15 .....9 H5
Stoford Cl WIM/MER SW19 .....25 F1
Stoke Rd KUTN/CMB KT2 .....31 F2
Stokesby Rd CHSGTN KT9 .....41 G5
Stonecot Cl MRDN SM4 .....39 F5
Stonecot Hl MRDN SM4 .....39 F5
Stone Crs EBED/NFELT TW14 .....10 A5
Stonehill Cl MORT/ESHN SW14 .....15 G3
Stonehill Rd CHSWK W4 .....7 H1
MORT/ESHN SW14 .....15 G3
Stoneleigh Av WPK KT4 .....43 F2
Stoneleigh Broadway EW KT17 .....43 F4
Stoneleigh Crs HOR/WEW KT19 .....43 F4
Stoneleigh Park Rd
HOR/WEW KT19 .....43 E5
Stone Pl WPK KT4 .....43 E5
Stormont Wy CHSGTN KT9 .....40 D4
Stoughton Cl PUT/ROE SW15 .....24 B1
Stourhead Cl WIM/MER SW19 .....17 G3
Stourhead Gdns RYNPK SW20 .....32 B5
Stourton Av FELT TW13 .....19 G4
Strachan Pl RYNPK SW20 .....32 B2
Strafford Rd HSLW TW3 .....11 G1
TWK TW1 .....13 F5
Strand-on-the-Green
CHSWK W4 .....7 H2
Stratford Ct NWMAL KT3 .....37 G1
Stratford Gv PUT/ROE SW15 .....17 E2
Strathan Cl WAND/EARL SW18 .....17 F4
Strathearn Av WHTN TW2 .....20 B3
Strathearn Rd WIM/MER SW19 .....25 H5
Strathmore Rd TEDD TW11 .....20 D4
WIM/MER SW19 .....25 H3
Strathville Rd
WAND/EARL SW18 .....
WIM/MER SW19 .....33 G4
Stratton Cl HEST TW5 .....4 C4
Stratton Rd SUN TW16 .....26 A4
WIM/MER SW19 .....33 G4
Strawberry Hill Rd TWK TW1 .....21 E3
Strawberry V TWK TW1 .....21 E3
Stretton Rd RCHPK/HAM TW10 .....21 H2
Stroud Crs PUT/ROE SW15 .....24 A3
Stroudes Cl WPK KT4 .....38 A4
Stroud Rd WIM/MER SW19 .....25 H5
Stuart Gv TEDD TW11 .....20 D5
Stuart Rd RCHPK/HAM TW10 .....21 G2
WIM/MER SW19 .....25 H3
Stucley Rd ISLW TW7 .....5 H4
Studland Rd KUTN/CMB KT2 .....30 B1
Sudbrook Gdns
RCHPK/HAM TW10 .....22 B3
Sudbrook La
RCHPK/HAM TW10 .....22 B1
Sudlow Rd WAND/EARL SW18 .....17 H2
Suffolk Rd BARN SW13 .....9 E3
WPK KT4 .....
Suffolk Vls WAND/EARL * SW18 .....17 H5
Sugden Rd THDIT KT7 .....35 F5
Sulivan Rd FUL/PGN SW6 .....17 H1
Sullivan Cl E/WMO/HCT KT8 .....28 A5
Summer Av E/WMO/HCT KT8 .....34 D2
Summerfield La SURB KT6 .....41 E1
Summer Gdns E/WMO/HCT KT8 .....34 D2
Summerhouse Av HEST TW5 .....4 B4
Summer Rd E/WMO/HCT KT8 .....34 C2
Summer Trees SUN TW16 .....26 C3
Summerwood Rd TWK TW1 .....13 E4
Sunbury Av MORT/ESHN SW14 .....15 G2
Sunbury Ct SUN TW16 .....26 D4
Sunbury Court Rd SUN TW16 .....26 D4
Sunbury Rd FELT TW13 .....18 B3
Sunbury Wy FELT TW13 .....18 D5
Sunmead Rd SUN TW16 .....26 B5
Sunna Gdns SUN TW16 .....26 C3
Sunningdale Av FELT TW13 .....19 F2
Sunningdale Cl SURB KT6 .....41 F1
Sunnycroft Rd HSLW TW3 .....5 E5
Sunnymead Rd PUT/ROE SW15 .....16 C3
Sunnyside WIM/MER SW19 .....33 F1
Sunnyside Rd TEDD TW11 .....19 H5
Sunray Av BRYLDS KT5 .....42 A1
Sunrise Cl FELT TW13 .....19 G3
Sunset Rd WIM/MER SW19 .....24 D5
Surbiton Ct SURB KT6 .....35 H3
Surbiton Crs KUT KT1 .....36 B1
Surbiton Hall Pk BRYLDS KT5 .....36 C2
Surbiton Hill Pk SURB KT6 .....36 C2
Surbiton Hill Rd SURB KT6 .....36 C2
Surbiton Rd KUT KT1 .....36 A1
Surrey Crs CHSWK W4 .....7 F1
Sussex Av ISLW TW7 .....12 D1
Sussex Cl NWMAL KT3 .....38 B2
TWK TW1 .....13 G4
Sussex Gdns CHSGTN KT9 .....40 D5
Sussex Pl HMSMTH W6 .....9 H1
NWMAL KT3 .....37 H1

Sussex Rd NWMAL KT3 .....37 H1
Sutherland Av SUN TW16 .....26 A4
Sutherland Gdns
MORT/ESHN SW14 .....15 H1
SUN TW16 .....26 A4
WPK KT4 .....38 C5
Sutherland Gv TEDD TW11 .....20 D5
WAND/EARL SW18 .....17 G5
Sutherland Rd CHSWK W4 .....8 B2
Sutton Cl CHSWK * W4 .....8 B2
Sutton Common Rd
CHEAM SM3 .....39 G4
Sutton Ct CHSWK * W4 .....8 B2
Sutton Court Rd CHSWK W4 .....8 B2
Sutton Dene HSLW TW3 .....5 E4
Sutton Hall HEST TW5 .....4 D3
Sutton La HSLW TW3 .....4 B1
HSLW TW3 .....
Sutton La South CHSWK W4 .....8 B2
Sutton Rd HEST TW5 .....4 D4
Sutton Sq HEST TW5 .....4 C4
Sutton Wy HEST TW5 .....4 C4
Swan Cl FELT TW13 .....19 F4
Swan Island TWK * TW1 .....21 F3
Swan Pl BARN SW13 .....9 E5
Swan Rd FELT TW13 .....19 F4
Swanscombe Rd CHSWK W4 .....8 B2
Swan St ISLW TW7 .....13 G1
Swanton Gdns WIM/MER SW19 .....25 E1
Swanwick Cl PUT/ROE SW15 .....16 A5
Swift Rd FELT TW13 .....19 E4
Swinburne Rd PUT/ROE SW15 .....16 B2
Swinfield Cl FELT TW13 .....19 F4
Sycamore Cl TEDD TW11 .....18 B3
Sycamore Gv NWMAL KT3 .....31 F5
Sycamore Rd WIM/MER SW19 .....32 D1
Sycamore Wy TEDD TW11 .....20 D1
Sydney Rd EBED/NFELT TW14 .....18 B1
RCH/KEW TW9 .....14 B2
RYNPK SW20 .....33 E4
TEDD TW11 .....21 E5
Sydney Ter ESH/CLAY * KT10 .....40 A5
Sylvan Gdns SURB KT6 .....36 A4
Syon Gate Wy BTFD TW8 .....6 B3
Syon La ISLW TW7 .....6 C1
Syon Pk ISLW * TW7 .....13 G1
Syon Park Gdns ISLW TW7 .....6 C1

T

Tabor Gv WIM/MER SW19 .....33 F2
Tachbrook Rd
EBED/NFELT TW14 .....10 A5
Tadworth Av NWMAL KT3 .....38 A1
Talbot Rd ISLW TW7 .....13 F2
WHTN TW2 .....20 D1
Talma Gdns WHTN TW2 .....12 D5
Tamesis Gdns WPK KT4 .....42 D1
Tamian Wy HSLWW TW4 .....10 D2
Tangier Rd RCHPK/HAM TW10 .....14 D2
Tanglewood Wy FELT TW13 .....18 C3
Tangley Gv PUT/ROE SW15 .....16 A5
Tangley Park Rd HPTN * TW12 .....19 G5
Tangmere Gv KUTN/CMB KT2 .....22 A5
Tankerton Rd SURB KT6 .....41 G1
Tapping Cl KUTN/CMB KT2 .....3 G1
Taunton Av HSLW TW3 .....5 F5
RYNPK SW20 .....32 C4
Taunton Cl CHEAM SM3 .....39 H5
Tawny Cl FELT TW13 .....18 B3
Tayben Av WHTN TW2 .....12 D4
Taylor Av RCH/KEW TW9 .....8 A5
Taylor Cl HOR/WEW KT19 .....45 H4
HPTN TW12 .....20 B5
HSLW TW3 .....5 G3
Taylors Ct FELT TW13 .....18 B2
Tealing Dr HOR/WEW KT19 .....42 D4
Teck Cl ISLW TW7 .....6 B5
Tedder Cl CHSGTN KT9 .....40 D4
Teddington Pk TEDD TW11 .....21 E4
Teddington Park Rd
TEDD TW11 .....21 E4
Teesdale Cl ISLW TW7 .....6 B4
Teesdale Gdns ISLW TW7 .....6 B4
Telegraph La ESH/CLAY KT10 .....40 A3
Telegraph Rd PUT/ROE SW15 .....16 C5
Telford Rd HSLWW TW4 .....11 H1
Templar Pl HPTN TW12 .....27 H2
Templecombe Wy MRDN SM4 .....39 F2
Temple Rd HSLW TW3 .....12 A2
RCH/KEW TW9 .....7 G5
Temple Sheen Rd
MORT/ESHN SW14 .....15 F2
Tennyson Av NWMAL KT3 .....38 C2
TWK TW1 .....21 E1
Tennyson Cl EBED/NFELT TW14 .....10 A4

Tennyson Rd HSLW TW3 .....5 F5
Terrace Gdns BARN SW13 .....9 E5
Terrace La RCHPK/HAM TW10 .....14 B4
The Terrace BARN SW13 .....8 D5
Terrace Vls HMSMTH * W6 .....9 F1
Terrac St RCH/KEW TW9 .....14 C2
Thackeray Cl ISLW TW7 .....6 B5
WIM/MER SW19 .....33 E2
Thames Bank
MORT/ESHN SW14 .....8 B5
Thames Cl HPTN TW12 .....28 A4
Thames Down Link
CHSGTN KT9 .....42 B3
Thames Eyot TWK * TW1 .....21 F2
Thamesgate Cl
RCHPK/HAM TW10 .....21 G4
Thameside TEDD TW11 .....30 A2
Thames Meadow
E/WMO/HCT KT8 .....27 H5
RCH/KEW TW9 .....9 E4
WOT/HER KT12 .....26 D5
Thames Pth CHSWK W4 .....9 E4
RCH/KEW TW9 .....9 E4
WOT/HER KT12 .....26 D5
Thames Pl PUT/ROE SW15 .....17 E1
Thamespoint TEDD * TW11 .....30 A1
Thames Reach KUT * KT1 .....2 A2
Thames Rd CHSWK W4 .....8 A2
Thames Side KUTN/CMB KT2 .....2 B3
THDIT KT7 .....35 G3
Thames St HPTN TW12 .....28 A4
KUT KT1 .....2 B4
SUN TW16 .....26 C5
Thamesvale Cl HSLW TW3 .....4 D5
Thames Village CHSWK W4 .....8 B4
Thatchers Wy ISLW TW7 .....12 C3
Thaxted Pl RYNPK SW20 .....33 E2
The Beverly MRDN SM4 .....39 E3
Thelma Gv TEDD TW11 .....29 F1
Thetford Rd NWMAL KT3 .....37 G3
Third Cl E/WMO/HCT KT8 .....34 A1
Third Cross Rd WHTN TW2 .....20 C2
Thistledene THDIT KT7 .....34 D3
Thistleworth Cl ISLW TW7 .....5 G3
Thompson Av RCH/KEW TW9 .....15 E1
Thompson Rd HSLW TW3 .....12 A2
Thorkhill Gdns THDIT KT7 .....35 F5
Thorkhill Rd THDIT KT7 .....35 G5
Thornbury Av ISLW TW7 .....5 G3
Thornbury Rd ISLW TW7 .....5 G3
Thorncliffe Rd NWDGN UB2 .....4 C1
Thorndon Gdns HOR/WEW KT19 .....42 D3
Thorne St BARN SW13 .....15 H1
Thornhill Av SURB KT6 .....41 F1
Thornhill Rd SURB KT6 .....41 F1
Thornton Hl WIM/MER SW19 .....33 F2
Thornton Rd MORT/ESHN SW14 .....15 G1
WIM/MER SW19 .....33 F1
Thorpe Rd KUTN/CMB KT2 .....30 B2
Thrigby Rd CHSGTN KT9 .....41 G5
Thurleston Av MRDN SM4 .....39 E4
Thursley Gdns WIM/MER SW19 .....25 E2
Thurstan Rd RYNPK SW20 .....32 C2
Tibbets Cl WIM/MER SW19 .....25 E1
Tibbet's Ride PUT/ROE SW15 .....17 E1
Tideswell Rd PUT/ROE SW15 .....16 D2
Tideway Cl RCHPK/HAM TW10 .....21 G4
Tildesley Rd PUT/ROE SW15 .....16 D4
Tilford Gdns WIM/MER SW19 .....25 E1
Timbercroft HOR/WEW KT19 .....42 D3
Tintern Cl PUT/ROE SW15 .....17 F3
Titan Ct BTFD TW8 .....7 G1
Tithe Barn Cl KUTN/CMB KT2 .....3 G1
Tiverton Rd HSLW TW3 .....5 E5
Tiverton Wy CHSGTN KT9 .....40 D4
Tivoli Rd HSLWW TW4 .....11 H3
Toad La HSLWW TW4 .....11 G2
Toby Wy SURB KT6 .....42 A1
Toland Sq PUT/ROE SW15 .....16 B3
Tolson Rd ISLW TW7 .....13 F1
Tolverne Rd RYNPK SW20 .....32 D3
Tolworth Cl SURB KT6 .....37 E5
Tolworth Park Rd SURB KT6 .....41 G1
Tolworth Ri North BRYLDS KT5 .....37 F4
Tolworth Ri South BRYLDS KT5 .....37 F5
Tolworth Rd SURB KT6 .....41 F1
Tomlinson Cl CHSWK W4 .....8 A1
Tonfield Rd CHEAM SM3 .....39 G5
Topiary Sq RCH/KEW TW9 .....14 C1
Torrington Wy MRDN SM4 .....39 H4
Torwood Rd PUT/ROE SW15 .....16 B3
Tower Gdns ESH/CLAY KT10 .....44 C1
Tower Ri RCH/KEW TW9 .....14 B1
Tower Rd WHTN TW2 .....20 D3
Towers Pl RCHPK/HAM TW10 .....14 B3
Towfield Rd FELT TW13 .....19 G2
Town End Pde KUT * KT1 .....2 B6
Town Field Wy ISLW TW7 .....6 B5
Townhall Av CHSWK W4 .....8 C1
Town Meadow BTFD TW8 .....7 E3

Townmead Rd *RCH/KEW* TW9 ....8 A5
Townshend Rd *RCH/KEW* TW9 ......14 C2
Townshend Ter *RCH/KEW* TW9 .....14 C2
Town Whf *ISLW* * TW7 ....13 G1
Toynbee Rd *RYNPK* SW20 ....33 F3
Trafalgar Av *WPK* KT4 ....39 E5
Trafalgar Rd *WHTN* TW2 ....20 C2
Tranmere Rd *WHTN* TW2 ....12 A5
Transport Av *BTFD* TW8 ....6 B1
Traps La *NWMAL* KT3 ....31 H4
Tree Cl *RCHPK/HAM* TW10 ....22 A1
Treen Av *BARN* SW13 ....15 H1
Tregaron Gdns *NWMAL* KT3 ....37 H1
Trehern Rd *MORT/ESHN* SW14......15 C1
Trentham St *WAND/EARL* SW18......25 H1
Trent Wy *WPK* KT4 ....43 H2
Treville St *PUT/ROE* SW15 ....16 C5
Trevithick Cl *EBED/NFELT* TW14 ....18 A1
Trevor Cl *ISLW* TW7 ....13 E3
Trevor Rd *WIM/MER* SW19 ....33 F2
Trewenna Dr *CHSGTN* KT9 ....41 E4
Trewince Rd *RYNPK* SW20 ....32 D3
The Triangle *NWMAL* KT3 ....31 F4
Trinity Church Rd *BARN* SW13 ....9 E4
Trinity Cl *HSLWW* TW4 ....11 F1
Trinity Pde *HSLW* * TW3 ....12 A1
Trinity Rd *RCH/KEW* TW9 ....14 C1
   WIM/MER SW19 ....33 H1
Trotter Wy *HOR/WEW* KT19 ....45 H5
Trowlock Av *TEDD* TW11 ....29 H1
Trowlock Island *TEDD* TW11 ....30 A1
Trowlock Wy *TEDD* TW11 ....29 H1
Trystings Cl *ESH/CLAY* KT10 ....40 B5
Tudor Av *HPTN* TW12 ....27 H2
   WPK KT4 ....43 G2
Tudor Cl *CHSGTN* KT9 ....41 F4
   HPTN TW12 ....20 B5
Tudor Dr *KUTN/CMB* KT2 ....22 B5
   MRDN SM4 ....39 E5
Tudor Gdns *BARN* SW13 ....15 H1
   TWK TW1 ....21 E1
Tudor Rd *HPTN* TW12 ....27 H2
   HSLW TW3 ....12 C2
   KUTN/CMB KT2 ....3 C1
Tufton Gdns *E/WMO/HCT* KT8 ......28 A4
Tulip Cl *HPTN* TW12 ....27 C1
Tunworth Crs *PUT/ROE* SW15 ....16 A4
Turner Av *WHTN* TW2 ....20 B3
Turner Rd *NWMAL* KT3 ....37 C4
Turnpike Wy *ISLW* TW7 ....6 D4
Turpin Rd *EBED/NFELT* TW14 ....10 A4
Twickenham Br *TWK* TW1 ....13 H3
Twickenham Rd *FELT* TW13 ....19 F4
   ISLW TW7 ....13 G3
   TEDD TW11 ....21 F4
Twining Av *WHTN* TW2 ....20 B3
Tybenham Rd *WIM/MER* SW19 ......33 H5
Tynan Cl *EBED/NFELT* TW14 ....18 B1

U

Udney Park Rd *TEDD* TW11 ....21 F5
Ullswater Rd *KUTN/CMB* * KT2 ......23 C4
Ullswater Crs *PUT/ROE* SW15 ....23 C4
Ullswater Rd *BARN* SW13 ....9 F3
Ulva Rd *PUT/ROE* SW15 ....16 B4
Umbria St *PUT/ROE* SW15 ....16 B4
Union St *KUT* KT1 ....2 B4
Unwin Rd *ISLW* TW7 ....12 A1
Uplands Cl *MORT/ESHN* SW14 ......15 E3
Upper Brighton Rd *SURB* KT6 ....36 A3
Upper Butts *BTFD* TW8 ....6 D2
Upper Grotto Rd *TWK* TW1 ....21 E2
Upper Ham Rd
   RCHPK/HAM TW10 ....22 A4
Upper Ml *HMSMTH* W6 ....9 F1
Upper Park Rd
   KUTN/CMB KT2 ....30 D1
Upper Richmond Rd
   PUT/ROE SW15 ....16 C2
Upper Richmond Rd West
   RCHPK/HAM TW10 ....14 D2
Upper Sq *ISLW* TW7 ....13 F1
Upper Sunbury Rd *HPTN* TW12.......27 C3
Upper Sutton La *HEST* TW5 ....4 D4
Upper Teddington Rd *KUT* KT1 ......29 H3
Upton Rd *HSLW* TW3 ....11 H1
Urmston Dr *WIM/MER* SW19 ....19 E1
Uxbridge Rd *FELT* TW13 ....19 E2
   SURB KT6 ....36 A1

V

The Vale *EBED/NFELT* TW14 ....10 C4
Vale Cl *TWK* * TW1 ....21 F3
Vale Cottages *PUT/ROE* * SW15 ....23 H3
Vale Crs *PUT/ROE* SW15 ....23 H4
Vale Cft *ESH/CLAY* KT10 ....44 A1
Vale Rd *HOR/WEW* KT19 ....43 E3
Vale Rd North *SURB* KT6 ....41 F1
Vallis Wy *CHSGTN* KT9 ....41 E5
Valonia Gdns *WAND/EARL* SW18 ...17 G4
Vancouver Rd *RCHPK/HAM* TW10...21 H4
Van Dyck Av *NWMAL* KT3 ....37 G4
Vandyke Cl *PUT/ROE* SW15 ....16 D5
Vanneck Sq *PUT/ROE* * SW15 ....16 B3
Varna Rd *HPTN* * TW12 ....28 A3
Varsity Dr *ISLW* TW7 ....12 D3
Varsity Rw *MORT/ESHN* SW14 ....8 B5
Vaughan Rd *THDIT* KT7 ....35 G4
Vencourt Pl *HMSMTH* W6 ....9 F1
Verbena Gdns *HMSMTH* W6 ....9 F1
Verdun Rd *BARN* SW13 ....9 F3
Vereker Dr *SUN* TW16 ....26 B5
Vernon Av *RYNPK* SW20 ....33 E4
Vernon Cl *HOR/WEW* KT19 ....42 B5
Vernon Rd *FELT* TW13 ....18 A2
   MORT/ESHN SW14 ....15 G1
Verona Dr *SURB* KT6 ....41 F1
Vicarage Cl *WPK* KT4 ....37 H5
Vicarage Dr *MORT/ESHN* SW14 .....15 G3
Vicarage Farm Rd *HEST* TW5...........4 B4
Vicarage Ms *CHSWK* * W4 ....8 D2
Vicarage Rd *E/WMO/HCT* KT8 ....29 H5
   KUT KT1 ....1 B4
   MORT/ESHN SW14 ....15 G1
   SUN TW16 ....18 A5
   TEDD TW11 ....21 F5
   WHTN TW2 ....12 B4
   WHTN TW2 ....20 B4
Victoria Av *E/WMO/HCT* KT8 ....28 A5
   HSLWW TW4 ....11 H3
   SURB KT6 ....36 A3
Victoria Cl *E/WMO/HCT* KT8 ....28 A5
Victoria Cottages *RCH/KEW* TW9 .....7 G4
Victoria Crs *WIM/MER* SW19 ....33 G2
Victoria Dr *WIM/MER* SW19 ....17 E5
Victoria Gdns *HEST* TW5 ....4 B4
Victoria Pde *RCH/KEW* * TW9 ....7 H4
Victoria Pl *RCHPK/HAM* TW10 ....14 A4
Victoria Rd *FELT* TW13 ....18 C1
   KUT KT1 ....3 F5
   MORT/ESHN SW14 ....15 G1
   SURB KT6 ....36 A4
   TEDD TW11 ....29 F1
   TWK TW1 ....13 G5
Victoria Vls *RCH/KEW* TW9 ....14 C1
Victor Rd *TEDD* TW11 ....20 D5
Victors Dr *HPTN* * TW12 ....27 F1
Viewfield Rd *WAND/EARL* SW18 .....17 G4
Villiers Av *BRYLDS* KT5 ....36 C2
   WHTN TW2 ....19 G1
Villiers Cl *BRYLDS* KT5 ....36 C1
Villiers Rd *ISLW* TW7 ....5 H5
   KUT KT1 ....3 E7
Vincam Cl *WHTN* TW2 ....11 H5
Vincent Av *BRYLDS* KT5 ....36 C5
Vincent Rd *HSLWW* TW4 ....11 E1
   ISLW TW7 ....5 H5
   KUT KT1 ....3 H6
Vincent Rw *HPTN* TW12 ....28 B1
Vine Cl *BRYLDS* KT5 ....36 C3
Vine Pl *HSLW* TW3 ....12 A2
Vine Rd *BARN* SW13 ....16 A1
   E/WMO/HCT KT8 ....28 B5
Vine Rw *RCHPK/HAM* * TW10 ....14 B3
The Vineyard *RCHPK/HAM* TW10 ...14 A4
   SUN TW16 ....26 B5
Vineyard Cl *KUT* KT1 ....2 D7
Vineyard Hill Rd *WIM/MER* SW19 ...25 H4
Vineyard Pth *MORT/ESHN* SW14.....15 G1
Vineyard Rd *FELT* TW13 ....18 B3
Vineyard Rw *RCH/KEW* KT8 ....29 F3
Viola Av *EBED/NFELT* TW14 ....10 D4
Virginia Cl *NWMAL* KT3 ....37 F1
Vivien Cl *CHSGTN* KT9 ....45 F1
Vivienne Cl *TWK* TW1 ....14 A4
Voewood Cl *NWMAL* KT3 ....38 A3

W

Wade's La *TEDD* TW11 ....21 F5
Wadham Rd *PUT/ROE* SW15 ....17 F2
Waights Ct *KUTN/CMB* KT2 ....2 C2
Wainford Cl *WIM/MER* SW19 ....25 E1
Wainwright Gv *ISLW* TW7 ....12 C2
Wakefield Rd
   RCHPK/HAM TW10 ....14 A3
   HEST TW5 ....4 B2
   SUN * TW16 ....26 B1
Vale Cl *TWK* * TW1 ....21 F3
Waldeck Rd *CHSWK* W4 ....7 H2
   MORT/ESHN SW14 ....15 F1
Waldegrave Gdns *TWK* TW1 ....21 E2
Waldegrave Pk *TWK* TW1 ....21 E4
Waldegrave Rd *TWK* TW1 ....21 E4
Waldemar Rd *WIM/MER* SW19 ....25 H5
Walham Ri *WIM/MER* SW19 ....33 F1
Walker Cl *EBED/NFELT* TW14 ....10 A5
   HPTN TW12 ....27 G1
Walker's Pl *PUT/ROE* * SW15 ....17 F2
Wallorton Gdns
   MORT/ESHN SW14 ....15 G2
Walnut Tree Cl *BARN* SW13 ....9 E4
Walnut Tree Rd *BTFD* TW8 ....7 E4
   HEST * TW5 ....4 C2
Walpole Av *RCH/KEW* TW9 ....7 G5
Walpole Crs *TEDD* TW11 ....21 E5
Walpole Gdns *CHSWK* W4 ....8 B1
   WHTN TW2 ....20 D2
Walpole Pl *TEDD* TW11 ....21 E5
Walpole Rd *SURB* KT6 ....36 B4
   TEDD TW11 ....21 E5
   WHTN TW2 ....20 D2
Walsham Rd *EBED/NFELT* TW14 ....10 C5
Walsingham Gdns
   HOR/WEW KT19 ....42 D3
Walter St *KUTN/CMB* KT2 ....2 C3
Walton Av *NWMAL* KT3 ....38 A1
Walton Gdns *FELT* TW13 ....18 A4
Wanborough Dr *PUT/ROE* SW15.....24 C1
Wandle Ct *HOR/WEW* KT19 ....42 B3
Wandsworth High St
   WAND/EARL SW18 ....17 H3
Warbank La *KUTN/CMB* KT2 ....32 A2
Warboys Ap *KUTN/CMB* KT2 ....31 E1
Warboys Rd *KUTN/CMB* KT2 ....31 E1
Warburton Rd *WHTN* TW2 ....20 A1
The Wardrobe *RCH/KEW* * TW9 .....14 A4
Wareham Cl *HSLW* TW3 ....12 A3
Warfield Rd *HPTN* TW12 ....28 A3
Warkworth Gdns *ISLW* TW7 ....6 B3
Warner Cl *HPTN* TW12 ....19 G5
The Warren *HEST* TW5 ....4 C3
   HOR/WEW KT19 ....42 C5
Warren Av *RCHPK/HAM* TW10 ....10 A5
Warren Cutting *KUTN/CMB* KT2 .....31 G2
Warren Dr North *BRYLDS* KT5 ....37 E5
Warren Dr South *BRYLDS* KT5 ....37 F5
Warren Pk *KUTN/CMB* KT2 ....31 F1
Warren Ri *NWMAL* KT3 ....31 G3
Warren Rd *KUTN/CMB* KT2 ....31 F1
   WHTN TW2 ....12 C4
Warrington Rd
   RCHPK/HAM TW10 ....14 A3
Warwick Cl *HPTN* TW12 ....28 B2
Warwick Dr *BARN* SW13 ....16 C1
Warwick Gdns *THDIT* KT7 ....35 E2
Warwick Gv *BRYLDS* KT5 ....36 C4
Warwick Pl *THDIT* * KT7 ....35 F3
Warwick Rd *HSLWW* TW4 ....10 C1
   KUT KT1 ....29 H3
   NWMAL KT3 ....31 H5
   THDIT KT7 ....35 E2
   WHTN TW2 ....20 D1
Washington Rd *BARN* SW13 ....9 G5
   KUT KT1 ....3 G5
   WPK KT4 ....43 G1
Watchfield Ct *CHSWK* * W4 ....8 B1
Waterfield Cottages
   MORT/ESHN SW14 ....15 E2
Water La *KUT* KT1 ....2 B3
   RCH/KEW TW9 ....14 A3
   TWK TW1 ....13 H4
Waterloo Cl *EBED/NFELT* TW14 .....18 A1
Waterloo Pl *RCH/KEW* TW9 ....7 H2
Watermans Cl *KUTN/CMB* * KT2 ......2 C1
Waterman St *PUT/ROE* SW15 ....17 F1
Watermill Rd *RCHPK/HAM* TW10 ...21 H3
Water Mill Wy *FELT* TW13 ....19 G2
Watersedge *HOR/WEW* KT19 ....42 B3
Waterside Cl *SURB* KT6 ....41 F1
Watersplash Cl *KUT* KT1 ....2 C6
Waters Rd *KUT* KT1 ....3 J5
Waters Sq *KUT* KT1 ....3 J6
Watery La *RYNPK* SW20 ....33 G4
Watney Rd *MORT/ESHN* SW14.......15 F1
Watt's La *TEDD* TW11 ....21 F5
Watts Rd *THDIT* KT7 ....35 F4
Wavendon Av *CHSWK* W4 ....8 C1
Waverley Av *BRYLDS* KT5 ....37 E3
   WHTN TW2 ....19 G1
Waverley Rd *EW* KT17 ....43 G4
Wayside *MORT/ESHN* SW14 ....15 F1
Wayside Ct *TWK* TW1 ....13 H4
Weavers Cl *ISLW* TW7 ....12 D3
Weimar St *PUT/ROE* SW15 ....17 F1
Weiss Rd *PUT/ROE* SW15 ....17 E1
Welbeck Cl *NWMAL* KT3 ....38 A2
Welford Pl *WIM/MER* SW19
Wellesley Crs *WHTN* TW2
Wellesley Pde *WHTN* * TW2
Wellesley Rd *CHSWK* W4 ....
   WHTN TW2
Wellington Av *HSLWW* TW4 ....
   WPK KT4 ....
Wellington Crs *NWMAL* KT3 ....
Wellington Gdns *HPTN* TW12 ....
Wellington Rd *HPTN* TW12 ....
   WIM/MER SW19 ....
Wellington Rd North
   HSLWW TW4 ....
Wellington Rd South
   HSLWW TW4 ....
Well La *MORT/ESHN* SW14 ....
Wellside Gdns
   MORT/ESHN SW14 ....
Weltje Rd *HMSMTH* W6 ....
Welwyn Av *EBED/NFELT* TW14 .....
Wembley Rd *HPTN* TW12 ....
Wendover Dr *NWMAL* KT3 ....
Wensleydale Gdns *HPTN* TW12 .....
Wensleydale Rd *HPTN* TW12 ....
Wentworth Cl *MRDN* SM4 ....
   SURB KT6 ....
Werter Rd *PUT/ROE* SW15 ....
Wesley Av *HSLW* TW3 ....
Wessex Av *WIM/MER* SW19 ....
Wessex Cl *KUTN/CMB* KT2 ....
Westbank Rd *HPTN* TW12 ....
West Barnes La *NWMAL* KT3 ....
   RYNPK SW20 ....
Westbourne Rd *FELT* TW13 ....
Westbrook Av *HPTN* TW12 ....
Westbrook Rd *HEST* TW5 ....
Westbury Av *ESH/CLAY* KT10 ....
Westbury Pl *BTFD* TW8 ....
Westbury Rd *FELT* TW13 ....
   NWMAL KT3 ....
Westcliffe Vls *KUT* * KT1 ....
Westcoombe Av *RYNPK* SW20 ......
Westcroft Gdns *MRDN* SM4 ....
West Cross Wy *BTFD* TW8 ....
Western Ter *HMSMTH* * W6 ....
Westfield Rd *SURB* KT6 ....
Westfields *BARN* SW13 ....
Westfields Av *BARN* SW13 ....
West Hall Rd *RCH/KEW* TW9 ....
Westhay Gdns
   MORT/ESHN SW14 ....
West Hl *PUT/ROE* SW15 ....
   WAND/EARL SW18 ....
West Hl Rd *WAND/EARL* SW18 ......
Westhorpe Rd *PUT/ROE* SW15 .....
West House Cl *WIM/MER* SW19 .....
Westleigh Av *PUT/ROE* SW15.........
Westmacott Dr
   EBED/NFELT TW14 ....
West Md *HOR/WEW* KT19 ....
Westmead *PUT/ROE* SW15 ....
Westminster Cl
   EBED/NFELT TW14 ....
   TEDD TW11 ....
Westmoreland Rd *BARN* SW13 ......
Westmorland Cl *TWK* TW1 ....
Weston Av *ESH/CLAY* KT10 ....
Weston Gdns *ISLW* TW7 ....
Weston Gn *THDIT* KT7 ....
Weston Green Rd
   ESH/CLAY KT10 ....
Weston Pk *KUT* KT1 ....
   THDIT KT7 ....
Weston Park Rd *THDIT* * KT7 ....
Weston Rd *THDIT* KT7 ....
West Park Av *RCH/KEW* TW9 ....
West Park Rd *HEST* TW5 ....
West Park Rd *HOR/WEW* KT19 ......
   RCH/KEW TW9 ....
West Pl *WIM/MER* SW19 ....
West Rd *CHSGTN* KT9 ....
   KUTN/CMB KT2 ....
West Sheen V *RCH/KEW* TW9 ....
West Side Common
   WIM/MER SW19 ....
West Temple Sheen
   MORT/ESHN SW14 ....
Westville Rd *THDIT* KT7 ....
West Wy *HEST* TW5 ....
Westway *RYNPK* SW20 ....
Westway Rd *RYNPK* SW20 ....
Westways *HOR/WEW* KT19 ....
Westwood Gdns *BARN* SW13 ....
Westwood Rd *BARN* SW13 ....
Wetherby Wy *CHSGTN* KT9 ....
Wey Ct *HOR/WEW* KT19 ....
Weydown Cl *WIM/MER* SW19 ....
Wharf Bridge Rd *ISLW* TW7 ....

f La *TWK* TW1 ....21 F1
ley Av *RYNPK* SW20 ....33 E5
tfield Wy *KUT* KT1 ....2 C6
tlands *HEST* TW5 ....4 D2
tley Rd *ISLW* TW7 ....13 E1
tsheaf La *FUL/PGN* SW6 ....9 H3
e Bridge Cl
PD/NFELT TW14 ....10 A4
efield Cl *WAND/EARL* SW18 ....17 F4
hall Crs *CHSGTN* KT9 ....41 E4
hall Gdns *CHSWK* W4 ....8 A2
hall Park Rd *CHSWK* W4 ....8 A2
Hart La *BARN* SW13 ....8 D5
Heron Ms *TEDD* * TW11 ....29 E1
leys Wy *FELT* TW13 ....19 H3
estile Rd *BTFD* TW8 ....6 D1
ock Dr *WIM/MER* SW19 ....17 F5
ell Wy *PUT/ROE* * SW15 ....16 D3
aker Av *RCH/KEW* * TW9 ....14 A3
on Dene *HSLW* TW3 ....12 B4
on Manor Rd *ISLW* TW7 ....12 B4
TN TW2 ....12 A1
on Waye *HSLW* TW3 ....11 H4
ecroft *HEST* TW5 ....4 A3
iam Av *CHEAM* SM3 ....43 H4
iam Cl *NWMAL* KT3.....................38 A2
Rd *TEDD* TW11 ....29 G2
y Rd *FELT* TW13 ....19 E1
rforce Wy
M/MER SW19 ....33 E1
x Rd *TEDD* TW11........................20 C4
roft Rd *PUT/ROE* SW15 ....16 D5
ilderness
MO/HCT* KT8................................24 A2
N * TW12 ....20 A4
cks Cl *CHSGTN* KT9 ....41 F2
m Evans Rd
/WEW* KT19 ....45 H4
e Gdns *PUT/ROE* SW15.............16 C3
m Rd *WIM/MER* SW19 ....33 F2
ms Gv *SURB* KT6 ....35 H3
ms La *MORT/ESHN* SW14 ....15 F1
gham Wy *KUT* KT1 ....3 G5
ighby Rd *KUTN/CMB* KT2 ....3 G5
K TW1 ....13 H3
v Av *BARN* SW13.........................9 E5
brook *HPTN* * TW12 ....20 A5
v Cl *BTFD* TW8 ....6 D2
dene Cl *WHTN* TW2 ....12 B5
hayne Gdns *WPK* KT4 ....43 H1
w Rd *NWMAL* KT3 ....37 F1
w Wy *HOR/WEW* KT19 ....42 A1
TN TW2 ....20 A2
n *HSLW* TW3 ....12 A4
er Cl *RCHPK/HAM* TW10...........22 C5
er Crs *RCHPK/HAM* TW10.........22 C5
ngton Av *CHSWK* W4 ....8 C3
n Rd *CHSGTN* KT9 ....41 G5
n *CHSWK* W4 ....8 D1
n Crs *WIM/MER* SW19 ....33 G3

Wilton Gdns *E/WMO/HCT* KT8 ......27 H5
Wilton Gv *NWMAL* KT3 ....38 A3
WIM/MER SW19 ....33 G2
Wilton Rd *HSLWW* TW4 ....11 E1
Wilton Wk *FELT* * TW13 ....18 C2
Wiltshire Gdns *WHTN* TW2 ....20 B1
Wilverley Crs *NWMAL* KT3 ....37 H3
Wimbledon Br *WIM/MER* SW19 ...33 G1
Wimbledon Hill Rd
WIM/MER SW19 ....33 F1
Wimbledon Park Rd
WIM/MER SW19 ....25 F3
Wimbledon Park Side
WIM/MER SW19 ....25 E2
Wimborne Cl *WPK* KT4 ....38 D5
Wimpole Cl *KUT* KT1 ....3 F5
Wincanton Rd
WAND/EARL SW18......................17 G5
Winchelsea Cl *PUT/ROE* SW15 ...17 H5
Winchendon Rd *TEDD* TW11 ....20 C4
Winchester Av *HEST* TW5..............4 C2
Winchester Cl *KUTN/CMB* KT2 ...31 E2
Winchester Rd *FELT* TW13 ....19 G3
TWK TW1 ....13 G4
Winchilsea Crs *E/WMO/HCT* KT8 ...28 B4
Windermere Rd *PUT/ROE* SW15 ...23 H4
Windham Rd *RSH/KEW* TW9 ....14 C1
Windlesham Gv
WIM/MER SW19 ....25 E1
Windmill Cl *SURB* KT6 ....35 H5
Windmill La *THDIT* KT7 ....35 H4
Windmill Ri *KUTN/CMB* KT2 ....31 E2
Windmill Rd *HPTN* TW12 ....20 A5
WIM/MER SW19 ....24 C5
Windrush *NWMAL* KT3 ....37 H5
Windrush Cl *CHSWK* * W4 ....8 B3
Windsor Av *E/WMO/HCT* KT8......27 F1
NWMAL KT3 ....37 F2
Windsor Rd *KUTN/CMB* KT2 ....2 C1
RCH/KEW TW9 ....14 C2
SUN TW16 ....26 B2
TEDD TW11 ....20 C5
WPK KT4 ....43 H1
Windy Ridge Cl *WIM/MER* SW19 ...25 E5
Winery La *KUT* KT1 ....3 G4
Winey Cl *CHSGTN* KT9 ....44 D1
Wingfield Rd *KUTN/CMB* KT2 ......30 C1
Wingrave Rd *HMSMTH* W6...........9 H2
Winifred Rd *HPTN* TW12 ....12 A4
WIM/MER SW19 ....33 H4
Winslow Rd *HMSMTH* W6..............9 H2
Winslow Wy *FELT* TW13 ....19 E3
Winston House *SURB* * KT6 ....36 B2
Winter Box Wk
RCHPK/HAM TW10....................14 C3
Winterfold Cl *WIM/MER* SW19......25 F2
Winters Rd *THDIT* KT7 ....35 G4
Winthorpe Rd *PUT/ROE* SW15 ...17 F2
Witham Rd *ISLW* TW7 ....5 H4
Wittering Cl *KUTN/CMB* KT2........22 A5
Wivenhoe Ct *HSLWW* TW4 ....11 G2
Woffington Cl
E/WMO/HCT KT8.......................29 H2

Woking Cl *PUT/ROE* SW15 ....16 A2
Wolseley Av *WAND/EARL* SW18 ...25 H2
Wolseley Gdns *CHSWK* W4 ....8 A2
Wolsey Cl *WIM/MER* SW19 ....12 B2
KUTN/CMB KT2 ....3 K3
RYNPK SW20 ....32 C2
WPK KT4 ....43 F3
Wolsey Crs *MRDN* SM4 ....39 G4
Wolsey Dr *KUTN/CMB* KT2...........22 B5
Wolsey Rd *E/WMO/HCT* KT8 ....34 C1
HPTN TW12 ....28 A1
SUN TW16 ....26 A2
Wolsey Wy *CHSGTN* KT9 ....41 H4
Wolverton Av *KUTN/CMB* KT2.......3 H2
Wonford St *NWMAL* KT3 ....31 H3
Woodall Cl *CHSGTN* KT9 ....41 E5
Woodberry Cl *SUN* TW16 ....26 B1
Woodbine Cl *WHTN* TW2..............20 C2
Woodbine La *WPK* KT4 ....43 G2
Woodbines Av *KUT* KT1.................2 B7
Woodborough Rd
PUT/ROE SW15 ....16 C2
Woodbourne Dr
ESH/CLAY KT10 ....40 A5
Woodcote Cl *KUTN/CMB* KT2......22 C5
Woodfield Gdns *NWMAL* KT3 ......38 A2
Woodfield Rd *ESH/CLAY* KT10 .....40 A1
Woodgate Av *CHSGTN* KT9 ....41 E4
Woodhayes Rd *RYNPK* SW20 ......32 C5
Woodland Gdns *ISLW* TW7 ....12 D1
The Woodlands *ISLW* TW7 ....6 A5
Woodlands *RYNPK* SW20 ....38 D1
Woodlands Av *NWMAL* KT3 ....31 G3
WPK KT4 ....43 E1
Woodlands Cl *ESH/CLAY* KT10 ....44 A1
Woodlands Dr *SUN* TW16 ....26 D4
Woodlands Gv *ISLW* TW7 ....5 H5
Woodlands Rd *BARN* SW13 ....16 A1
ISLW TW7 ....12 D1
SURB KT6 ....35 E5
Woodlands Wy *PUT/ROE* SW15 ...17 G3
Woodland Wk *HOR/WEW* KT19 ...41 H5
Woodland Wy *BRYLDS* KT5 ....42 A1
MRDN SM4 ....39 G1
Wood La *ISLW* TW7 ....5 H2
Woodlawn Cl *PUT/ROE* SW15 .....16 E6
Woodlawn Crs *WHTN* TW2 ....20 A2
Woodlawn Dr *FELT* TW13 ....19 E2
Woodside *WIM/MER* SW19...........25 C5
Woodside Av *ESH/CLAY* KT10 .....34 D4
Woodside Cl *BRYLDS* KT5 ....37 F4
Woodside Rd *KUTN/CMB* KT2 ....2 C1
NWMAL KT3 ....31 G4
Woodspring Rd
WIM/MER SW19 ....25 F2
Woodstock Av *CHEAM* SM3 ....39 G4
ISLW TW7 ....13 F3
Woodstock La North *SURB* KT6....40 D1
Woodstock La South
ESH/CLAY KT10 ....40 C4
Woodstock Ri *CHEAM* SM3..........39 G5
Woodstone Av *EW* KT17 ....43 F4

Wood St *CHSWK* W4 ....8 D1
KUT KT1 ....2 B4
Woodthorpe Rd *PUT/ROE* SW15 ...16 C2
Woodview *CHSGTN* KT9 ....44 D5
Woodview Cl *KUTN/CMB* KT2 ......23 C4
Woodville Cl *TEDD* TW11 ....21 F4
Woodville Gdns *SURB* * KT6 ....36 A4
Woodville Rd *MRDN* SM4 ....39 H1
RCHPK/HAM TW10....................21 G3
Woodward Cl *ESH/CLAY* KT10 .....40 A5
Wool Rd *RYNPK* SW20 ....32 C1
Worcester Gdns *WPK* KT4 ....42 D2
Worcester Park Rd *WPK* KT4 ....42 B2
Worcester Rd *WIM/MER* SW19 ....25 G5
Wordsworth Dr *CHEAM* SM3 ....43 H3
Wordsworth Rd *FELT* TW13 ....19 G4
Worlidge St *HMSMTH* W6 ....9 H1
Worple Av *ISLW* TW7 ....13 F3
WIM/MER SW19 ....33 E2
Worple Rd *ISLW* TW7 ....13 F2
RYNPK SW20 ....32 D4
Worple Road Ms
WIM/MER SW19 ....33 G1
Worple St *MORT/ESHN* SW14 ......15 G1
Worple Wy *RCHPK/HAM* TW10....14 B3
Worthing Rd *HEST* TW5 ....4 C1
Worthington Rd *SURB* KT6 ....36 C5
Worton Gdns *ISLW* TW7 ....5 G5
Worton Rd *ISLW* TW7 ....13 E1
Worton Wy *ISLW* TW7 ....5 G5
Wraysbury Cl *HSLWW* TW4 ....11 F3
Wyatt Cl *FELT* TW13 ....19 E1
Wyatt Dr *BARN* SW13 ....9 G2
Wychwood Cl *SUN* TW16 ....26 B1
Wydell Cl *MRDN* SM4 ....38 D3
Wyke Cl *ISLW* TW7 ....6 A2
Wyke Rd *RYNPK* SW20 ....32 D4
Wymond St *PUT/ROE* SW15 ....16 D1
Wyndham Crs *HSLW* TW4 ....11 G4
Wyndham Rd *KUTN/CMB* KT2 .....30 C1
Wyvern Est *NWMAL* * KT3...........32 B5

Y

Yale Cl *HSLWW* TW4 ....11 G3
Yenston Cl *MRDN* SM4 ....39 H3
Yeovilton Pl *KUTN/CMB* KT2 ....22 A5
Yew Tree Cl *WPK* KT4 ....37 H5
Yew Tree Wk *HSLWW* TW4 ....11 G3
York Av *MORT/ESHN* SW14 ....15 F3
York Pde *BTFD* * TW8 ....7 E1
York Rd *BTFD* TW8 ....7 E1
HSLW TW3 ....12 A1
KUTN/CMB KT2 ....2 E1
RCHPK/HAM TW10....................14 C3
TEDD TW11 ....20 D4
York St *TWK* TW1 ....21 F1
York Wy *CHSGTN* KT9 ....45 E1
FELT TW13 ....19 G3

Index - featured places

inema
TN/CMB* KT2 ....2 D4
T/ROE* SW15 ....17 F1
Road Health Clinic
TN/CMB* KT2 ....2 E1
echnology College
T/ROE* SW15 ....17 G3
ale Physiotherapy Clinic
SWK* W4 ....9 E1
harle Primary School
M/MER* SW19 ....25 F2
ndra Infant School
TN/CMB* KT2 ....3 G1
ndra Junior School
LW* TW3 ....5 E5
l England Lawn Tennis &
quet Club
M/MER* SW19 ....25 E3
nts CE Primary School
T/ROE* SW15 ....16 D1
lton School
T/ROE* SW15 ....16 A5
ndrew Ewing
mary School
ST* TW5 ....4 C3
Retail Park
.T* TW13 ....19 G3
olic Nuncio
M/MER* SW19 ....24 D3

Archdeacon Cambridge's CE
Primary School
WHTN TW2.................................20 D2
Arndale Health Centre
WAND/EARL SW18 ....17 H4
Arts Theatre
PUT/ROE SW15 ....17 E2
Ashton House School
ISLW TW7 ....5 G4
Assembly Rooms
KUT KT1 ....36 B1
Aston Clinic
NWMAL KT3 ....37 H1
Athelstan House School
HPTN TW12 ....27 H3
Atkinson Morley Hospital
RYNPK SW20 ....32 C2
Auriol Junior School
HOR/WEW KT19 ....43 E3
Back Care Clinic
WPK KT4 ....38 B5
Barn Elms Athletics Track
BARN SW13 ....9 G5
Barn Elms Water Sports Centre
BARN SW13 ....9 H5
Barnes Hospital
MORT/ESHN SW14 ....15 H1
Barnes Sports Club
BARN SW13 ....9 E4
Barwell Business Park
CHSGTN KT9..............................45 E1

Beauclerc Infant School
SUN TW16 ....26 D5
The Beavers Community
Primary School
HSLWW TW4 ....10 D1
Bective House Clinic
PUT/ROE SW15 ....17 G2
Bedelsford Special School
KUT KT1 ....2 C7
Berkeley Primary School
HEST TW5 ....4 A2
Beverley School
NWMAL KT3 ....38 B2
Beverley Trading Estate
MRDN SM4 ....39 E4
Bishop Gilpin Primary School
WIM/MER SW19 ....25 G5
Bishop Perrin CE
Primary School
WHTN TW2 ....12 B4
Bishop Wand CE
Secondary School
SUN TW16 ....26 A4
Brandlehow Primary School
PUT/ROE SW15 ....17 G2
Brentford Business Centre
BTFD TW8 ....6 D3
The Brentford Clinic
BTFD TW8 ....7 F2

Brentford County Court
BTFD TW8 ....7 E3
Brentford FC (Griffin Park)
BTFD TW8 ....7 E2
Brentford Fountain
Leisure Centre
CHSWK W4..................................7 H1
Brentford Health Centre
BTFD TW8 ....6 D2
Brentford Medical Centre
BTFD TW8 ....7 E3
Brentford School for Girls
BTFD TW8 ....7 E2
Brentwaters Business Park
BTFD TW8 ....6 D3
Brewery Mews Business Centre
ISLW TW7 ....13 E1
Broadway Shopping Centre
HMSMTH W6...............................9 H1
Brookfield Primary School
CHEAM SM3...............................39 F5
Brook Lane Business Centre
BTFD TW8 ....7 E1
Broomfield House School
RCH/KEW TW9 ....7 G4
Brunel University
ISLW TW7 ....5 H3
TWK TW1 ....13 G2
Brunel University
(Osterley Campus) Track
ISLW TW7 ....5 H3

Buckingham Primary School
  HPTN TW12 .... 19 G5
Buckland Infant School
  CHSGTN KT9 .... 41 G4
Buddhapadipa Temple
  WIM/MER SW19 .... 25 E4
Burlington Primary School
  NWMAL KT3 .... 38 A1
Bushey Middle School
  RYNPK SW20 .... 32 C5
Butterfly House
  BTFD TW8 .... 6 C4
Cambridge Park Bowling &
  Sports Club
  TWK TW1 .... 13 H4
Campion House College
  ISLW TW7 .... 5 C3
Canbury Business Centre
  KUTN/CMB KT2 .... 2 D3
Canbury 2000 Business Park
  KUTN/CMB KT2 .... 2 D3
Canbury Medical Centre
  KUTN/CMB KT2 .... 2 E2
Canbury School
  RCHPK/HAM TW10 .... 31 E1
Cardinal Road Infant School
  FELT TW13 .... 18 C1
Carlisle Infant School
  HPTN TW12 .... 28 A1
The Cassel Hospital
  RCHPK/HAM TW10 .... 22 A4
Cavendish Primary School
  CHSWK W4 .... 8 D3
Centaurs Business Centre
  BTFD TW8 .... 6 B2
  ISLW TW7 .... 6 B2
Centaurs RFC
  ISLW TW7 .... 6 A2
Centre Court Shopping Centre
  WIM/MER SW19 .... 33 G1
Charrington Bowl
  SURB KT6 .... 42 A1
Chartfield School
  PUT/ROE SW15 .... 16 C3
Chase Bridge Primary School
  WHTN TW2 .... 12 D4
Chatsworth J & I School
  HSLW TW3 .... 12 B2
Cheam Common Infant School
  WPK KT4 .... 43 G1
Cheam Common Junior School
  WPK KT4 .... 43 G2
Chennestone Community School
  SUN TW16 .... 26 C4
Chessington Community College
  CHSGTN KT9 .... 45 E1
Chessington Cricket Club
  CHSGTN KT9 .... 44 D1
Chessington Golf Club
  CHSGTN KT9 .... 45 E1
Chessington World
  of Adventures
  CHSGTN KT9 .... 44 D3
Chiswick Community School
  CHSWK W4 .... 8 C3
Chiswick House
  CHSWK W4 .... 8 C2
Christ Church CE Infant School
  NWMAL KT3 .... 31 H5
Christ Church CE Junior School
  NWMAL KT3 .... 31 G5
Christ Church CE
  Primary School
  BRYLDS KT5 .... 36 D3
Christs School
  RCHPK/HAM TW10 .... 14 C3
Chrysanthemum Clinic
  CHSWK W4 .... 8 B3
Churchill College
  RYNPK SW20 .... 32 D4
The Churchill Medical Centre
  KUTN/CMB KT2 .... 3 G3
The Church School
  BTFD TW8 .... 7 F2
Cineworld Cinema
  FELT TW13 .... 18 C2
Clarendon Special School
  HPTN TW12 .... 28 A1
Collis Primary School
  TEDD TW11 .... 29 G1
Coombe Girls School
  NWMAL KT3 .... 31 G4
Coombe Hill Golf Club
  KUTN/CMB KT2 .... 31 G2
Coombe Hill J & I School
  NWMAL KT3 .... 31 G3
Coombe Wood Golf Club
  KUTN/CMB KT2 .... 3 K1
Corinthian Casuals FC
  CHSGTN KT9 .... 41 H2

Crane Infant School
  FELT TW13 .... 19 G2
Crane Junior School
  FELT TW13 .... 19 F2
Cuddington Cemetery
  WPK KT4 .... 43 G1
Cuddington CP School
  HOR/WEW KT19 .... 43 E2
Darell Primary School
  RCH/KEW TW9 .... 14 D1
Denmead School
  HPTN TW12 .... 27 H2
Deutsche Schule
  RCHPK/HAM TW10 .... 22 A1
Diana Fountain
  E/WMO/HCT KT8 .... 29 E4
Dockwell's Industrial Estate
  EBED/NFELT TW14 .... 10 C3
Dorchester Primary School
  WPK KT4 .... 38 D5
Douglas Bader Foundation
  PUT/ROE SW15 .... 16 B4
Dundonald First School
  WIM/MER SW19 .... 33 G2
Dysart School
  KUTN/CMB KT2 .... 22 A4
Dysart Special School
  SURB KT6 .... 36 B4
Ealing Road Trading Estate
  BTFD TW8 .... 7 E1
East Molesey Cricket Club
  E/WMO/HCT KT8 .... 28 B5
East Sheen Cemetery
  RCHPK/HAM TW10 .... 14 D3
East Sheen Primary School
  MORT/ESHN SW14 .... 15 H2
Eden Walk Shopping Centre
  KUT KT1 .... 2 C5
Ellingham Primary School
  CHSGTN KT9 .... 45 E1
Elliott Foundation School
  PUT/ROE SW15 .... 16 D4
Ember Sports Club
  ESH/CLAY KT10 .... 34 B5
Epsom & Ewell High School
  HOR/WEW KT19 .... 42 B5
Esher College
  THDIT KT7 .... 34 D4
Evolution House
  RCH/KEW TW9 .... 7 F5
Ewell Athletics Track
  HOR/WEW KT19 .... 42 C5
Fairfield Industrial Estate
  KUT KT1 .... 3 F7
Farnell House Medical Centre
  HSLW TW3 .... 5 E4
Feltham Airparcs
  Leisure Centre
  FELT TW13 .... 19 E2
Feltham Athletics Arena
  EBED/NFELT TW14 .... 10 B5
Felthambrook Industrial Estate
  FELT TW13 .... 18 C3
Feltham Community College
  FELT TW13 .... 18 D2
Feltham Hill Junior School
  FELT TW13 .... 18 A3
Feltham & Hounslow Boro FC
  EBED/NFELT TW14 .... 10 B5
Feltham Superbowl
  FELT TW13 .... 18 C2
Fern Hill Primary School
  KUTN/CMB KT2 .... 30 B1
Film House Cinema
  RCH/KEW TW9 .... 14 A3
Five Ways Business Centre
  FELT TW13 .... 18 C3
The Foot Clinic
  WIM/MER SW19 .... 25 F5
Forge Lane Primary School
  FELT TW13 .... 19 F5
Freehold Industrial Centre
  HSLWW TW4 .... 10 D3
Froebel College
  PUT/ROE SW15 .... 16 B4
Fulham FC (Craven Cottage)
  BARN SW13 .... 9 H4
Fuller Smith & Turner
  Sports Club
  CHSWK W4 .... 8 D4
Fulwell Golf Club
  HPTN TW12 .... 20 C4
Gaflac Sports Ground Pavilion
  SUN TW16 .... 26 B3
The Garth Road Industrial Centre
  MRDN SM4 .... 38 D4
Gleen Lecky Health Centre
  PUT/ROE SW15 .... 17 E2
Glenlyn Medical Centre
  E/WMO/HCT KT8 .... 34 B2

Glenthorne High School
  CHEAM SM3 .... 39 H5
Gosbury Hill Health Centre
  CHSGTN KT9 .... 41 F3
Granard Primary School
  PUT/ROE SW15 .... 16 C4
Grand Avenue Primary School
  BRYLDS KT5 .... 37 F4
Grasshoppers RFC
  ISLW TW7 .... 6 A2
Grassroots School
  HPTN TW12 .... 27 H3
Great West Trading Estate
  BTFD TW8 .... 6 C2
Green Dragon School
  BTFD TW8 .... 7 F1
Green Lane Primary School
  WPK KT4 .... 38 C4
Greenmead Primary School
  PUT/ROE SW15 .... 16 C3
The Green School for Girls
  ISLW TW7 .... 6 B3
Grey Court School
  RCHPK/HAM TW10 .... 21 H3
Grist Memorial Sports Club
  E/WMO/HCT KT8 .... 34 D2
Grove Park Primary School
  CHSWK W4 .... 8 B2
Grove Road Primary School
  HSLW TW3 .... 11 H2
The Groves Medical Centre
  NWMAL KT3 .... 31 H5
Guildhall
  KUT KT1 .... 2 B5
Guildhall Annex
  KUT KT1 .... 2 B5
Gumley House Convent School
  ISLW TW7 .... 13 F1
Gunnersbury Catholic School
  BTFD TW8 .... 6 D1
Hall School Wimbledon
  PUT/ROE SW15 .... 24 B3
Ham Health Clinic
  RCHPK/HAM TW10 .... 21 H1
Ham House (NT)
  RCHPK/HAM TW10 .... 21 H1
Hammersmith Apollo
  HMSMTH W6 .... 9 H1
Hammersmith Industrial Estate
  HMSMTH W6 .... 9 H2
Hammersmith New Cemetery
  RCH/KEW TW9 .... 8 A5
Ham & Petersham Cricket Club
  RCHPK/HAM TW10 .... 22 A4
Hampton Cemetery
  HPTN TW12 .... 27 H2
Hampton Community College
  HPTN TW12 .... 19 H5
Hampton Court Palace
  E/WMO/HCT KT8 .... 29 E5
Hampton Farm Industrial Estate
  FELT TW13 .... 19 F3
Hampton FC
  HPTN TW12 .... 28 A3
Hampton Hill Junior School
  HPTN TW12 .... 20 B5
Hampton Infant School
  HPTN TW12 .... 27 G2
Hampton Junior School
  HPTN TW12 .... 27 H3
The Hampton Medical Centre
  HPTN TW12 .... 27 H2
Hampton School
  HPTN TW12 .... 19 H5
Hampton Swimming Baths
  HPTN TW12 .... 28 B2
Hampton Wick Infants School
  KUT KT1 .... 29 H2
Hanworth Trading Estate
  FELT TW13 .... 19 F3
Harrodian School
  BARN SW13 .... 9 E3
Haslemere Industrial Estate
  EBED/NFELT TW14 .... 10 B3
Hawkedale Gm School
  SUN TW16 .... 26 A5
Hawkins Clinic
  PUT/ROE SW15 .... 17 E2
  RYNPK SW20 .... 32 A3
Hazelhurst School
  RYNPK SW20 .... 33 E3
Heath Business Centre
  HSLW TW3 .... 12 B2
Heathfield Primary School
  WHTN TW2 .... 19 H1
Heathland School
  HSLWW TW4 .... 11 G4
Heathmere Primary School
  PUT/ROE SW15 .... 24 B1

Heathrow International
  Trading Estate
  HSLWW TW4 ....
Helston Court Business Centre
  WIM/MER SW19 ....
Heston Community School
  HEST TW5 ....
Heston Industrial Mall
  HEST TW5 ....
Heston Infant School
  HEST TW5 ....
Heston Junior School
  HEST TW5 ....
Heston Park Cricket Club
  HEST TW5 ....
Heston Swimming Baths
  HEST TW5 ....
Hillcroft College
  SURB KT6 ....
Hinchley Wood School
  ESH/CLAY KT10 ....
Hogarth Business Park
  CHSWK W4 ....
Hogarth Primary School
  CHSWK W4 ....
Hogarth's House
  CHSWK W4 ....
The Hollyfield School
  SURB KT6 ....
Hollymount Primary School
  RYNPK SW20 ....
Holy Cross Convent School
  NWMAL KT3 ....
Holy Cross Preparatory School
  KUTN/CMB KT2 ....
Holy Trinity CE First School
  WIM/MER SW19 ....
Holy Trinity CE Primary School
  RCHPK/HAM TW10 ....
Home Park Golf Club
  E/WMO/HCT KT8 ....
Hook Rise South Industrial Park
  CHSGTN KT9 ....
Horton Country Park
  HOR/WEW KT19 ....
Hotham Primary School
  PUT/ROE SW15 ....
Hounslow Business Park
  HSLW TW3 ....
Hounslow Cemetery
  HSLWW TW4 ....
Hounslow College
  Independent School
  FELT TW13 ....
Hounslow Cricket Club
  HSLW TW3 ....
Hounslow Heath Golf Club
  HSLWW TW4 ....
Hounslow Heath Infant School
  HSLWW TW4 ....
Hounslow Heath Junior School
  HSLWW TW4 ....
Hounslow Manor School
  HSLW TW3 ....
Hounslow Manor Sports Hall
  HSLW TW3 ....
Hounslow Town
  Primary School
  HSLW TW3 ....
Hurlingham Business Park
  FUL/PGN SW6 ....
Hurlingham & Chelsea School
  FUL/PGN SW6 ....
Hurlingham House
  FUL/PGN SW6 ....
Hurst Park School
  E/WMO/HCT KT8 ....
Ibstock Place School
  PUT/ROE SW15 ....
Imber Court Trading Estate
  E/WMO/HCT KT8 ....
Inwood Business Centre
  HSLW TW3 ....
The Islamic Grammar School
  WAND/EARL SW18 ....
Isleworth Baths
  ISLW TW7 ....
Isleworth Blue CE
  Primary School
  ISLW TW7 ....
Isleworth Cemetery
  ISLW TW7 ....
Isleworth & Syon School for Boys
  ISLW TW7 ....
Isleworth Town Primary School
  ISLW TW7 ....
Ivybridge Primary School
  TWK TW1 ....
Ivybridge Retail Park
  ISLW TW7 ....

Royal Hospital
RCH/KEW TW9 .... **14** B1
Royal Hospital for
Neuro-Disability
PUT/ROE SW15 .... **17** F4
Royal Hospital & Home
PUT/ROE SW15 .... **16** C5
Royal Mid-Surrey Golf Club
RCH/KEW TW9 .... **14** A1
Royal Wimbledon Golf Club
WIM/MER SW19 .... **24** C5
The Russell JMI School
RCHPK/HAM TW10 .... **22** A2
The Russell School
RCHPK/HAM TW10 .... **22** A1
Rutlish School
RYNPK SW20 .... **33** G4
Sacred Heart RC
Primary School
NWMAL KT3 .... **38** B1
TEDD TW11 .... **29** G2
St Agathas RC Primary School
KUTN/CMB KT2 .... **30** C1
St Albans RC Aided
Primary School
E/WMO/HCT KT8 .... **34** A2
St Anthonys Hospital
WPK KT4 .... **39** E5
St Catherines RC Middle School
NWMAL KT3 .... **38** D2
St Catherines School
TWK TW1 .... **21** E2
St Clare Business Park
HPTN TW12 .... **28** B1
St Edmunds RC Primary School
WHTN TW2 .... **12** A5
St Elizabeths RC
Primary School
RCHPK/HAM TW10 .... **14** C4
St Georges Industrial Estate
KUTN/CMB KT2 .... **22** A5
St Ignatius RC Primary School
SUN TW16 .... **26** B3
St James Independent School
TWK TW1 .... **21** F2
St James RC Primary School
WHTN TW2 .... **20** D3
St John Fisher RC
Primary School
NWMAL KT3 .... **38** D2
St Johns CE Primary School
KUT KT1 .... **2** D7
St John the Baptist CE
Junior Sch
KUT KT1 .... **2** A1
St Josephs Primary School
PUT/ROE SW15 .... **17** H3
St Josephs RC Primary School
KUT KT1 .... **2** E5
St Lawrence Business Centre
FELT TW13 .... **18** C2
St Lawrence Catholic School
FELT TW13 .... **18** C2
St Lawrence Junior School
E/WMO/HCT KT8 .... **28** C5
St Lukes CE Primary School
KUTN/CMB KT2 .... **2** E2
St Margarets Business Centre
TWK TW1 .... **13** F5
St Marks RC School
HSLW TW3 .... **11** G1
St Mary CE Primary School
PUT/ROE SW15 .... **17** E1
St Mary Magdalens RC
Primary School
MORT/ESHN SW14 .... **15** G1
St Marys CE Junior School
THDIT KT7 .... **35** C5
St Marys CE Primary School
CHSGTN KT9 .... **41** F5
TWK TW1 .... **13** F5
St Marys RC Primary School
CHSW W4 .... **8** C1
ISLW TW7 .... **13** F1
WIM/MER SW19 .... **33** H2
St Marys & St Peters CE Primary
School
TEDD TW11 .... **20** D5
St Marys University College
TWK TW1 .... **21** E3
St Matthews CE Primary School
RYNPK SW20 .... **32** B3
SURB KT6 .... **36** B4
St Michaels and St Martins RC
Primary School
HSLWW TW4 .... **11** G1
St Michaels CE Primary School
WAND/EARL SW18 .... **17** G5
St Osmunds RC Primary School
BARN SW13 .... **9** E4

St Pauls Catholic College
SUN TW16 .... **26** B3
St Pauls CE Junior School
KUTN/CMB KT2 .... **3** H1
St Pauls CE Primary School
BTFD TW8 .... **7** E2
CHSGTN KT9 .... **41** F3
St Pauls Preparatory School
BARN SW13 .... **9** H1
St Paul's Primary School
HMSMTH W6 .... **9** H1
St Pauls RC Primary School
THDIT KT7 .... **34** D4
St Peters CE Primary School
HMSMTH W6 .... **9** F1
St Philips School
CHSGTN KT9 .... **41** E5
St Richards with St Andrews CE
Primary School
RCHPK/HAM TW10 .... **21** G3
St Stephens CE Junior School
TWK TW1 .... **13** F4
School of Art
RCH/KEW TW9 .... **14** B2
Shannon Corner Retail Park
NWMAL KT3 .... **38** B1
Sheen Lane Health Centre
MORT/ESHN SW14 .... **15** F1
Sheen Mount Primary School
RCHPK/HAM TW10 .... **15** E3
Sheen School
MORT/ESHN SW14 .... **15** H2
Sheen Sports Centre
MORT/ESHN SW14 .... **15** H2
Sheringdale Primary School
WAND/EARL SW18 .... **25** G1
Shrewsbury House School
SURB KT6 .... **41** E1
Silverglade Business Park
CHSGTN KT9 .... **44** D5
Smallberry Green
Primary School
ISLW TW7 .... **6** B5
Southborough School
SURB KT6 .... **41** F2
The Southfields Clinic
WAND/EARL SW18 .... **17** H4
Southfields Community School
WAND/EARL SW18 .... **25** H1
Southlands College
PUT/ROE SW15 .... **16** A2
Southmead Primary School
WIM/MER SW19 .... **25** F1
South Thames College
PUT/ROE SW15 .... **17** E3
South Thames College/
Wandsworth Adult College
PUT/ROE SW15 .... **16** A4
Southville Junior School
EBED/NFELT TW14 .... **18** A1
South West Middlesex
Crematorium
FELT TW13 .... **19** F1
Sparrow Farm County
Junior School
EW KT17 .... **43** C4
Sparrow Farm Junior School
EBED/NFELT TW14 .... **10** D5
Sparrow Farm Nursery School
EBED/NFELT TW14 .... **10** D5
Spring Grove Primary School
ISLW TW7 .... **5** C5
Springwell Infant School
HEST TW5 .... **4** B3
Springwell Junior School
HEST TW5 .... **4** B3
Squash and Badminton Club
WIM/MER SW19 .... **33** F2
Staines School
FELT TW13 .... **18** B5
Stanley Infant School
TEDD TW11 .... **20** D4
Stanley Junior School
WHTN TW2 .... **20** D4
Strand on the Green
J & I School
CHSW W4 .... **7** H2
Strathmore School
RCHPK/HAM TW10 .... **22** A1
Strawberry Hill Golf Club
WHTN TW2 .... **20** D3
The Study Preparatory School
WIM/MER SW19 .... **25** E5
The Study School
NWMAL KT3 .... **37** H2
Summit Business Park
SUN TW16 .... **26** B2
Sunbury Court
SUN TW16 .... **27** E4

Sunbury Health Centre
SUN TW16 .... **26** B4
Sunbury Leisure Centre
SUN TW16 .... **26** A3
Sunbury Lock
WOT/HER KT12 .... **26** C5
Sunbury Manor School
SUN TW16 .... **26** A3
Sun Life Trading Estate
EBED/NFELT TW14 .... **10** B1
Surbiton Business Centre
SURB KT6 .... **36** A3
Surbiton Cemetery
BRYLDS KT5 .... **36** D1
Surbiton Golf Club
ESH/CLAY KT10 .... **40** C3
Surbiton High School
KUT KT1 .... **36** B1
Surbiton Hospital
SURB KT6 .... **36** B3
Surbiton Natural Health Centre
SURB KT6 .... **36** B3
Surrey County Hall
KUT KT1 .... **2** B7
Swedish School
BARN SW13 .... **9** F2
Syon House
BTFD TW8 .... **6** D4
Syon Park
BTFD TW8 .... **6** D5
Syon Park School
ISLW TW7 .... **6** C4
Tamian Industrial Estate
HSLWW TW4 .... **10** D2
TAVR Centre
KUT KT1 .... **36** A1
Teddington Business Park
TEDD TW11 .... **21** E5
Teddington Cemetery
WHTN TW2 .... **20** D4
Teddington Clinic
TEDD TW11 .... **28** D1
Teddington Lock
TEDD TW11 .... **21** G4
Teddington Memorial Hospital
TEDD TW11 .... **28** D1
Teddington School
TEDD TW11 .... **30** A1
Teddington Swimming Pool
TEDD TW11 .... **21** F5
The Teddington Theatre Club
E/WMO/HCT KT8 .... **34** C2
Temperate House
RCH/KEW TW9 .... **7** C5
Thames Ditton Infant School
THDIT KT7 .... **35** E3
Thames Ditton Junior School
THDIT KT7 .... **35** E4
Theatre of the Dispossessed
WIM/MER SW19 .... **25** E1
Tiffin Girls School
KUTN/CMB KT2 .... **30** B1
Tiffin School
KUTN/CMB KT2 .... **2** E4
Tolworth CP School
SURB KT6 .... **36** C5
Tolworth Girls School & Centre
for Continuing Education
CHSGTN KT9 .... **41** G2
Tolworth Recreation Centre
CHSGTN KT9 .... **41** G2
Tolworth Tower
SURB KT6 .... **42** A1
Tower House School
MORT/ESHN SW14 .... **15** F2
Trafalgar Primary School
WHTN TW2 .... **20** C2
The Treaty Centre
HSLW TW3 .... **12** A1
Tudor Lodge Health Centre
WIM/MER SW19 .... **17** E5
Twickenham Cemetery
WHTN TW2 .... **20** A1
Twickenham Golf Club
FELT TW13 .... **19** H3
Twickenham Park
Health Centre
TWK TW1 .... **13** H4
Twickenham Stadium
WHTN TW2 .... **12** D4
Twickenham Trading Estate
TWK TW1 .... **13** E4
Unicorn School
RCH/KEW TW9 .... **7** G4
United Services Sports Ground
CHSW W4 .... **8** D4
University of London
Athletics Ground
NWMAL KT3 .... **38** B2

University of Westminster
CHSW W4 ....
Ursuline High School
RYNPK SW20 ....
Victoria Junior School
FELT TW13 ....
Victory Business Centre
ISLW TW7 ....
The Vine Clinic
KUTN/CMB KT2 ....
Vine Medical Centre
E/WMO/HCT KT8 ....
The Vineyard Primary School
RCHPK/HAM TW10 ....
The Waldegrave Clinic
TEDD TW11 ....
Waldegrave Girls School
WHTN TW2 ....
Wallbrook Business Centre
HSLWW TW4 ....
Wandsworth County Court
PUT/ROE SW15 ....
Watermans Arts, Cinema &
Theatre Centre
BTFD TW8 ....
Waterside Business Centre
ISLW TW7 ....
Wellington Primary School
HSLW TW3 ....
West Ewell County
Infant School
HOR/WEW KT19 ....
Westfields Primary School
BARN SW13 ....
West Hill Primary School
WAND/EARL SW18 ....
West Middlesex
University Hospital
ISLW TW7 ....
Westmoor Community Clinic
PUT/ROE SW15 ....
Weston Green School
THDIT KT7 ....
West Park Hospital
HOR/WEW KT19 ....
West Thames College
ISLW TW7 ....
The Wetlands Centre
BARN SW13 ....
Whitton Health Centre
WHTN TW2 ....
Whitton Health Clinic
WHTN TW2 ....
Whitton School
WHTN TW2 ....
Willington School
WIM/MER SW19 ....
Wimbledon Chase
Middle School
RYNPK SW20 ....
Wimbledon College
High School
WIM/MER SW19 ....
Wimbledon Common
Golf Club
WIM/MER SW19 ....
Wimbledon Common
Pre-Preparatory School
WIM/MER SW19 ....
Wimbledon High School
WIM/MER SW19 ....
Wimbledon House School
WIM/MER SW19 ....
Wimbledon Magistrates Court
WIM/MER SW19 ....
Wimbledon Park
Athletics Track
WIM/MER SW19 ....
Wimbledon Park Golf Club
WIM/MER SW19 ....
Wimbledon Park
Primary School
WIM/MER SW19 ....
Wimbledon RFC
RYNPK SW19 ....
Wimbledon School of Art
WIM/MER SW19 ....
WIM/MER SW19 ....
Wimbledon School of English
WIM/MER SW19 ....
Wimbledon Theatre
WIM/MER SW19 ....
Wolfson Medical Centre
RYNPK SW20 ....
Worple Primary School
ISLW TW7 ....
Worton Hall Industrial Estate
ISLW TW7 ....
Wyke Green Golf Club
ISLW TW7 ....

 **QUESTIONNAIRE**

Dear Atlas User
Your comments, opinions and recommendations are very important to us.
So please help us to improve our street atlases by taking a few minutes
to complete this simple questionnaire.

You do NOT need a stamp (unless posted outside the UK). If you do not want to remove this page from your street atlas, then photocopy it or write your answers on a plain sheet of paper.

Send to: The Editor, AA Street by Street, FREEPOST SCE 4598,
Basingstoke RG21 4GY

ABOUT THE ATLAS...

Which city/town/county did you buy?

Are there any features of the atlas or mapping that you find particularly useful?

Is there anything we could have done better?

Why did you choose an AA Street by Street atlas?

Did it meet your expectations?

Exceeded ☐   **Met all** ☐   **Met most** ☐   **Fell below** ☐

Please give your reasons

ML

continued overleaf

Where did you buy it?

For what purpose? (please tick all applicable)

To use in your own local area ☐   To use on business or at work ☐

Visiting a strange place ☐   In the car ☐   On foot ☐

Other (please state)

LOCAL KNOWLEDGE...

Local knowledge is invaluable. Whilst every attempt has been made to make the information contained in this atlas as accurate as possible, should you notice any inaccuracies, please detail them below (if necessary, use a blank piece of paper) or e-mail us at *streetbystreet@theAA.com*

ABOUT YOU...

Name (Mr/Mrs/Ms)

Address

Postcode

Daytime tel no

E-mail address

Which age group are you in?

Under 25 ☐   25-34 ☐   35-44 ☐   45-54 ☐   55-64 ☐   65+ ☐

Are you an AA member?   YES ☐   NO ☐

Do you have Internet access?   YES ☐   NO ☐

Thank you for taking the time to complete this questionnaire. Please send it to us as soon as possible, and remember, you do not need a stamp (unless posted outside the UK).

ML